- "兴滇英才支持计划"教学名师专项（高等教育领域）（YNWR-JXMS-2019-065）
- 2022年云南省高等教育本科教学成果立项培育项目：教育滋兰树蕙，尽显一流专业担当——云南大学旅游管理专业实践教学体系构建探索
- 2022年云南大学校级教改项目：应用型本科专业社会实践一流课程建设路径研究——以旅游管理专业为例（2022Y28）

普通高等学校"十四五"规划旅游管理类精品教材
旅游管理双语系列教材
总主编◎史 达

TOURISM DESTINATION MANAGEMENT

旅游目的地管理
（双语版）

TOURISM DESTINATION MANAGEMENT (BILINGUAL EDITION)

主　编◎赵书虹
副主编◎梁春媚　王　静　钟喆鸣

华中科技大学出版社
http://press.hust.edu.cn
中国·武汉

内容提要

本书从概念体系、基础理论,到旅游目的地管理的利益相关群体,再到旅游目的地的管理实践,建构起对旅游目的地管理的认知逻辑链条,以帮助读者逐步建立对旅游目的地管理的感知,并且通过案例来解读相关概念和方法的实际运用场景。本书在每章开头用思维导图呈现出该章知识强化点及各要点间的逻辑关系,便于读者对本书的全面掌握。此外,每章的学习目标和关键词(中英文对照),也在章节开头作了说明,便于使用本书的读者进行对照学习。

Abstract

This book constructs the cognitive logic chain of tourism destination management from the concept system and basic theory to the stakeholders , and then to the management practice of tourism destination, so as to help readers gradually establish their perception of tourism destination management, and interpret the practical application scenarios of relevant concepts and methods through cases. At the beginning of each chapter, the knowledge strengthening points of this chapter and the logical relationship among the points are listed with a knowledge graph, so that readers can fully master the book. In addition, the learning objectives and technical words (in Chinese and English) of each chapter are also indicated at the beginning of the chapter, which is convenient for readers who use the book to learn by comparison.

图书在版编目(CIP)数据

旅游目的地管理:双语版/赵书虹主编.—武汉:华中科技大学出版社,2023.7
ISBN 978-7-5680-9609-6

Ⅰ.①旅… Ⅱ.①赵… Ⅲ.①旅游地-旅游资源-资源管理-双语教学-高等学校-教材 Ⅳ.①F590.3

中国国家版本馆 CIP 数据核字(2023)第 138185 号

旅游目的地管理(双语版) 赵书虹 主编
Lüyou Mudidi Guanli (Shuangyu Ban)

策划编辑:王　乾
责任编辑:王雅琪　王　乾
封面设计:原色设计
责任校对:刘小雨
责任监印:周治超
出版发行:华中科技大学出版社(中国•武汉)　　电话:(027)81321913
　　　　　武汉市东湖新技术开发区华工科技园　　邮编:430223
录　　排:孙雅丽
印　　刷:武汉科源印刷设计有限公司
开　　本:787mm×1092mm　1/16
印　　张:16.75
字　　数:512千字
版　　次:2023年7月第1版第1次印刷
定　　价:59.80元

本书若有印装质量问题,请向出版社营销中心调换
全国免费服务热线:400-6679-118　竭诚为您服务
版权所有　侵权必究

总 序

华中科技大学出版社出版的旅游管理类专业的双语教材,首套包含《旅游消费者行为》《旅游学概论》《旅游目的地管理》《中国旅游文化》《旅游资源学》五本教材,由分别来自东北财经大学、山东大学、云南大学、西安外国语大学、北京第二外国语学院等多所在旅游管理国际化办学方面有较多经验积累的高校的三十多名教师合作完成。

我们都知道,旅游业是中国1978年改革开放后,较早对外开放的一个行业。旅游业的特性也决定了它始终具有国际化发展的元素和内在动因。从行业发展和顾客服务的角度来看,这个行业与人,比如国际游客的直接接触频率很高;对英文信息,比如各境外旅游目的地或英文版的旅游网站的搜索量很大。从语言要求上来看,英语是为大多数国际游客所能听懂的语言。在国内的很多知名旅游景点,我们会经常看到用熟练的外语给外国游客介绍中国历史文化景点的导游;在很多城市的街头巷角,会有一些当地居民用外语为外国旅客指路或者推介家乡的风土人情。他们亲切友善的表达,不仅传递了信息,还展现了一个国家的包容度和自信。所以,与其他服务业业态和商业业态相比,旅游业的国际化程度相对较高,对国际化人才的需求也更多。要想做到准确地把握不同国家旅游者的行为,达意地传递旅游和文化信息,就需要旅游业的从业者能够掌握和使用专业外语。

高等教育机构作为人才的提供者,要想满足行业对于国际化人才的需求,就需要从教师国际化和课程国际化等方面提供支撑。从目前高校发展的情况看,在经过多年教育国际化发展后,越来越多的教师已经具备较强的国际化视野和国际化沟通能力。但是课程国际化的关键环节——教材国际化却成为木桶上的短板。在国际化教材的使用方面,高校主要通过中国图书进出口(集团)有限公司来引进教材,或者由教师自制课程讲义和幻灯片。引进的教材几乎都为国外学者所著,里面的案例多以国外企业为样本,中国学生甚至教师对很多国外企业并不了解。特别是在新的旅游业态方面,中国的旅游业有着其他一些国家所没有的运营形态,比如数字化等,在这个层面上,中国的旅游业与国外存在较大程度的差异性。

而教师自制的讲义对于学生而言,其在课后很难进行阅读和复习。此外,随着中国教育改革和对外开放的不断深入,越来越多的国际留学生选择来华学习。这个时候再拿着境外的教材讲中国企业的案例,就显得有点不合时宜了。因此,由中国教师编著一套讲述"中国故事"的双语教材,让境外的读者也能更便捷地了解中国旅游业的实践与发展,就成为一项非常紧迫且有意义的工作了。首套五本教材涵盖了旅游管理类专业的三门核心课程,同时还包括"中国旅游文化""旅游资源学"两门非常有特点的课程,希望能够满足大多数读者的需求。

华中科技大学出版社是国内在旅游管理类教材出版方面的佼佼者。因为工作的关系,编者与李欢社长、王乾编辑在多次交流中碰撞出火花,并很快确定出版书目,组建写作团队。从筹备到五本教材全部完稿用时一年半。经历了严肃的周例会讨论、外审等多个环节,克服了各种困难,该系列教材终于能够与读者见面了,编者在内心充满了喜悦的同时,也有担心不能如读者所愿的不安。

因此,也希望读者在阅读过程中,如发现其中的问题或不足之处,能及时与我们进行沟通。编者将不断吸取读者的意见和建议,不断完善本套教材,以便能为旅游管理教育提供更多、更好的教材。

史达
2023年3月19日

Foreword

The first set of bilingual textbook on tourism management majors published by Huazhong University of Science and Technology Press includes five textbooks: *Tourism Consumer Behavior*, *Introduction to Tourism*, *Tourism Destination Management*, *Chinese Culture and Tourism*, and *Tourism Resources*, which were jointly written by over thirty teachers from such universities as Dongbei University of Finance and Economics, Shandong University, Yunnan University, Xi'an International Studies University, Beijing International Studies University as they have accumulated experiences of international education in the field of tourism management.

The tourism industry, as we know, was one of the earliest industries that opened up to the outside world after China put in place the policy of reform and opening up in 1978. The qualities of the industry determine that it always has attributes and dynamism from within to pick up an international characteristic in its development. From a perspective of industry development and customer service, this industry has a high frequency of direct contact with people, international tourists, for example; as for information in English on tourist destinations or travel websites, the search volume is large; when it comes to language accessibility, English is the language that most international tourists can understand. At many popular tourist attractions in China, it is common to see tour guides fluent in English or other foreign languages introducing historical and cultural sites to international tourists; locals give directions to international travelers or introduce local culture in the neighborhoods in English or other foreign languages. Their kind words convey more than information. They are showcasing openness and confidence of a nation. For all these reasons, the tourism industry has a higher degree of internationalization and demands more international talent than other service and business formats. It is required that industry employees be able to use a kind of foreign language for business purposes to effectively understand the behavior of tourists from different countries and precisely deliver tourism and cultural messages.

As talent suppliers, higher education institutions need to provide support by offering international faculty and courses to meet the industry's demand for international talent. Over the years of international practice, the current development of colleges and universities shows that an increasing number of teachers have gained global visions and international communication capabilities. Textbooks, however, turn out to be the short stave of the barrel, hindering international course development. The text materials in use were either imported from CNPIEC or handouts and slides produced by teachers themselves. Imported teaching materials were nearly all written by foreign scholars and packed with cases of foreign businesses, which Chinese students and sometimes even teachers have difficulty understanding very well. It is worth noting that the tourism industry in China has what is not common in other countries when it comes to a nascent business format, such as digitalization, where differences can be identified between China and other countries.

On the other hand, teachers' handouts make it hard for students to do extension reading and review after class. We also witness more international students coming to study with us when China's educational reform and opening up further advances. It is inconvenient to use foreign text materials while talking about cases of Chinese businesses. As a result, writing textbooks, telling Chinese stories and facilitating overseas readers to get insights into tourism practice and development in China has become an imperative and meaningful task for Chinese teachers. This initial five-volume set covers three core courses in the tourism management major and the two distinctive courses on "Chinese Culture and Tourism" and "Tourism Resources". We hope that these books can meet the needs of the majority of the readers.

Huazhong University of Science and Technology Press excels in publishing tourism management text materials. The inspiring work discussions between the authors, President Li Huan and editor Wang Qian kindled the spark to confirm the book list for publication and eventually have the writing team pulled together. It took one and a half years from preparation to completion of all five manuscripts. This textbook set finally made it to be put in print after we undertook discussions at weekly meetings, went through external reviews and overcame difficulties. While being full of joy, we are concerned about not being able to fulfil our readers' expectations.

We look forward to hearing from you if any mistakes or errors are spotted during your reading. Any of your opinions and suggestions will be welcome so that we will continue to improve and provide you with better textbooks.

Shi Da
March 19, 2023

前言

在东北财经大学萨里国际学院牵头组织的国内首批旅游管理类专业全英文教材编写工作中，我们有幸承担了《旅游目的地管理》这本教材的编写工作。选择全英文的方式出版教材，一是为了满足国内高校中外合作办学专业课程的全英文或者双语教学的要求，二是希望用我们的叙事手法向全世界讲好中国旅游发展故事，向全球传递中国旅游业发展方案和中国旅游管理智慧。本着这样的初衷，主编向兄弟院校发出邀请，最终由分别来自云南大学、东北财经大学、云南财经大学和上海商学院的四位教师组成了主创团队，经过近一年的共同努力，终于将书稿完成。

本书由云南大学工商管理与旅游管理学院的赵书虹教授担任主编，东北财经大学旅游与酒店管理学院梁春媚副教授、云南财经大学旅游与酒店管理学院王静副教授、上海商学院酒店管理学院的钟喆鸣博士担任副主编。具体分工如下：赵书虹负责本书大纲设计和前言的撰写，正文第1章和第5章的编写，以及书稿整体的统稿工作；梁春媚负责正文第6章和第8章的编写工作；王静负责正文第2章和第3章的编写工作；钟喆鸣负责正文第4章和第7章的编写工作。

在这耗时一年多的编写过程中，主创团队从教材大纲设计到样章编写，从初步合成书稿到按照出版社的要求一次次修订，克服了不能线下见面讨论以及日常繁重的教学科研任务及行政工作的困难，一次次的线上沟通，一次次的私信讨论，包括改标题、加思维导图、补充案例等，没有一位教师掉队，最终得以将书稿完成。感谢主创团队四位教师的精诚团结和倾情付出，感谢出版社编辑的认真编校，感谢东北财经大学萨里国际学院的牵头组织和鼎力支持。此外，同样感谢参与书稿思维导图制作、案例编写、资料收集等工作的云南大学工商管理与旅游管理学院硕士研究生杨雨婷、杨越琴，云南财经大学旅游与文化产业研究院硕士研究生孙蓉蓉、刘小琴，东北财经大学旅游与酒店管理学院硕士研究生陈建霞、李妍、冯仕佳。

  本书引用和借鉴了众多专家学者的研究成果,这些研究已经在参考文献部分罗列出来。如有遗漏,敬请谅解,在此一并感谢。尽管编者从事旅游管理专业教学科研多年,尽管我们在教材编写过程中用心撰写、认真修订,但水平有限,难免有错漏之处,还请多多批评指正。

赵书虹
2023年1月

Preface

In the compilation of the first batch of all-English textbooks for the major of tourism management in China, led by Surrey International Institute of Dongbei University of Finance and Economics, we had the honor to undertake the compilation of the book *Tourism Destination Management*. The book is published in English. First, it is aimed at Chinese-foreign cooperatively-run majors in domestic universities and meets the requirements of English or bilingual teaching of specialized courses. Second, it is hoped that we can tell the story of China's tourism development to the whole world with our narrative technique, and pass on China's tourism development program and China's tourism management wisdom to the whole world. In line with this original intention, the editor-in-chief sent an invitation to peer colleges and universities, and finally four teachers from Yunnan University, Dongbei University of Finance and Economics, Yunnan University of Finance and Economics and Shanghai Business School formed a creative team. After nearly one year's joint efforts, the manuscript was finally completed.

This book is edited by Professor Zhao Shuhong from School of Business and Tourism Management of Yunnan University, and written by Associate Professor Liang Chunmei from School of Tourism and Hotel Management of Dongbei University of Finance and Economics, Associate Professor Wang Jing from School of Tourism and Hotel Management of Yunnan University of Finance and Economics, and Dr. Zhong Zheming from School of Hotel Management of Shanghai Business School. The specific division of labor is as follows: Zhao Shuhong is in charge of Chapters 1 and 5, Liang Chunmei is in charge of Chapters 6 and 8; Wang Jing is in charge of Chapters 2 and 3; Zhong Zheming is in charge of Chapters 4 and 7, and Zhao Shuhong is in charge of writing the outline, preface and unified manuscript.

In the process of writing for more than a year, from the book outline design to sample chapter writing, from preliminary synthesis of the manuscript to revision according to the requirements of the publishing house, the creative team overcame the difficulty of meeting, discussing offline, and overcome the difficulties of daily teaching and research tasks and heavy administrative work. Through repeated online communication and private message discussions, changing the title, adding mind maps, and supplementing cases, the manuscript was finished with no one left behind finally. I would like to thank the four teachers of the creative team for their sincere solidarity and dedication, the editors of the publishing house for their careful proofreading and guidance, the Surrey International Institute of Dongbei University of Finance and Economics for their leading organization and full support. I also give thanks to Yang Yuting and Yang Yueqin, the postgraduates of the School of Business and Tourism Management of Yunnan University, Sun Rongrong and Liu Xiaoqin, the postgraduates of the Tourism and Cultural Industry Research Institute of Yunnan University of Finance and Economics, and Chen Jianxia, Liyan and Feng Shijia, the postgraduates of the School of Tourism and Hotel Management in Dongbei University of Finance and Economics, who participated in the collection of manuscripts and unified formats.

The book quotes and draws lessons from the research results of many experts and scholars, and has been listed in the reference section. If there are any omissions, thank you here. Although the author has been engaged in teaching and scientific research of tourism management major for many years, and although we have carefully written and revised the textbook in the process of compiling, the level is limited, and there are inevitably some mistakes and omissions. Please make more criticisms and corrections.

Zhao Shuhong
January, 2023

目录
Contents

Chapter 1 Introduction / 001

1.1 Conceptual System of Tourism Destination Management / 002
1.1.1 Tourism Destination / 002
1.1.2 Tourism Destination System / 004
1.1.3 Types of Tourism Destination / 006

1.2 Theoretical System of TourismDestination Management / 009
1.2.1 Place Theory / 009
1.2.2 Tourism Destination Competitiveness Theory / 013
1.2.3 Tourism Destination Life Cycle Theory / 018
1.2.4 Criticism and Revision of Life Cycle Theory / 022

1.3 The Significance of Tourism Destination Management / 026
1.3.1 Call from the Social Needs / 026
1.3.2 Call from the Environmental Needs / 026
1.3.3 Call from the Cultural Needs / 027

Chapter 2 The Community Management of Tourism Destination / 029

2.1 The Community Management Model and Experience of Tourism Destination / 030
2.1.1 Community and Tourism Destination Community / 031
2.1.2 Tourism Destination Community Management Model / 033
2.1.3 Tourism Destination Community Management Experience / 037

2.2 Promotion of Community Participation in Tourism Destination / 041
- 2.2.1 Introduction / 041
- 2.2.2 The Present Situation of Community Tourism Development in China / 045
- 2.2.3 Countermeasures to Promote Effective Community Participation / 047

Chapter 3　The Tourist Management of Tourism Destination / 052

3.1 Motivation and Behavior of Tourists in Tourism Destination / 053
- 3.1.1 Tourist Motivation / 054
- 3.1.2 Tourist Behavior / 057

3.2 Overview of Tourist Management in Tourism Destination / 061
- 3.2.1 Origin and Development of Tourist Management / 062
- 3.2.2 Current Situation of Tourist Management in Tourism Destination / 063

3.3 Content of Tourist Management / 065
- 3.3.1 Tourist Carrying Capacity Management / 065
- 3.3.2 Tourist Experience Management / 072
- 3.3.3 Tourist Uncivilized Behavior Management / 075
- 3.3.4 Tourist Satisfaction Management / 076

Chapter 4　Service Management of Tourism Destination / 079

4.1 Management of Tourism Destination Service Enterprise / 081
- 4.1.1 Definition of Management of Tourism Destination Service Enterprise / 081
- 4.1.2 Main Content of Management of Tourism Destination Service Enterprise / 081
- 4.1.3 Corporate Social Responsibility of Tourism Destination Service Enterprise / 083

4.2 Service Quality Management of Tourism Destination / 085
- 4.2.1 Service Quality / 085
- 4.2.2 Service Quality Problems Recognition and Correction / 086
- 4.2.3 Service Quality Measurement / 088
- 4.2.4 Integrated Quality Management of Tourism Destination / 089

4.3 Safety Management of Tourism Destination Services / 092
- 4.3.1 Safety of Tourism Destination / 092
- 4.3.2 Safety Precautions and Responses for Tourism Destination / 094

4.3.3 Tourism Destination Crisis / 097
4.3.4 Tourism Destination Crisis Management / 100

Chapter 5　Tourism Destination Planning and Development Management / 104

5.1 Tourism Destination Planning and Management / 105
5.1.1 Rural Tourism Destination Planning and Management / 105
5.1.2 Urban Tourism Destination Planning and Management / 109
5.1.3 Scenic Tourism Destination Planning and Management / 111

5.2 Tourism Destination Development Management / 114
5.2.1 Tourism Destination Project Planning / 114
5.2.2 Tourism Destination Product Development / 117

Chapter 6　Tourism Destination Marketing Management / 124

6.1 Tourism Destination Marketing Strategy / 125
6.1.1 Tourism Destination Marketing Overview / 126
6.1.2 Theories of Tourism Destination Marketing / 131
6.1.3 Strategy Design of Tourism Destination Marketing / 134

6.2 Brand Management of Tourism Destination / 150
6.2.1 Concept of Tourism Destination Brand / 150
6.2.2 Marketing of Tourism Destination Brand / 151
6.2.3 Management of Tourism Destination Brand / 157

Chapter 7　Intelligent Management of Tourism Destination / 166

7.1 Informatization Construction of Tourism Destination / 167
7.1.1 Introduction of Tourism Destination Informatization / 167
7.1.2 Informatization Management of Tourism Destination / 170
7.1.3 Tourism Destination Information System / 175

7.2 Intelligent Tourism / 177
7.2.1 Introduction of Intelligent Tourism / 177

7.2.2 Intelligent Tourism Destination / 181

Chapter 8　Sustainable Development of Tourism Destination / 186

8.1 Environment Management of Tourist Destination / 188

8.1.1 Overview / 188
8.1.2 Research Trend of Sustainable Tourism at Home and Abroad / 189
8.1.3 Research Trend of Tourism Environment Management at Home and Abroad / 191
8.1.4 Sustainable Tourism and Tourism Destination Environment Management / 192
8.1.5 Tourism Destination Environment Management Content / 192
8.1.6 Environment Management Characteristics of Tourism Destination / 195
8.1.7 Basic Functions of Tourism Environment Management / 197
8.1.8 Ways to Achieve Tourism Destination Management / 199

8.2 Tourism Destination Industry Management / 201

8.2.1 Overview / 201
8.2.2 Tourism Destination Industry System / 208
8.2.3 Tourism Destination Industry Layout / 215
8.2.4 Tourism Destination Industry Integration / 223
8.2.5 Principles of Sustainable Development of the Tourism Destination Industry / 226

8.3 Development Trend of Tourism Destination / 233

8.3.1 Development of Tourism Destination in the New Era / 233
8.3.2 Sustainable Development Paths for Tourism Destination / 240

参考文献 / 248

Chapter 1
Introduction

Knowledge Graph

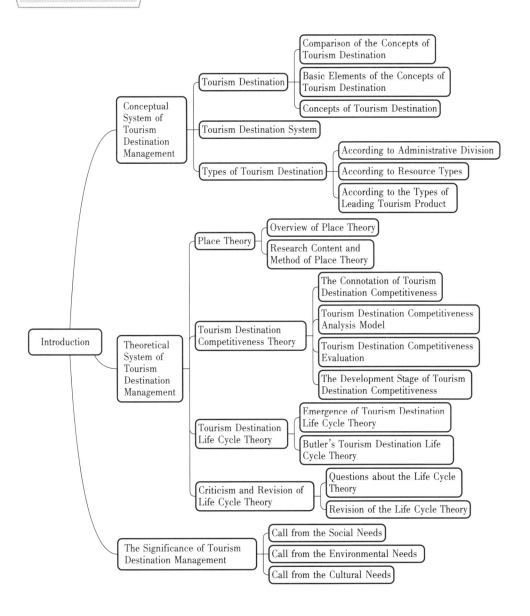

> **Learning Objectives**
>
> (1) Master the concepts and types of tourism destination management.
> (2) Be familiar with the basic theories of tourism destination management.
> (3) Understand the significance of tourism destination management.

Technical Words

English Words	中文翻译
the tourism destination system	旅游目的地系统
place theory	场所理论
tourism destination competitiveness theory	旅游目的地竞争力理论
tourism destination life cycle theory	旅游目的地生命周期理论
competitiveness analysis model	竞争力分析模型

1.1 Conceptual System of Tourism Destination Management

1.1.1 Tourism Destination

1) Comparison of the Concepts of Tourism Destination

The concepts of tourism destination are common at home and abroad. The study of foreign tourism destination began in the 1970s, and the original tourism destination was a geographical area. American scholar Gunn put forward the concept of "destination zone" in 1972. "Destination zone" includes main passages and entrances, communities (including attractions and infrastructure), attraction complexes, and connecting roads (communication channels between attraction complexes and communities).

Leiper (1995) thought that the tourism destination is a place where tourists come to experience some characteristics of attractive scenic spots.

British scholar Buharis (2000) thought that the tourism destination is a specific geographical area which is recognized as a complete individual by tourists and has a unified policy and judicial framework for tourism management and planning, that is, an area managed by a unified destination management agency.

Domestic scholars' attention to tourism destination originated in the middle and late 1990s. Among them, Bao Jigang et al. (1996), Cui Fengjun (2002), Zhang Hui (2002), Wei Xiaoan (2002), Zhang Liming, Zhao Liming (2005) and Lam Raymond (2005) all gave the definition of tourism destination. From the way and content of the definition, the above definitions are similar, but there are also some differences (as shown in Table 1-1). Zou Tongqian (2006) put forward that the tourism destination is a perceptual concept, which provides tourists with a composite product of products and services and a combined experience. There are two key elements of a tourism destination: one is tourist attraction, and the other is human settlement. There must be permanent or temporary accommodation facilities, and tourists usually stay for more than one night. General scenic spots should not be tourism destinations. Dong Guanzhi and Zhang Qiaoling (2008) believed that the tourism destination is the regional integration of tourism activities and tourism services with certain tourism resources as the core, comprehensive tourism facilities as the basis and accessibility as the premise, and it is the core carrier for tourists to stay and carry out tourism activities. The concept of tourism destination mainly includes three meanings: first, it has a certain scale and a relatively concentrated regional spatial scope; second, certain tourism resources have been developed and utilized, which has obvious tourism attraction functions; third, it has a comprehensive tourism industrial structure with close internal ties and relatively complete functions of amusement and reception services, so that tourism occupies a large proportion in the local economic structure.

Table1-1 Different definitions by domestic scholars

Author	Definition
Bao Jigang et al.	In a certain space, tourism resources, tourism facilities, tourism infrastructure and other related conditions organically gather, becoming the destination of tourists to stay and participate in activities, that is, the tourism destination.
Cui Fengjun	Tourism destination is an open system with a unified and integral image of tourism attraction system.
Zhang Hui	Tourism destination is a specific area with specific tourism resources and tourism attraction, which can attract a certain number of tourists to carry out tourism activities.
Wei Xiao'an	The simplest definition of tourism destination is a place or main activity location that can meet the ultimate purpose of tourists.

From the definitions of tourism destination given by domestic and foreign scholars in different periods, we can easily see that tourism destination must be located in a specific geographical space and have a certain resources base. These resources include natural resources and social and cultural resources, which can be developed and utilized by cultural tourism and attract tourists.

2) Basic Elements of the Concepts of Tourism Destination

From the comprehensive view of the above concepts of tourism destination, every tourism destination must have the following elements: specific geographical space, natural resources and social and cultural resources base, supporting service facility, community and resident, tourism factor supply department and even the formation of industry. These basic elements constitute a relatively complete system, which is mature and perfect in the process of continuous promotion and attraction of the tourism market. If the tourism destination is regarded as a complete system, it should at least include three parts: foundation system, power system and support system. Among them, the foundation system is composed of space, industry and community resident. The power system includes endogenous power and exogenous power, and the support system mainly refers to the government and policy.

3) Concepts of Tourism Destination

Tourism destination is a complete system with geographical space, community, resident and tourism industry as its development foundation, tourism market and innovation as its external driving force, and main capacity and industrial organization as its internal driving force. Its operation conforms to the law of tourism industry development, and its development benefits are constrained or supported by all parts of the system, and also feed back to them, thus forming a positive cycle in the same direction or a negative cycle in different directions.

1.1.2 Tourism Destination System

Gunn(1976) thought that a region that can truly become a tourism destination should have the following conditions: a tourism market with a certain distance; development potentiality and condition; reasonable accessibility to potential market; social and economic foundation with the minimum level that can support the development of tourism; a certain scale with many communities.

Tourism destination is generally composed of destination space with natural and social elements, community, industry, facilities, indigenous people, etc. Therefore, in this system, Buhalis thought there should be "6A" and Cooper thought there should be "4A". However, they have not reflected the interrelation of these elements and their roles in the whole tourism destination. The composition and development of tourism destination itself are carried out in the form of system. Therefore, this book proposes that tourism destination should be regarded as an industrial system, and its operation needs the cooperation of foundation system, power system and support system. Among them, the foundation system includes the geographical space of the tourism destination, the natural and social cultural resources in this space, and the community residents and their main livelihood constitute the industrial development foundation of the touristm destination. The power system includes industrial organizations such as trade association and the participation and support of community and resident, which can constitute the endogenous motive force of the system. It also needs external power from the market and drives development through innovation. So there should also be a strong support system from a government, including policy support, which is very important for the overall development of tourism destination.

The foundation of tourism destination system includes industry, geographical space, community and its resident. First of all, industry is the foundation for the development of tourism destination. Whether it is a city or a country, the prosperity of urban and rural areas can be achieved only when industry is prosperous. Most tourism destinations rely on traditional industry to form a "tourism+" development model, which is supported by the main emerging industry. Secondly, geographic space is the spatial carrier of tourism destination industry development. The location and style of this carrier are important components of tourist attractions, and also the main support for the development of tourism industry. The space carrier of tourism destination should be the space where tradition and modernity, nature and culture are organically integrated. Therefore, we should not only consider the greening and ecologicalization of the space, but also improve the accessibility of the space through the construction of public service facility. What's more, we can integrate the regional cultural characteristic and modern construction technique into the ecological design of tourism destination, so as to highlight the attractiveness of livable tourism destination and jointly support the development of high-quality tourism product and the innovation of tourism format. Thirdly, the community and its resident are the main body of tourism destination development. Resident can either directly participate in or indirectly contribute to the development of tourism industry, and there can be no development of tourism and related industry in tourism destination without the participation of community and resident. Especially, the tolerance, sharing, coordination and enthusiasm of the community and resident can promote the development of local tourism and attract more tourists.

Tourism destination also needs a power system which includes exogenous power and endogenous power. Only when the exogenous and endogenous forces form a joint force can the tourism destination operation system be effectively activated. Among them, driven by the demand of scale market and innovative development, the inexhaustible driving force for tourism to move towards high-quality development is the exogenous driving force. At the same time, efforts should be made to cultivate the endogenous power of tourism. On the one hand, it is necessary to continuously improve the service ability and service level of the main body of tourism development, pay attention to updating the concept of business main body and empower it with new technology. On the other hand, it is necessary to gradually cultivate tourism destination operation organization according to the actual development of tourism destination industry, and promote tourism to achieve "self-organization and marketization" development by setting up tourism industry association.

The support system includes the design of public service provided by the government, the effective guidance of the government, the ability to mobilize organization and attract investment, etc., which can support and encourage more tourism destination organization and resident to participate in tourism development. In addition, the government's effective implementation of relevant policy and governance of the community environment will also help attract social capital to invest in tourism development and meet the funding needs of tourism innovation and development.

To sum up, the foundation system is the development support, the power system leads the development, and the support system creates the development environment and condition. If the three systems are coordinated in the same direction, the tourism destination will move towards high-quality development. The lack of power system, the failure to consolidate the foundation system, the absence of surpport system and the failure of synergy among the three elements will lead to poor development benefit of tourism destination.

1.1.3 Types of Tourism Destination

Tourism destination has strong comprehensiveness with multiple tourism resources, attractions, products and services, so it is very hard to summarize. There is no mutual recognition about how to classify tourism destination by far. Most of the classification bases on tourism resources or attractions. This book will mainly introduce three types of tourism destination.

1) According to Administrative Division

Tourism destination is usually managed by administrative region, so the most common classification of tourism destination is on the basis of administrative division.

(1) National destination.

National destination regards a country as a destination. In general, national destination is combined with many regional destinations. The main function of a national destination is to set up convenient international air transports with the main tourist source markets to distribute tourists to domestic destinations.

(2) Regional destination.

In international market perspective, a regional destination might include several countries with similar tourism resources and characteristics, such as Caribbean area. In national space perspective, a regional destination is combined with some cities, villages, towns and several attractions. The regional service system is centered in main domestic airports and railways hubs. Good accessibility and convenient tourism distribution system are the major economic features. For example, there are the Yangtze River Delta tourism area and Bohai Sea ring area in China.

(3) Urban destination.

An urban destination is combined with several tourist attractions with a clear overall image. It not only has the function of visiting or sightseeing, but also takes the supporting function of tourism transport, accommodation, recreation and service system.

(4) Village and town destination.

Some villages and towns have distinctive characteristic or are rich in cultural deposit, and they can be developed into tourism destination. For example, China's famous historic and cultural towns and villages which are issued by the Ministry of Housing and Urban-Rural Development and the National Cultural Heritage Administration are representatives of this type of destination.

(5) Scenic spot destination.

Scenic spot (or tourism attraction) is the minor unit of tourism destination. Not all the scenic spots accord with the features of tourism destination. Only those large or super large scenic spots with a certain scale of source market, specific attractiveness, comprehensive service and facility can be taken as tourism destination.

2) According to Resource Types

(1) Mountain tourism destination.

Mountain tourism destination refers to the area that people rely on mountains and the highland gradient effect to carry out travel, leisure and outdoor activities within the nature and human integrated regional ecosystem in their spare time (IMTA[①], 2020). In the broad sense, a mountain destination includes both the areas that all kinds of mountain leisure experience activities rely on and the supporting activity areas. In the narrow sense, a mountain tourism destination mainly refers to the core region for travel and leisure activity.

(2) Water-based tourism destination.

Water-based tourism destination is the place mainly with water scenery attraction. It

---

① The International Mountain Tourism Alliance (IMTA) is a non-government, non-profit international organization established with the approval of the State Council of the People's Republic of China, and voluntarily formed by destination management agencies, private tourism organizations, groups, enterprises and individuals of major mountainous countries and regions in the world.

can be segmented into lake tourism destination, coastal tourism destination and river tourism destination.

(3) Forest ecological tourism destination.

Forest ecological tourism destination takes forest vegetation and natural ecology as main attractions, such as forest park, natural reserve and wetland park.

(4) Urban business tourism destination.

This type of tourism destination takes modern urban landscape, urban culture and business activity as the main attractions, such as Beijing, Shanghai, Guangzhou, Shenzhen and Wuhan.

(5) Rural tourism destination.

Rural landscape and life are the main attractions of rural tourism destination. Some famous historic and cultural villages are also rural tourism destinations, such as Wuyuan in Jiangxi Province, Xidi and Hongcun in Anhui Province.

(6) Religious historical tourism destination.

Religious historical tourism destination takes religious architecture as tourist attraction. Religious tourism is one of the oldest forms of tourism in the world. Religious believers go to this type of destination because of faith, well-known ancient temple, church or other religious architecture. They are keen on the activities which can realize their purposes of religious belief and bring happiness in the traveling.

(7) Ethnic customs tourism destination.

Ethnic customs and activities are the dominant attractions of ethnic tourism destination. Local customs and living habits are quite different among different ethnic groups. Tourists would like to have diverse culture experience in different places. The concentration place of minorities in China such as Guangxi, Yunnan, Tibet, Xinjiang, Inner Mongolia and Ningxia can be this type of destination.

(8) Ancient town and ancient village tourism destination.

Clearly, ancient town and ancient village are the main attractions. For example, the ancient town of Lijiang, the ancient village of Xidi and Hongcun of Anhui are some of them.

(9) Theme park tourism destination.

It refers to the destination with main attractions of comprehensive recreations. For example, Happy Valley Theme Park, Shanghai Disneyland, Universal Beijing Resort and Guangzhou Chimelong Tourist Resort are the favorite destinations in Chinese market.

3) According to the Types of Leading Tourism Product

(1) Sightseeing destination.

This type of destination mainly depends on sightseeing product. Some places are suitable for developing sightseeing product because of the feature of the tourism resources. Sightseeing destination is a traditional type, and it takes an important position in tourism activities in the world.

(2) Vacation destination.

Vacation destination is to provide leisure vacation product and function that can meet the tourists' demand for leisure and vacation. According to the characteristics of the product, it can be divided into coastal resort, spa resort, ski resort, mountain resort, village resort, etc.

(3) Business destination.

Business communication and MICE① market take predominance in business destination.

(4) Special need destination.

This type of destination can meet the demand for medicine, wellness, adventure, photography, birdwatching and any other special segment markets.

1.2 Theoretical System of Tourism Destination Management

1.2.1 Place Theory

In the 1970s, under the influence of phenomenology, existentialism and other philosophical trends, human geography developed vigorously. Since human geographer Yi-Fu Tuan first proposed "place" and "sense of place" in 1976, western scholars have put forward "locality spirit" (or spirit of place) centering on these two core concepts. "Placelessness" "place attachment" "place dependence" "place identity" "place making" and other concepts which constitute the theory of place together explain the relationship between human and place from different perspectives such as human feeling, psychology, social culture, ethic and morality, which constitute the theory of place together.

1) Basic concepts

(1) Place.

Yi-Fu Tuan (1976) starting from the research point of view of phenomenology space put forward the concept of "place" namely "where will become meaningful through human activity" and "where is the foundation of human life, and at the same time provides all of the background of human life, or gives a sense of security to the individual and collective identity". In his book *Place and Placelessness*, Edward C. Relph pointed out that physical environment, functional activity and sense of place (meaning) are the three basic elements

---

① MICE: Meeting, Incentive, Convention, Exhibition.

to identify a place, and this classification is the cornerstone of theory although it is simple. At the first level, place can be regarded as a physical entity composed of building and natural environment. The second level sees place as tool for social relation, where a rigorous and objective researcher can observe human behavior using the way an entomologist observes ant. At the third level, the person who is experiencing the environment or activity sees much more than that. He has his own opinion of things: beauty and ugliness, promotion and hindrance, love and loathing, closeness and alienation, in a word, it is meaningful (as shown in Figure 1-1).

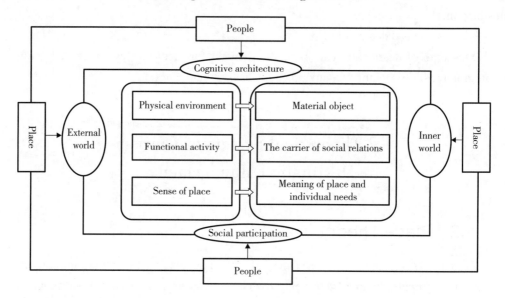

Figure 1-1　Local connotative structure

(2) Sense of place.

The sense of place is a reaction generated by the interaction between people's emotion and the environment they are in. Because people's emotional factors such as memory, feeling and value interact with the landscape environment in an emotional sense, individuals will have the behavior of attaching to the place. Yi-fu Tuan pointed out that a place can have a spirit or a character, but only people have a sense of place. The sense of place is an experience generated by a place and endowed by people.

(3) Locality and placelessness.

Locality is the characteristic that distinguishes a place from another place. It is the concentrated embodiment of local characteristics and endows a place with specific emotion and personality. In some places, because of its unique physical property, image, or a real and important event, myth is seen as a special and memorable scenic spot, such as the Potala Palace, the Forbidden City in Beijing, the Temple of Heaven, the Terracotta Army in Xi'an, etc., the mystery of these places has a strong spirit and unique significance. Even if people have not experienced these places themselves, they can feel a strong sense of place. Usually these places as tourism destinations are unique with the tourism brand image and the tourism development is quite successful.

Placelessness is the opposite of locality. Relph (1976) inherited the views of Heidegger (1962). He proposed that with the popularity of modernist standardized urban design, the monotonous modern architectural style and chain store operation mode resulted in the loss of a large number of "real gestures" that represented pre-industrial and manual culture, and created a sense of place. And the loss of local diversity portends an even greater loss of meaning. Commercialized tourist landscape, man-made park, suburb, and international style in architecture are all examples of non-locality and "unreal gesture".

(4)Place attachment.

Place attachment is a kind of connection between people and place based on emotion (feeling), cognition (thought, knowledge, belief) and practice (action, behavior), among which emotional factor is the first. Hammitt and Stewart classified local attachment into five levels: sense of familiarity, sense of belonging, sense of identity, sense of local dependence and deep-rooted local sense.

Place attachment constructs the structure of place dependence (PD) and place identity (PI). "Place dependence" refers to a kind of functional dependence, which depends on local resources and facilities to carry out certain activities. "Place identity" refers to a kind of spiritual dependence, which refers to a dependent relationship between individual and objective environment[①].Whether intentionally or not, this kind of relationship is formed by a comprehensive complex formed by an individual's thought, belief, preference, feeling, value, goal, behavioral trend and skill related to the environment. This emotion mainly comes from cognition and practice.

2) Research Content and Method of Place Theory

(1) Local theory.

Yi-fu Tuan (1977) believed that on the basis of the physical environment, a place can have a kind of character or spirit with the development of history and the accumulation of various events and the precipitation of culture. In this way, place is not only a symbol on a map, but also seen as a meaningful value center and an emotional attachment point with locality.

Locality is the synthesis of all kinds of objective features (nature, history, folk culture) of place itself, and the space spirit (meaning) is the inner meaning of these features. Unique local meaning can make a place competitive, unique and identifiable, and become an attractive tourism destination. It is generally believed that local composition includes the following five categories.

---

① Vorkinn M, Riese H. Environmental Concern in a Local Context: the Significance of Place Attachment[J]. Environmentand Behavior,2001,33(2):249-363.

① Natural conditions.

Natural conditions such as climate and scenery constitute the vast majority of natural aesthetic.

② Local culture.

Local culture which can reflect the living and working conditions of local residents brings knowledge satisfaction to tourists.

③ Activities.

A variety of activities can make tourists have a sense of participation, travel experience, and also can stimulate tourists' emotions.

④ Local special events.

Local special events such as cultural celebrations, arts and performances add the dynamic and unique nature to the place.

⑤ Upper facilities.

Upper facilities refer to the buildings and facilities that serve tourists, including hotels, restaurants, consulting centers, etc. Some facilities themselves are tourism attractions, such as the Eiffel Tower and the Statue of Liberty. Upper facilities are the foundation of local dependence.

(2) Space attachment theory.

Space attachment theory is about a reaction generated by the interaction between people's emotion and their environment. Because people's emotional factors such as memory, feeling and value interact with local resources (tourism resources) in an emotional sense, individuals will have attachment behaviors to places. Hummon (1992) believed that people's attachment behavior plays an important role in connecting people and places. Once consumers form an attachment to a destination, they will be loyal to it and pay a higher price for it.

(3) Place creation theory.

Place creation is the application of place theory in tourism. Gunn believed that place creation is to give more natural and psychological meanings to places while maintaining the essence of places. It is to provide tourists with more meaningful environment and functional space on the basis of maintaining and strengthening localism, so as to enhance tourists' sense of place. From the perspective of place creation theory, tourism planning is a process of showing locality and creating a meaningful place to enhance tourists' sense of place. Tourism planning is not only about planning buildings and tourism resources, but also about creating a sense of place. Gunn pointed out that "local alignment" is a fundamental principle of all tourism planning.

Place building emphasizes that place is a complex social structure with a wide range of meaning. Place building can guide the psychological cognitive process of tourists, publicize local meaning and shape the image of tourism destination by creating human-place perception system.

If the brand positioning of tourism destination is mainly based on the "local" formed in regional history and modern times, and the local spirit of tourism destination is explored through "local", then the local construction of tourism destination is based on the social audience. Through the integration of local resources it arouses their cognitive resonance and triggers the motivation of buying and traveling.

1.2.2 Tourism Destination Competitiveness Theory

1) Connotation of Tourism Destination Competitiveness

(1) Competitiveness.

According to *Concise Oxford English Dictionary*, "competitiveness" means striving to be superior in a particular quality. Competitiveness theory can be traced back to classical economics, its representative is the Ricardian theory of comparative advantage and the Marshall gathered advantage theory. The theoretical framework clearly reveals the international division of labor among countries under the system of the formation mechanism of absolute advantage and comparative advantage, which is regarded as the basis of the theory of competitiveness. It was not until the 1980s that a complete theoretical system or evaluation system emerged to reveal the formation and evolution of competitiveness. It mainly includes the competitive advantage theory of industrial organization school, firm resource basis theory, firm capability theory, competitive dynamics theory and international competitiveness theory.

(2) Tourism destination competitiveness.

The main body of tourism destination competitiveness (TDC) is tourism destination, namely service and facility centers that meet the needs of tourists. Its direct goal is to meet the needs of tourists and provide them with a satisfactory tourism experience, so as to achieve the economic goals of tourism destination. Tourism destination competitiveness is not only a concept in the "economic sense", it needs to consider environmental protection, sustainable use of resources and other content, so as to protect the long-term interests of tourism destination residents and other stakeholders. In other words, tourism destination competitiveness includes the ability to provide tourists with a satisfactory tourism experience and improve the quality of life of residents and the welfare of other stakeholders in tourism destination.

Tourism destination competitiveness is also a comparative concept, which also needs corresponding performance indicators. Market share, tourism income and other economic indicators can be used for reference here. Moreover, relevant studies have proved that satisfied tourism experience has a positive impact on the recommendation intention of tourists and shows a strong positive correlation. At the same time, there is a positive correlation between perceived quality and re-visiting, that is, the higher the perceived quality of tourists they have, the more likely the tourists choose to return. That is to say, on the one hand, tourists with satisfactory travel experience can bring new customers

Practical Application1-1

Lili Ancient Town in Jiangsu

through word-of-mouth publicity; on the other hand, these tourists tend to return to the destination in the future. Both the new customers brought by word-of-mouth effect and the old customers returning are conducive to the improvement of market share, that is, the market share can effectively reflect the satisfaction of tourists' tourism experience on the whole. In addition, tourism income can be used as a supplementary index of the market share, which can reflect the competitiveness of tourism destination more comprehensively. The life quality of residents in tourism destination and the welfare of other stakeholders are relatively difficult to measure without an intuitive indicator. Since the improvement of the life quality of residents in tourism destination and the welfare of other stakeholders which may depend on the satisfied tourism experience of tourists, this book takes the market share and tourism income as indirect indicators to reflect the life quality of residents in tourism destination.

To sum up, destination competitiveness can be defined as: the tourism destination should continuously provide tourists with tourism experience, improve the quality of tourism destination residents and other stakeholders' welfare, and form a common goal among tourism destinations in the size of the market share and market tourism revenue.

2) Tourism Destination Competitiveness Analysis Model

(1) C-R model.

Crouch and Ritchie established the famous tourism destination competitiveness analysis model (as shown in Figure 1-2①) on the basis of Michael Porter's diamond model. The model determines two important components of tourism destination competitiveness, namely micro environment and macro environment. Micro environment created among destinations directly participate in the competitive environment, including members of the tourism trade (wholesalers, suppliers, retailers, marketing and sales promotion personnel) destination, tourism market, the number of competitors and the public or stakeholders (residents and tourism practitioners, citizen action groups, media, financial and investment institutions, government departments). Macro environment refers to external factors that have an impact on tourism destination, including natural environment, political situation, economic structure, scientific and technological progress, cultural diversity, etc. Crouch and Ritchie pointed out that these macro and micro factors simultaneously act on four main components of tourism destination: qualification factors, core resources and attractions, supporting factors and resources, and destination management.

---

① Crouch G I, Ritchie J R B. Tourism, Competitiveness, and Social Prosperity[J]. Journal of Business Research, 1999, 44(3):137-152.

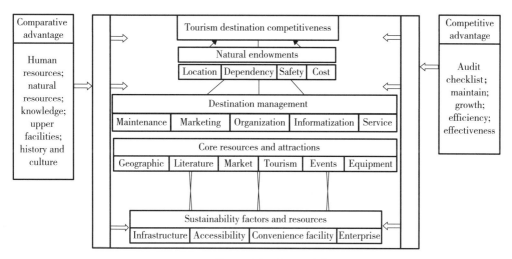

Figure 1-2　C-R model

(2) D-K model.

Dwyer and Kim (2003) proposed a new tourism destination competitiveness analysis model based on the C-R model (as shown in Figure1-3[①]). They believed that endowment resources, man-made resources and supporting factors and resources jointly determine the different characteristics that affect the attraction of tourism destination. They are the premise for the successful operation of tourism industry and fundamental to the competitiveness of tourism destination. Destination management factors can improve the attractiveness of core resources, strengthen the quality and effectiveness of supporting factors and resources, and make destinations better adapt to various situational conditions (Crouch and Ritchie, 1999). This includes destination management organization, destination marketing management, destination policy formulation, planning and development, human resource development, environmental management and other activities. The demand conditions of destination mainly include tourism demand, consciousness, perception and preference. Situational conditions can alter destination competitiveness by filtering the influence of other factors. The competitiveness of tourism destination has a direct impact on the social and economic prosperity of destination, which means that improving the competitiveness of tourism destination is only an intermediate goal, and the more important goal is to promote the development of destination and seek benefits for the residents of destination. Each goal has a corresponding metric. For example, there are many indicators of tourism destination competitiveness, including both subjective aspects (such as attractiveness of the destination, scenery) and objective aspects (destination market share, tourism foreign exchange income). Indicators of social and economic prosperity of a country or region include productivity level, overall employment

---

① Dwyer L, Kim C. Destination Competivieness: Determinants and Indicators[J]. Current Issues in Tourism, 2003, 6(5):369-414.

level, per capita income, economic growth rate, etc.

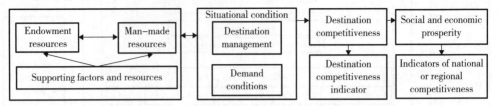

Figure 1-3　D-K model

3) Tourism Destination Competitiveness Evaluation

The competitiveness of tourism destination is based on all the resources of tourism destination, including all kinds of tourism natural resources, reception facilities, human resources and capital resources, which is the basic input of tourism destination to provide tourists with tourism experience and improve the quality of life of residents in tourism destination. The final performance of competition is the satisfaction of tourists' needs and the corresponding benefits obtained through this satisfaction. The difference in final performance depends on the utilization efficiency of different tourism destinations, and the efficiency reflects the competitiveness. Obviously, tourism destination competitiveness is the ability to obtain the maximum and optimal output under a certain input. This ability can only be determined by comparing the actual input and output, which also shows that the competitiveness of tourism destination is a practical ability that has been demonstrated.

Based on the above analysis, the tourism destination competitiveness evaluation model is a model similar to the input and output of an enterprise. The resource endowment of tourism destination and various supporting facilities are the input part of the tourism destination system. The tourist flow attracted by the tourism destination, the income and the welfare brought by the local residents are the output of the tourism destination. The management and operation process of tourism destination is a production process. The efficiency between tourism destination's input and output is the most intuitive performance of competitiveness. Accordingly, we can build a model of tourism destination competitiveness based on input-output efficiency, namely the I-O model, the input and output of tourism destination competitiveness is simplified to two systems and its internal relations can illustrate the ultimate goal of tourism destination competition and basic condition, which can automatically make category analysis carried out on the tourism destination from the aspects of foundation. The scope of basic strength of destination should be clearly defined, and the one-sidedness of taking influencing factors as evaluation factors of tourism destination competitiveness should be avoided. The conceptual model of tourism destination competitiveness based on input and output is shown in Figure 1-4[①].

[①]冯学钢,沈虹,胡小纯.中国旅游目的地竞争力评价及实证研究[J].华东师范大学学报,2009,41(5):101-107.

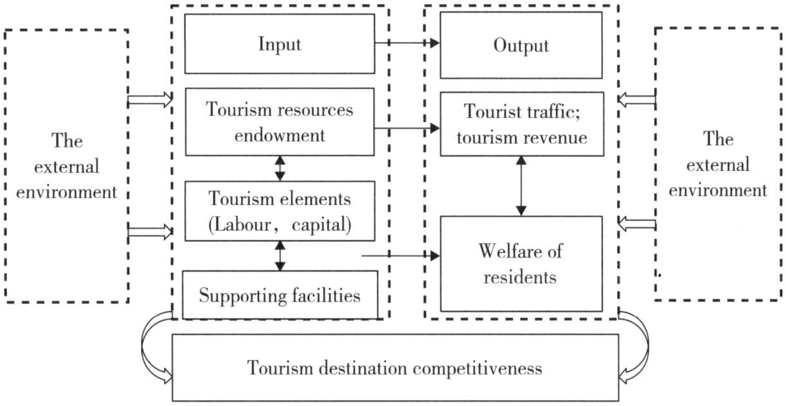

Figure 1-4　I-O model

4) Development Stage of Tourism Destination Competitiveness

(1) Exploitation stage—give play to your strengths.

A tourism destination in the development stage can be called a stage of exploiting its own advantages. At this stage, the development of tourism destination does not take into account the development of other related destinations, let alone the market demand, but their own resource endowment and leadership are the dominant factors of development. Tourism destination in this stage can only be competitive with high-quality tourism resources and attractions.

(2) Development stage— give play to comparative advantages.

At this stage, tourism destination have realized that blind development that only gives play to their own advantages cannot bring lasting benefits to tourism destination.

It is the main feature of this stage to study the advantages of tourism destination compared with other destinations, dig out their own characteristics and focus on development. The advantages of tourism destination in this stage over other destinations mainly come from their own resource endowments, such as beautiful natural tourism resources or profound cultural tourism resources, which become the driving force of their tourism development. Tourism destination in the development stage can be called the stage of exerting comparative advantages or resource-oriented stage. At this stage, tourism destination considers their own resource endowments, taps their potentials, gives full play to their advantages and forms their own competitiveness from a regional perspective.

(3) Mature stage—give play to competitive advantages.

With the development of a large number of tourism destination with regional resource advantages, the homogenous development among tourism destination becomes more and more serious, forming vicious competition. At this time, market-oriented and consumer-oriented tourism development emerged at the historic moment. In this stage of development, tourism destination mainly considers market acceptance and consumer demand preference, and tourism destination that is not suitable for market competition rules will eventually be eliminated.

The mature stage of tourism destination can be called the stage of building the competitive advantage of tourism destination. At this stage, the market plays a leading role in the development of tourism destination, and the resource endowment of tourism destination is no longer the first determining factor. Only by comprehensively enhancing its competitive advantages can tourism destination achieve sustainable competitiveness in the market.

In general, the three stages of the formation and development of tourism destination competitiveness are also the three stages of the development of tourism destination. Although tourism destination is divided into the exploitation stage, the development stage and the mature stage, tourism destination does not necessarily develop strictly in this order. The three stages of tourism destination development are a total developmental process, which is both a diachronic concept and a synchronic concept. A region may include three different stages at the same time. Taking China as an example, generally speaking, the western region is still in the exploitation stage as tourism destination, the central region has entered the development stage as tourism destination, and the eastern region now begins to build its competitive advantages.

The factors affecting the competitiveness of tourism destination are also different in different development stages. In short, the main factors affecting the competitiveness of tourism destination in the exploitation stage are the own resource endowment and the will of developers; the main factor affecting the competitiveness of tourism destination in the development stage is the resource endowment relative to other destinations. The main factor affecting the competitiveness of tourism destination in the mature stage is the ability of tourism destination to cater to the market.

1.2.3 Tourism Destination Life Cycle Theory

1) Emergence of Tourism Destination Life Cycle Theory

Tourism destination life cycle theory is usually used to describe the evolution of tourism destination and is one of the main contributions of geography to tourism research. Life cycle was first applied in the field of biology to describe the evolution of an organism from emergence to extinction. Later, the term has been used in many disciplines to describe a similar process of change, such as the product life cycle in marketing, which refers to the process of a product from putting on the market to removing from the market.

The origin of tourism life cycle is generally believed to have been put forward by Walter Christaller in 1963 when he studied the development of tourism in Europe. In his paper *Some Considerations of Tourism Location in Europe: the Peripheral Regions -*

Practical Application 1-2

Sichuan Daocheng Builds Astronomy Technology Tourism Destination

Undeveloped Countries-Recreation Areas, he proposed that all tourism destinations would undergo an evolutionary process of discovery, growth and decline. Another widely accepted life cycle model was also proposed by Plog in 1973. In 1978, Stansfield proposed a similar pattern through his study of Atlantic City's rise and fall. In 1980, Butler reformulated the cycle theory systematically. He divided the life cycle of a tourism destination into six stages: exploration, involvement, development, consolidation, stagnation, decline or rejuvenation. And he introduced the use of extensive "S" shaped curve to express (as shown in Figure 1-5[①]). Foreign scholars often use this six-stage model in quoting and researching cycle theory.

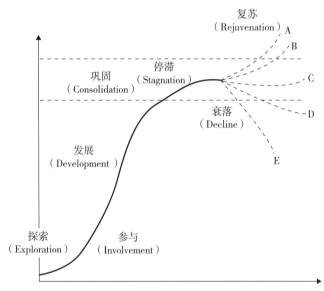

Figure 1-5　Tourism destination life cycle curve

2) Butler's Tourism Destination Life Cycle Theory

Butler, in his article *Overview of Tourism Destination Life Cycle*, used the product life cycle model to describe the evolution process of tourism destination and put forward the tourism destination life cycle theory.

(1) Overview.

Butler argued that destination, like product, undergoes a "life-to-death" process, with the number of tourists replacing the number of products sold. The destination is constantly evolving and changing as a result of various factors such as the changing tourist preferences and needs, the continuous degradation of physical facility and equipment, and the change or extinction of original natural and cultural attraction, which are the original attraction of the region.

---

①Butler R W. The Concept of a Tourist Area Cycle of Evolution: Implications for Management of Resources[J]. Canadian Geographer, 1980, 24(1):5-12.

(2) Description of each phase of the life cycle.

① Exploration stage.

The exploration stage is characterized by the scattered distribution of only a small number of exploratory tourists who have frequent contact with local residents. The natural, social, economic and cultural environment of the destination have not been altered by these visitors.

② Involvement stage.

In the involvement stage, the number of tourists gradually increases, and tourists still frequently communicate with local residents. In order to attract tourists, local residents begin to provide some simple facilities for tourists. The tourism season is taking shape, advertising begins to appear, and the scope of the tourism market has been defined.

③ Development stage.

In the development stage, a huge and perfect tourism market has been formed, attracting a large number of foreign investment. The number of tourists continues to rise, even surpassing the number of permanent residents at its peak. Transportation conditions, local facilities, etc., have been greatly improved, advertising and promotion efforts have been greatly enhanced, and large-scale, modern facilities provided by foreign companies have changed the image of the destination. Tourism has grown so fast that it is partly dependent on foreign labour and facilities. Excessive misuse of facilities should be prevented at this stage, so national or regional schemes are particularly important.

④ Consolidation stage.

At this stage, the economic development of tourism destination is closely related to tourism. The growth rate of tourists has decreased, but the total number of visitors will continue to increase and exceed the number of permanent residents. In order to expand the market scope, prolong the tourist season and attract more long-distance tourists, the scope of advertising promotion has been further expanded. The local residents have turned against the arrival of tourists, and the former facilities are now downgraded to secondary facilities, so the tourism destination is no longer a desirable place.

⑤ Stagnation stage.

At this stage, the capacity of tourism environment has reached or exceeded the maximum, resulting in many economic, social and environmental problems. Tourism destination has a perfect image of destination, but it is no longer popular. The number of tourists reaches the maximum, making the tourism market largely depend on repeat tourists, convention tourists, etc. With natural or cultural attractions replaced by man-made landscapes, and a surplus of reception facilities, the image of the tourism destination is divorced from the geography.

⑥ Decline or rejuvenation stage.

In the decline stage, tourists are attracted to other new destinations, and the original destination faces a shrinking market in both space and number, leaving only weekend vacationers or non-overnight visitors. A large number of tourist facilities have been replaced by other facilities, and the degree of resale of real estate is quite high. During this period, local residents' involvement in tourism can increase again through buying tourist facilities at very low prices. Tourism destination may become so-called "tourism slum", or even completely disconnected from tourism; another possibility is that tourism destination is recovering after a period of stagnation. There are two ways to get into recovery: one is to create a new set of man-made landscapes, but this strategy will be much less effective if neighboring areas or competitors copy this model; the second is to explore the advantages of undeveloped natural tourism resources and carry out marketing promotion activities to attract the original and future tourists. Thus, during recovery, new attractors replace existing attractors or new natural resources are developed.

Butler also pointed out that the overall quality and attractiveness of travel eventually decrease after a destination reaches maximum capacity. Therefore, for tourism planners, developers and managers, it must be clear that tourism attractions are not infinite, they should be treated as limited and non-renewable tourism resources, which should be carefully protected and preserved. The development of tourism destination should be kept within an affordable range so that their potential competitiveness can last.

It is important to note that not every tourism destination has gone through every stage of its life cycle, although it is an ideal concept to continue to develop tourism destination. The shape of life cycle curve may change due to different characteristics of different tourism destination, such as development rate, number of tourists, accessibility, government policies and homogeneous competition.

(3) The main factors influencing the life cycle of tourism destination.

Xu Zhiyun and Lu Lin summarized the factors that influence the life cycle of tourism destination proposed by foreign scholars, mainly including the following 15 factors: ①environmental quality and capacity; ②over-commercialization; ③good location; ④traffic condition; ⑤infrastructure; ⑥richness of tourism resources; ⑦residents' support; ⑧ tourism image; ⑨ competitiveness of tourism destination; ⑩ speed of tourism development; ⑪external investment; ⑫role of the government and tourism operator; ⑬change in external competition; ⑭change in customer market; ⑮external political environment.

(4) Tourism destination life cycle of the various stages of judgment and evaluation.

To judge the life cycle stage of tourism destination, the following factors should be investigated and comprehensively evaluated based on relevant researches: ①development time of tourism destination; ②tourism structure and function of tourism destination; ③ types of tourism product in tourism destination; ④ tourism format of tourism destination; ⑤change in the number of tourists received by tourism destination each year; ⑥ annual growth rate of tourists in tourism destination; ⑦ change of investment scale of foreign investors in tourism destination; ⑧ change in employment status of community residents in tourism destination; ⑨ change in the attitude of local residents towards investor and tourist; ⑩ damage to the community environment in tourism destination; ⑪ change in demand and supply of tourist facility in tourism destination.

We can compare the life cycle curve of the destination and the description of the characteristics of each stage to judge through the systematic investigation and analysis of the above factors; and then the stages of the life cycle of the tourism destination are obtained, and the corresponding counter measures are made.

1.2.4 Criticism and Revision of Life Cycle Theory

1) Questions about the Life Cycle Theory

(1) The question of cycle division stage.

Butler believed that the development of tourism destination will go through six stages: exploration, involvement, development, consolidation, stagnation, decline or rejuvenation. Most scholars found that the process of tourism destination undergo like that, but their empirical study results showed that very few tourism destination life cycle completely conforms to the Butler model described by the standard of "S" shape curve (especially those in the rear part of the decline and stagnant stage, as shown in Figure 1-6[①]). Cooper believed that the change in the shape of the life cycle curve of tourism destination is related to supply factors such as development speed, accessibility, government policies and competitors, and demand factors such as types of tourists and travel motivations, and any change of these basic factors will have a significant impact on tourism destination. In addition, the development of tourism destination is susceptible to major events, leading to the incomparability of data collected before and after major events. For example, the 2008 Beijing Olympic Games let more foreign tourists know China, so Beijing tourism can develop rapidly.

Getz (1992) pointed out that for Niagara Falls, there is no clear boundary between the initial stage and the development stage, and there is no single and complete stage of consolidation, stagnation, decline and recovery. They coexist under the pressure of competition and stagnation, and decline will not be allowed to exist for long in order to make profits. Either at the micro or macro level, there will always be efforts to make it revive.

---

① Stansfield C A. Atlantic City and the Resort Cycle Background to the Legalization of Gambling[J]. Annals of Tourism Research,1978(5) : 238-251.

Butler R W. The Concept of a Tourist Area Cycle of Evolution: Implications for Management of Resources[J]. Canadian Geographer,1980,24(1):5-12.

Hovinen G R. A Tourist Cycle in Lancaste County Pennsylvania[J].Canadian Geographer,1981(25):283-286.

Haywood M.Can the Tourist Area Cycle of Evolution Be Made Operational?[J].Tourism Management,1986 (7):154-167.

In spite of these doubts about the division of periodic stages, Butler's s-shaped curve model is not completely rejected, but only proved to be an ideal model, and all the anomalies mentioned are complementary to it.

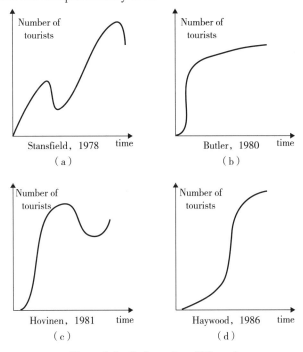

Figure 1-6 Deformation of life cycle curve

(2) Doubt about the potential of theoretical application.

The case study of Cooper and Jackson (1989) showed that the evolution of man's island is very consistent with the cycle theory model, but they pointed out that the cycle concept can also be applied to the development and evolution of a certain facility and administrative structure. Therefore, there is no single metric that can effectively sum up all aspects of the evolution of a tourism destination, or identify the current stage of the cycle of any tourism destination. In addition, for a specific tourism destination, its life cycle reflects policy decisions, and the turning points among cycle stages can only be determined after the event rather than predicted in advance. Just because of these, the life cycle of a tourism destination varies from place to place. As a result, they concluded that the cyclical model is useless for forecasting, only for describing and analyzing the trajectories of tourism destination.

Domestic scholar Yang Senlin questioned the life cycle theory of tourism product. Yu Shuwei refuted Yang's question and pointed out that the basic proposition of tourism destination life cycle theory is correct. Xu Chunxiao discussed the prediction function of tourism product life cycle theory and its falsification and verification. Yan Youbing discriminated the truth and science of the theory of tourism destination life cycle and pointed out that it is a specious theory. Zou Tongqian pointed out the following problems in the tourism destination life cycle theory. First, there are obvious differences in the life cycle of different tourism destinations, such as theme parks and nature tourism destinations. Second, life cycle curve has strong externality and is vulnerable to external influence such as market competition, price of substitute, consumer demand and government policy. Life cycle theory regards destination as a single product, but in fact it should be a complex of various factors. Third, the theory of tourism destination life cycle cannot be a perfect forecasting tool because of its long time span, many influencing factors and difficulty in determining the turning point of stages. Fourth, in marketing, the theory does not take into account the factors of market segmentation.

2) Revision of the Life Cycle Theory

(1) Division of life cycle stage.

Many scholars have modified Butler's theory in light of destination realities. Ioannides (1992) studied the development of tourism in Cyprus and pointed out that although the island tourism is largely influenced by multinational companies, the local government plays an important role in its development model. He stressed that the actions of government agencies and their relationship with foreign travel agencies play a significant role in the development and life cycle of tourism destination. Getz (1992) discussed the potential relationship between destination life cycle and tourism planning. Getz described the tourism development process of Niagara Falls in detail, pointing out that the tourism destination of Niagara Falls has entered the permanent mature stage of tourism, that is to say, its consolidation stage, stagnation stage, decline stage and recovery stage have been integrated and intertwined.

Debbage (1990) took Paradise Island in Bahamas as a case to study the impact on the life cycle of tourism destination when a few people control the market in the tourism market. He pointed out that, under the control of a tour operator, reducing visitor numbers in tourism destination often happens. This kind of situation makes this part of the operators obtain huge profits, so that they only care about the market possession and stability in the competition, and neglect for new product introduction and innovation. In reality, many resorts have a small number of multinational companies controlling the destination's operation, which can seriously affect the life cycle of the destination.

Priestley and Mundet (1998) pointed a new concept called the "post‐stagflation phase", which describes the life-cycle phenomenon of many competitive resorts that were unbeaten for a long time. After experiencing the general growth process and reaching the highest level of development, tourism destination did not decline immediately, but experienced a long period of stable development stage.

(2) Practicability of life cycle.

Zou Tongqian (1996) made a detailed analysis of the efficacy, defects and applications of tourism destination life‐cycle on the basis of a large number of foreign literature, and drew a conclusion: the life-cycle is affected by destination itself and the external factor and varies with the destination, so we can not sure the specific shape of cycle curve and time span to make regular summary of each phase, what's more, a tourist destination life-cycle theory cannot be applied to another destination, so it is more as a explanatory tool. It plays an important role in understanding the development of tourism destination and helps destination make long-term development plans. The tourism destination life-cycle combines the different factors that influence the destination, which can be a good descriptive tool. Because it includes all the factors related to tourism demand, supply and organization of tourism destination, the tourism destination life-cycle theory is of greater significance to tourism researchers than to tourism practitioners.

Haywood (1986) made a detailed and comprehensive discussion on the application potential of life-cycle theory. He pointed out that:

First of all, the following five concepts and measurements need to be considered to make the cycle theory model workable: unit of analysis (how to define a "tourist place", be it a region, a town, a specific area within a town, or a hotel, etc.); appropriate source market (refers to the whole source market as a homogeneous market, or should be divided into market segments); models and stages of tourism destination life cycle (there are various models of tourism destination life cycle. Haywood also pointed out that the existence of multiple models implies the existence of periodic stages different from the traditional ones); units of measurement selected (in addition to the commonly used unit of "number of tourists", we should also consider "length of stay, distribution of tourists in the tourism destination, characteristics of tourists, patronizing time", etc.); the appropriate time unit chosen(referring to annual data or quarterly data).

Second, the prediction using cycle model should be conditional prediction, that is, it should not only consider the relationship between the number of tourists or the expenditure and time, but also consider the heterogeneous source market, marketing strategy decision and the behavior of the competitive place.

Third, the marketing strategy that cycle theory should be adopted at different stages is only a hypothesis, which is basically not supported by empirical evidence. Moreover, the key of the problem is not what marketing strategy should be adopted by tourism destinations in different stages, but how to use the characteristics of cycle stages to form, develop and evaluate better marketing strategies.

Moreover, the evolution of tourism destination is the result of the comprehensive action of seven forces. Major changes in any of these forces will have a significant impact on the evolution of tourism destination. However, the description of the cycle theory makes people think that the evolution process of the tourism destination is determined in advance, so the significance of describing the evolution process of the tourism destination with the cycle theory is also doubted. Therefore, Haywood suggested using Darwinian models of natural selection to describe the evolution of tourism destination.

To conclude, Haywood pointed out that the cycle theory has nothing to do with the fact that "tourism destination will eventually decline". There is no meaning beyond the assumption of the base proposition. Tourism planners who want to fully understand how to manage an evolving destination should abandon the concepts of the destination life cycle.

1.3 The Significance of Tourism Destination Management

1.3.1 Call from the Social Needs

The 19th National Congress of the Communist Party of China (CPC) identified that now the principal contradiction facing Chinese society has evolved to be that between unbalanced and inadequate development and the people's ever-growing needs for a better life [1]. The historical change is strongly related to China's overall development.

Meanwhile, it marks that we must work hard to solve the problem of uneven and insufficient development on the basis of continuing to promote development. We should vigorously improve the quality and efficiency of development. We also must start from the diversity, level and incrementality of the people's needs for a better life, dynamically understand and grasp it in an all-round and multi-level manner, and do all the work in the future.

Tourism is one of the most influential aspects of the people's good life. If tourism needs can be better met, the provision of quantity and quality tourism and leisure products to serve will become a vital mission of tourism destination management. And it is also a new positioning of tourism destination management.

1.3.2 Call from the Environmental Needs

"Harmony between man and nature" is a major theme in ancient Chinese philosophy. Though it has been challenged by China's robust economic expansion over the past decades, it has always been in the mind and heart of Chinese[2]. Ecological civilization is a set of values and development concepts enshrined in the Constitution of the People's Republic of China (PRC) in 2018, and now a key driver in the country's transition to high quality development for the "New Era"[3]. Since 2007, the PRC has taken a plan that is potentially capable of establishing ecological integrity at many levels from local to global.

---

① http://chinaplus.cri.cn/opinion/opedblog/23/20171022/42529.html.
②http://www.chinatoday.com.cn/english/
③https://www.adb.org/

From that point, the PRC changed its intense focus for the past 40 years on high gross domestic product (GDP) growth to putting nature first. In order to embrace the ecological civilization, in the future management of tourism destination, we should emphasize more on the social responsibilities of environment and resource management, tourism companies, tourists and other stakeholders.

1.3.3 Call from the Cultural Needs

In 2021, the General Office of the CPC Central Committee and the General Office of the State Council jointly released *the Opinions on Further Strengthening Protection of Intangible Cultural Heritage* (ICH). It clearly defined the development goals between 2025 and 2035, such as building a workable ICH protection and inheritance system, strengthening such protection and inheritance as well as relevant public education programs[①]. A principal from the Ministry of Culture and Tourism said to the press that the *Opinions on Further Strengthening Protection of Intangible Cultural Heritage* (ICH) was based on the strategic height of consolidating the cultural confidence and realizing the Chinese dream and the rejuvenation of the great Chinese nation, it clarified the overall objectives and main tasks of ICH protection at present and in the future, setting up a baseline for ICH protection in the new era.

Over five thousand years long history has bred countless cultural treasures in China with 42 recognized by the United Nations Educational, Scientific and Cultural Organization (2020). Culture is the blood of a nation and the spiritual home of the people. Cultural self-confidence is a more basic, deeper and more lasting force. The unique idea, wisdom, tolerance, and charm of Chinese culture have added to the confidence and pride of the Chinese people and the Chinese nation. Nowadays, the revival of traditional culture is accelerating. As a significant part of tourism destination attractions, the cultural attractions of tourism destinations continue to be enriched and improved, and the requirements for cultural experience management of tourism destinations will also continue to rise. Meanwhile it poses new challenges for future tourism destination management.

Case Study

Sanya Becomes the Most Popular Tourism Destination

Case Analysis

Exercises

Chapter Summary

This chapter introduces the concepts and types of tourism destination management, provides the basic theory of tourism destination management, and helps students to understand how to carry out tourism destination management and grasp the significance of tourism destination management.

---

① http://www.iprchn.com/cipnews/news_content.aspx?newsId=130674

Issues for Review and Discussion

1. What are the types of tourism destination?
2. According to this chapter, discuss about your understanding of the tourism destination.

Chapter 2
The Community Management of Tourism Destination

Knowledge Graph

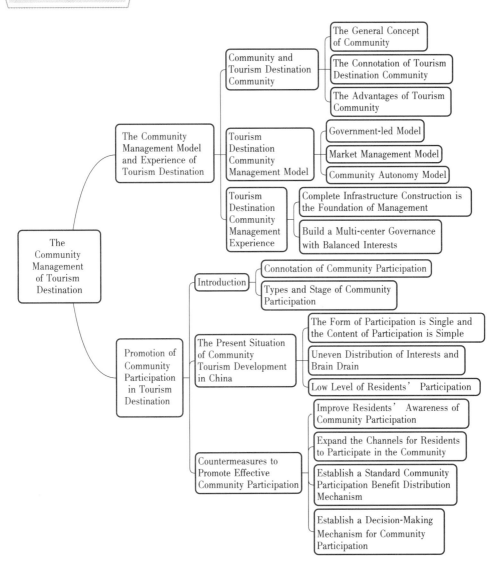

Learning Objectives

(1) Understand the meaning of destination community.

(2) Master the characteristics and advantages or disadvantages of different community management models.

(3) Summarize and learn tourism destination community management experience.

(4) Understand the connotation, types and stages of community participation in tourism.

(5) Know the development status of Chinese community participation in tourism.

(6) Master several strategies to promote effective community participation.

Technical Words

English Words	中文翻译
tourist destination community	旅游目的地社区
management model	管理模式
management experience	管理经验
community participation	社区参与
participation in promotion	参与推广

Introduce Case

Community-based Management of the USAT Liberty, Bali, Indonesia: Pathways to Sustainable Cultural Heritage Tourism

2.1 The Community Management Model and Experience of Tourism Destination

Tourism destination community is an important component of tourism destination, and the management of tourism destination cannot be separated from the management of tourism community. Therefore, on the basis of introducing basic concepts, this section also summarizes several typical tourism destination community management models gradually formed since the rapid development of tourism industry, and extracts some management experience from them in order to achieve better and more efficient management of tourism destination community in the future.

2.1.1 Community and Tourism Destination Community

The word "community" first appeared in the book *Community and Society* published by Ferdinand Tonnies, a German sociologist, in 1887. The Chinese word "Shequ" was freely translated from the English word "community" by Chinese sociologist Fei Xiaotong in the 1930s, which later became a common term in Chinese sociology. Tourism destination community is a social entity formed by the development of community tourism or tourism industry. Community and tourism destination community are different and related.

1) The General Concept of Community

Community is a sociological concept, which refers to the living community formed by people living in a certain area. From a sociological point of view, community is mainly composed of population, economy, region, specialization and interdependence of community, common cultural system of community resident, public facility shared by community resident, cohesion and sense of belonging of community resident. As a great union with a social nature and a regional nature, a community, as large as a country or as small as a community, it is not only the basic content of a social organism, but also the epitome of a macro society.

2) The Connotation of Tourism Destination Community

In recent years, with the rapid development of tourism, community tourism gradually developed into a new way of tourism. Compared with traditional tourism and ecological tourism, community tourism has its own characteristics not only in the content and focus of consideration, but also in the principle and core of development. For example, in order to better meet the diversified needs of tourists and let them enjoy multiple customs, under the background of "the coordinated development of Beijing, Tianjin and Hebei", Binhai new area has vigorously implemented the strategy of "full-area scenic spot, high-quality scenic spot, integration of industry and tourism, and diversification of business type". It has built a comprehensive tourism system integrating a prosperous and livable smart new city, profound cultural highland and romantic leisure resort. This move has greatly improved the tourism facility, scenic spot and taste creation of Binhai new area, turning it into a featured tourism destination in the Beijing-Tianjin-Hebei region.

Tourism carries out activities among communities which are the dependence of tourism development. Tourism destination community does not necessarily refer to a geographical territory, but mainly focuses on people living in tourism destination to strengthen their connection and sense of common based on their proximity. The community can achieve common interests or solve problems together through group living, cooperation, and public service system. A well-developed tourism community in which the residents have a strong sense of identity to the touristm destination have the spirit of cooperation and mutual assistance, this is the manifestation of "the sense of community", namely "the psychological community". " The sense of community" is an important factor to eliminate the sense of alienation in modern people. Tourism destination with a higher sense of community will have more sound community development, and these communities will be more cheerful, harmonious and hospitable in physical, psychological and social environment.

Murphy was the first to discuss the planning and development of tourism destination based on community[①]. He believed that "tourism is a method to build community". The diversity of economic structure will drive the reform of the social system, and the tourism community is the inevitable result of the evolution of the general community as the tourism attribute of the community becomes more and more prominent. Compared with general community, tourism destination community emphasizes more on the participation of the public, the sharing of responsibilities and achievements by stakeholders such as residents, community self-governing organizations, enterprises and social organizations.

3) The Advantages of Tourism Community

(1) Make tourism more experiential and participatory.

Tourism destination community is a holographic epitome of local ethnic or urban life. The communization of tourism can bring and show the life pattern of local cities, ethnic groups and even customs and culture to tourists. Community-based tourism can bring community activities into the tourism process, so that tourists can participate in the experience, or bring local characteristics of food or scenery to tourists, so that tourists can feel different local conditions and customs. Moreover, the development of homestay dwellings also brings tourists into real life, allowing them to personally feel the cultural differences of different regions.

(2) Make travel more real.

The authenticity of tourism lies in the genuine experience and feelings that tourists get by participating in and integrating into the tourism process. Traditional sightseeing tourism is more in "the seeing" efforts. Modern tourism also has many tourists around "the photo clock", a mere formality, and there is no actual acceptance and integration. Real tourism requires deep contact, practical appreciation and integration into the local social culture. The formation of a community in tourism destination can be a very good solution to this, whether it is the unique culture, architecture, or community lifestyle, economy, community service and other characteristics, tourists can truly enter the tourism destination, communicate with the local residents, participate in the activities of the local

① Murphy P E. Tourism: A Community Approach[M].New York: Methuen, 1985.

festival, intimate feeling of the local cultural charm.

(3) Have strong cultural feeling.

The community is also the witness and recorder of historical change and social development. For example, the buildings on the bund and left behind in the narrow alleys in Shanghai and the Siheyuan in Beijing are particularly dazzling in modern architecture. They are quietly telling about the change of the times, social reform and development. People can't help stopping and watching, causing contemplation and understanding from the bottom of heart. Compared with modern architecture, the change of people's living condition and the improvement of living standard show nakedly in front of our eyes.

(4) Promote the development of local community.

Tourism is inseparable from food, housing, transportation, tour, shopping and entertainment. The vigorous development of tourism will naturally bring economic income to various industries in tourism destination. The communization of tourism destination will promote the economic development of local community. Residents can take advantage of local cuisine and activity as one of the tourism projects to attract tourists, promote consumption and gain profits, which also solves the employment problem of residents to a certain extent. At the same time, it also brings convenience and joy to tourists. In order to attract tourists and generate income, the communalization of tourism destination will encourage local governments and planning developers to build community and improve living condition to attract tourists to the region. On the one hand, tourists can satisfy their own purpose. On the other hand, it promotes the development of the local area.

2.1.2 Tourism Destination Community Management Model

As early as 1991, the government put forward the idea of "community construction". Only by gradually reducing government intervention can residents take step and launch "mutual aid" of the residents within the community. Finally, if we need government guidance and social support, we cannot ignore "other help". Only when the community itself is strong, can resident' sense of community identity and sense of belonging be enhanced, and can community autonomy gradually get on the right track. More than 30 years have passed, China's exploration in community governance has not stopped, and a series of national experimental areas for community management and service innovation have emerged, providing a wide range of references and templates for different types of community development. How to manage the tourism destination community as a special object to achieve sustainable development of the destination is still an important topic. At present, tourism destination community management in China can be divided into the following three models.

1) Government-led Model

(1) Overview.

The government-led model is a model in which the government uses administrative means to lead the community public service, sustainable tourism development, ecological environment protection, and constantly improve the community residents' participation mechanism and tourism community governance framework. Through the establishment of various agencies, the government directly interferes with the management of communities, resulting in a strong administrative color of community autonomous organizations. This model has the following three characteristics: first, it has strong executive power. The operation model of government organization is copied into the process of community management, which can quickly mobilize various organizations; second, the authority is strong. Government departments plan, organize, coordinate, and exert strong institutional advantages to ensure community construction with coerciveness; third, the funds for community construction and management mainly come from the government. As the largest resource holder, the government has incomparable resource mobilization capacity.

Under the system of China, the vast majority of communities are obviously government-led model. For example, Shenzhen developed from a border fishing village into a modern city with prosperous economy, sound legal system, beautiful environment, civilization and harmony. The development of the city is inextricably linked with the strong promotion of the government. The "separate residential stations and multiple residential stations" implemented in Shenzhen in 2005 and the promotion of community service center in 2012 are typical government-led models. The administrative function of the neighborhood committee is transferred to the community workstation, and the government's management platform in the community is specified, and the community workstation implements the responsibility of community management and social service. With the support of the government, it introduces qualified social organization, improves the tourism infrastructure, and has an intelligent and information-based management of the tourism community in the form of the government purchasing services.

(2) Existing problems.

First, for tourism planning, travel and integrated community development which need the support of government policies, the harvest cycle is generally long, and relatively stable policy routes are needed in the process. This model inevitably relies too much on the personal charm of government leaders. With the replacement of each leadership group, the continuity and execution of policies will be affected, and there is an obvious phenomenon of "politics will be abolished with others". Second, direct government intervention runs counter to the essence of the market economy. When communities are used to passively accepting "offerings", their ability to rely on themselves will deteriorate, resulting in idle public service resources, insufficient tourism development vitality and inadequate participation of residents in decision-making. Third, government-led community management may lead to unequal distribution of decision-making power in communities, communities have to rely on the government, and it is difficult to carry out community autonomy. The lack of relative decision-making freedom will directly affect the play of advantages of social organizations.

2) Market Management Model

(1) Overview.

The market management model refers to the authorized enterprise operating, organizing and managing the tourism community by market means in accordance with laws and regulations, so this model is also called the enterprise-led model. In this model, the government's main function in tourism community affair is policy planning and supervision. Enterprise controls the main fields of community tourism operation, real estate development, property management and so on. The marketization degree of the tourism community directly affects tourism reception capacity and resource income scale.

In terms of tourism management, enterprise is based on its strong economic resources and directly responsible for the operation and performance of the entire tourism organization through the development of the public services and resources supply, while achieving comprehensive development of tourism and communities, improving community infrastructure, balancing community development goals, and affecting the effectiveness of community management in tourism destinations. In terms of tourism real estate, with tourism development as the main body and real estate as the extension, real estate enterprises are endowed with the tourism function to promote the development of tourism communities through the seamless connection between tourism and real estate. Market mechanism and competition mechanism play a leading role in promoting tourism community facilities and services to a relatively high level. In the actual management work, a large part is undertaken by the community property management enterprise which has the greatest ability to deploy community resources and has more direct contact with residents. To a certain extent, property management enterprise determines the management level of the tourism destination community and affects tourists' perception of the destination. In this model, as tourism attractions become more commercial and diversified, the market greatly alleviates the management pressure at the national grass-roots level.

(2) Existing problems.

First, the enterprise-led model operates on the basis of the market mechanism, and everything is based on the maximum benefit as the decision-making standard, which is easy to cause the neglect of tourism services. Relying solely on the market to play a role, it is easy to blindly pursue economic benefits and neglect to guard against market failure, that is, the market allocation of resources caused by monopoly, externality, incomplete information and other factors cannot achieve the optimal allocation of resources. Second, profit-oriented operators may not be able to objectively judge the priority of economic income generation and social responsibility. For some enterprises that cannot take the initiative to assume social responsibility, it is easy to lose the original intention and mission of building tourism destination communities in the pursuit of profits. Third, the development, utilization, organization and management of community resources cannot ensure that they pay enough attention to the sustainable development of community ecology and tourism, whether it is to "leave" after a short profit, or based on the long-term consideration of the sustainable development of the community, which depends on the attitude of tourism enterprises themselves. Without regulators to take good care of the legal system, it is difficult for tourism destination communities to go for a long time.

3) Community Autonomy Model

(1) Overview.

Community autonomy model is a management model of "weak government-strong society". The government does not directly intervene in community affairs but relies on community members to jointly manage public affairs. Through the formulation of laws and regulations, the government indirectly guides the community to absorb social forces to exercise autonomous power independently to make democratic decisions. First of all, in order to realize the harmony of the community and the equal distribution of interests, it is necessary to stimulate the subjective consciousness of the community residents. Community residents need to have a stronger sense of ownership and can actively express their demands to promote democratic decision-making in community affairs; secondly, the government is committed to providing environmental supervision and institutional guarantee for community governance after transforming its functions and delegating power; finally, community social organizations take the initiative to expand public space, strengthen the application of professional skills and improve governance performance based on consultation and cooperation.

(2) Existing problems.

The background of the formation of community autonomy model requires weak government capacity and more developed civil society, but Chinese environment management model is transformed from "strong government-weak society" to "strong government-strong society". Therefore, the realization of community complete autonomy has limitations. Even if the autonomy model satisfies the residents' desire for self-management and responsibility, the government is still the largest resource owner in

China, and the community cannot support the long-term development of the community simply by relying on the existing infrastructure conditions and natural resources, and also cannot be capable of providing public services independently at present. In addition, the self-management, self-service and self-education of Chinese social communities lack the mass foundation, the self-governance function is not strong, and there are widespread problems such as ineffective democratic elections. It can be said that the "soil" of community autonomy in China is not fertile. Therefore, the development of community autonomy model in China needs the government's policy support and resource input, so as to more smoothly absorb the participation of social organizations and residents, and achieve moderate community autonomy.

2.1.3 Tourism Destination Community Management Experience

Several main existing community management models have their unique advantages or disadvantages. The effective community management of tourism destinations can not only alleviate the contradictions of all parties, but also help to improve the vitality of community development, which is of great significance. Therefore, what we can do is to learn from the strengths and weaknesses of different management models on the basis of the complete construction of community hardware facilities.

1) Complete Infrastructure Construction is the Foundation of Management

Infrastructure construction is the cornerstone of tourism destination community development and an important guarantee for tourists and local residents to carry out tourism activity and live. Community as a tourism destination will be complete with the six key elements in tourism and its supporting facilities including beverage industry, traffic commuter network and hotel industry, consumer shopping, leisure and entertainment industry, scenic spot construction level, news media industry, information infrastructure network, bank financial system, medical treatment, etc. With the development of society and the progress of technology, we should also pay attention to the update of all kinds of hardware facilities, introduce modern information system technology, improve the function of tourism community, and create a comfortable, convenient, livable and healthy modern tourism destination community.

2) Build a Multi-center Governance with Balanced Interests

Tourism involves a wide range, which is a comprehensive and broad industry, tourism destination community management involves the interests of many parties. From the perspective of the previous management model, whether it is government-led, enterprise-led or community autonomy, there still are deficiencies to some extent.

Therefore, in the actual management, it is necessary to coordinate from multiple parties to promote the sustainable development of tourism destination communities.

Governance means that social management includes not only the government and social public institutions, but also civil organizations and various cooperative organizations. The responsibility initially undertaken by the government alone is gradually transferred to civil society, and its essence is cooperation based on market principles, public interests and identities. Under the guidance of the governance theory, a multi-center governance model with the government, community residents, tourism enterprises and tourists should be constructed, so as to effectively meet the interest demands of all stakeholders in tourism destination community. Polycentric governance has the following three characteristics: first, there is more than one stakeholder, including the relevant government departments of tourism community, tourism enterprise, community resident; second, all stakeholders cooperate with each other and form a model of operation with the same goal; third, all stakeholders hope to meet the demands of all parties on the premise of realizing the sustainable development of tourism in the destination community.

(1) The guiding role of the government.

Under the background of the reform of "delegating control and providing services", the role of the government in the management of tourism destination communities should be transformed from "leading" to "guiding", taking the road of service-oriented government, strengthening multi-party interaction with tourism enterprises, community residents and tourists, and standardizing the behavior in the governance of tourism communities. The government is the regulator of tourism development. In the process of developing community landscape and utilizing natural resources, the government should establish a scientific system, give full play to the role of industrial policies, and realize the coordination between economic and social development and ecological environment while improving the living conditions of community residents.

In guiding tourism enterprises, we should first make tourism enterprises in an open, orderly and fair competition environment through policies and systems. Second, we should cultivate enterprises' awareness of benign development and utilization of tourism resources. We should not take the way of "pollution first, treatment later". We should avoid malignant expansion caused by the short-term pursuit of interests, and establish a new development concept of "Clear waters and green mountains are as good as mountains of gold and silver". The government needs to build a timely feedback mechanism to understand local residents' views on tourism development guidance, actively listen to and respond to their requirements, master their ideological trends, and integrate their interest requirements and needs into the specific work of tourism destination community management. In addition, it is necessary to take measures to avoid some unreasonable and illegal acts of soliciting and blackmailing, which may damage the image of tourism destination, so as to effectively protect the interests of every stakeholder.

(2) The rights of community residents should be increased.

Local residents are the main body of the community, and they are most closely related to the local natural and cultural resources. Their support is crucial to the success or failure of tourism development. And in the future construction of tourism destination, community residents can be empowered from the following four aspects.

First, government departments should be open in the management process to ensure the right of speech of residents in the tourism community. At the community level the government should report for residents about the good of the people's livelihood, community construction and tourism development of policy information. Many residents organizations give opinions to the government departments in resources development and utilization, which should give full play to the community autonomy organization in ties with the masses, stimulate residents and community cohesion strength advantages. In addition, attention should be paid to the standardized management of tourism community consultation and co-governance organizations to ensure equal opportunities, effective procedures and efficiency of residents' participation in tourism community governance. Relevant consultation and supervision mechanism should be improved to ensure that residents can participate in tourism decision-making and have the rights to obtain benefits.

The second one is economic empowerment. First of all, families and individuals with low income and difficulty in employment should be targeted and supported by autonomous organizations of tourism communities. Residents with economic difficulties should be encouraged to actively participate in tourism services and production, so as to improve their income level and realize economic empowerment. Secondly, the development of social organizations in tourism communities should be cultivated. Through the introduction of project profits and social capital, residents in tourism communities should be given priority in employment, and the endogenous power to solve employment should be activated so that all audience groups can realize economic empowerment. Finally, the government and relevant departments should adopt the method of policy support and economy incentive. When residents' property is expropriated in tourism development, eligible residents can enjoy the policy of converting capital into share to ensure their equal status in the distribution of interests to realize economic empowerment.

The third one is psychological empowerment. The disturbance and influence of tourism development and planning on the life and environment of community residents, the excessive utilization of resources and the damage of public infrastructure caused by the surge in the number of tourists will all have an impact on the life and psychology of tourism community residents. There are two things we can do. On the one hand, we can strengthen the skills of tourism community resident education and employment guidance, such as holding the lecture and education activity with the local natural and cultural resources to make the residents inherit and carry forward the Hakka culture, strengthen the psychological sense of pride, and further seek education and training opportunities to improve employment and income situation; on the other hand, we should build a harmonious cultural environment, the management of tourism community cannot be completely guided by economic interests, it is essential to meet the needs of community residents, improve their living experience and enhance their cohesion.

The fourth one is social empowerment. Tourism destination community is a microcosm of macro society, community residents and their families should be encouraged to work together to create a successful tourism career, from individual to whole. Community residents and groups are encouraged to share the benefits brought by tourism and work together to create a harmonious social environment. Part of the income obtained can be used for community development, so as to improve community cohesion and maintain the balance between local ecology and environment.

(3) Participation of tourism enterprise.

Tourism enterprise refers to the tourism management practitioner in the community, the participation of tourism enterprise makes tourism destination market do research, release information, coordinate industry, creat image, etc. It also can effectively integrate the destination tourism products through the coordination and interaction among enterprises to promote tourism products and make the tourism destination "rise" and "go out". In addition, basic knowledge training and other activities of tourism enterprises can also provide employment information and help to local community residents, especially migrant workers, urban unemployed and college graduates.

In order for tourism enterprises to participate in community construction effectively, the government should pay attention to the adjustment of economic interests of tourism enterprises. First, it should select appropriate tourism enterprises according to the value of resources, so as to give full play to the role of tourism destination resources. Second, the government should use economic adjustment means of distribution of benefits to create favorable space for the development of tourism enterprises, because the market itself does not have individual marginal revenue subsidy and large resources of tourism enterprises. Government also should adjust, such as increasing funding, entitling to duty exemption or reduction, issuing small low-interest loan, etc., to ensure that tourism enterprises can obtain considerable profit from production and operation activity, and realize their own sustainable development. Finally, for the tourism enterprises that take the initiative to govern and protect the tourism environment and have good governance effects, the government should give subsidies in time to play an incentive effect.

(4) Restrictions of tourists.

Tourists are participants and experiences in tourism communities. Due to the temporary and nonresident nature of tourism, some tourists may bring their own bad habits to tourism destination, so they cannot consciously respect and maintain the local conditions, customs and cultural history of the tourism destination. Therefore, certain laws and regulations, media and public opinion should be adopted to restrict tourists so that they can respect local customs and promote cross-cultural understanding and appreciation through contacting with community residents in the process of tourism without affecting the natural environment adversely; after the end of tourism activities, the awareness of environment protection and cultural respect can be brought to real life to promote the protection of natural ecology and cultural diversity.

2.2 Promotion of Community Participation in Tourism Destination

In order to have a deeper understanding of community participation, this section first puts forward the connotation of community participation, and describes the relationship between community participation and tourism development, and then it talks about the type of community participation, and the last part is the stage of community participation in tourism development. On the basis of these understanding, combined with the current situation of community participation in our country, this book puts forward some countermeasures to promote effective community participation.

2.2.1 Introduction

Participation is a concept in sociology. It means to take part in, to participate in, to share, etc. In terms of scope, community participation is a part of the large system of public participation. There is widespread recognition of the importance of participation. In 1969, General Assembly of the United Nations issued *the Declaration on Social Progress and Development*, pointing out that civic participation is an integral part of the process of social development. *Extensive Participation* was published in 1971 and *Extensive Participation as a Strategy for Action and National Development at the Social Level* was published in 1981, which elaborated on community participation and reflected the strategic significance of community participation to community and national development. Tourism destination community is a unique social miniature, and whether residents participate or not even determines the success or failure of tourism destination development to a certain extent. Therefore, it is necessary to sort out the relevant content of community participation.

1) Connotation of Community Participation

Tourism destination of community participation is not only the ways and means of local government and non‑governmental organizations involved in community development process, but also refers to the community residents participating in the tourism development plans, projects and other kinds of behaviors and the process of public affairs and public welfare activities, which embodies the residents' shared responsibility and results for tourism destination community development. The subjects of community participation in tourism destination include four main social groups, namely, government organizations related to tourism, resident enterprises and legal entities, intermediary organizations (non‑profit institutions), and community residents (the most important subjects). The object of community participation refers to various affairs related to tourism development in the community, including political development, economic development, cultural development and social development centered on the development of community tourism. The psychological motivation of community participation is the spirit of public participation. The goal orientation of community participation is the development of tourism destination and human development. Community participation in tourism destination generally has the basic characteristics of universality, comprehensiveness, self-consciousness, autonomy, equality, relativity, hierarchy and dynamic development. Tourism is the pillar industry of the community's economic development, which supports the development of the whole community and permeates into various affairs of the community. Only the direct participation and governance of residents can cultivate residents' sense of community belonging, identity and community consciousness of tourism destination, and can effectively integrate and play various tourism resources of the community itself.

Since Murphy (1985), a major advocate of community participation, published his book *Tourism: A Community Approach* which makes community participation in tourism development become a research hotspot. And its importance has gradually been recognized by scholars at home and abroad. Akama (1996) believed that only by participating in economic, political, social and psychological activities can local residents fully share the benefits brought by tourism development and promote the sustainable development of tourism. Liza and Fallon et al. (2003) believed that only when communities participate in the infrastructure construction of ecotourism can various tourism reception facilities meet the requirements of ecotourism development and landscape ecology. Samantha Jones (2005) pointed out the importance of "social capital" in community tourism. Wen Jun (1998) emphasized the subjectivity of community residents in community development. Liu Weihua (2000) proposed that "community participation in tourism development" refers to incorporating the community as the subject of tourism development into the decision‑making and implementation system of tourism planning, tourism development and other major issues related to tourism development. Residents' participation in tourism mainly includes participation in tourism development decision-making, interest distribution and educational training.

Sustainable community is an essential element of sustainable tourism, and it is very necessary to get community support for tourism development, and local community participation is a very important way to obtain and maintain such support.

2) Types and Stage of Community Participation

(1) Types of community participation.

According to different classification criteria, community participation can be divided into different types.

① The willing of the participant.

According to the willing of participant, community participation can be divided into two types: absorbing participation and autonomous participation. Absorbing participation refers to the political system including community residents in the scope of participation through social mobilization. It is a passive participation model of "asking me to participate", which can be divided into two levels: obedience and compulsion. Autonomous participation refers to the active participation model of "I want to participate", which is characterized by the clear intention and active action of the participants. It can be divided into two levels of belief and distribution.

② The field of the participation.

According to the different areas of participation of community members, it can be divided into four categories: economic participation, political participation, social participation and psychological participation. Economic participation refers to the economic benefits brought by community and residents' participation in community tourism activities, such as providing food and accommodation which are shared among many families in the community and bring many visible improvements. Political participation refers to community residents participating in community development of destination tourism decision, which suggests that political institutions are fair representatives of the community collective interests and needs, and residents to community groups, including women, youth and the interests of other social vulnerable groups, or related tourism enterprises have decision-making opportunities. Social participation means that community residents and the collectivity share the benefits brought by tourism development, work together to create a civilized and harmonious social environment, and use part of tourism income to feed the community development. Psychological participation means that community members can improve their sense of accomplishment, self-esteem and self-identity through the participation of the first three items and the humanistic history and natural scenery of the community itself. Therefore, community members have a positive attitude towards the tourism destination community, so as to consciously build and promote the development of community tourism. In practice, this kind of division is used more often.

③ The organization form of the participant.

According to the organizational form of participant, it can be divided into two types: organizational participation and non‐organizational participation. Organizational participation means that community residents participate in community affairs through various regular organizations, such as residents representative meetings, residents' committees, volunteer groups, etc., which is suitable for communities with low awareness of residents' participation. Non‐organizational participation means that community residents voluntarily exercise their democratic rights or participate in community affairs without organization, such as neighborhood mutual aid, anonymous opinions or suggestions.

④ The level of the institutionalization.

According to the level of institutionalization, participation channels can be divided into institutionalized participation and non‐institutionalized participation. As the name implies, institutionalized participation refers to participation behavior supported by institutions, which can be carried out continuously and stably and promote the sustainable development of community tourism. Non‐institutionalized participation refers to the participation behavior without the support of the system. It may be huge, but it is easy to cause blind participation, and too hurried to last.

⑤ The contact form of participation.

According to the different contact forms between the participants and tourism development, it can be divided into direct participation and indirect participation. Direct participation refers to the participation directly involved in tourism development and directly benefiting from tourism development in the form of special accommodation reception, tourism commodity processing and sales, tourism transportation and tour guide. Indirect participation is not directly involved in tourism development activities, but to provide support for tourism participation, such as legal protection.

(2) Stages of community participation.

In the process of tourism development, community participation has experienced a process from simple economic participation to all‐round participation in economy, politics, social culture and psychology, from individual participation of residents to voluntary participation of the whole people. For this reason, community participation can be divided into four stages: individual participation, organizational participation, mass participation and full participation.

Individual participation means that community residents mainly engage in spontaneous and decentralized tourism commodity management and simple tourism services, and participate in a single form. Organizational participation means that community residents provide tourists with handicrafts, local specialties and other commodities, tour guides, transportation and other services in an organized way through community service agencies. The main form of participation is economic participation, and the goal of community participation is to obtain economic benefits. Mass participation refers to the active participation of foreign capital to build a large number of infrastructure and tourism service facilities, establish travel agencies, tourism companies and other service agencies, and participate in the formation of a complete tourism system. Community residents can operate independently or cooperate with foreign enterprises. Full participation has two meanings. First, participation is comprehensive, including tourism economic decision-making and practice, tourism planning and implementation, environmental protection, social and cultural progress, etc. Second, residents' participation is no longer aimed at employment and seeking economic income. Protecting the environment, maintaining traditional culture and seeking psychological satisfaction have become the needs and responsibilities of the community's own development, and the whole people consciously participate in the process of tourism development.

2.2.2 Present Situation of Community Tourism Development in China

According to Maslow's hierarchy of needs theory, people will seek higher-level needs only after the lower-level needs, such as physiological needs and safety needs, are satisfied. In our country, due to the influence of revolution and war, everything was waiting for prosperity in the early days of the founding of the People's Republic of China. As a luxury, tourism started relatively late, coupled with social, economic, scientific and technological constraints, resulting in many areas that need to be improved in tourism practice.

From the rise of tourism in the 1990s to the present in the 21st century, China's tourism industry has gradually entered the stage of universal participation, and has also developed a variety of types such as sightseeing tour, experience tour, health tour, community tour and so on. Tourism has gradually become colorful and personalized. However, in the process of community development of tourism destination, there are still some practical problems in community participation in tourism development, which are as follows.

1) The Form of Participation is Single and the Content of Participation is Simple

In China, most community residents participate in tourism mainly through economy participation. The purpose of participating in tourism activity is also to obtain economic benefit, increase income and improve their quality of life. Therefore, the form of participation is relatively simple, which is usually manifested as individual participation and part of the community organized participation. Generally speaking, it is still in the initial stage, and the degree of participation is not high. Most of them take families and individuals as units to participate in it individually and randomly, and the organizational form is relatively loose. The main content is to provide tourists with catering, hotel reception, transportation service and selling some local specialty, handicraft and so on. These business activities usually have less investment and higher income, so community residents have a strong willingness to participate. However, they lack awareness and ability to participate in some cultural and environmental affairs of the community, and they also lack a clear and full understanding of their position and role in tourism development and the impact of tourism activities on their production and life.

2) Uneven Distribution of Interests and Brain Drain

Undeniably, in the development of community tourism, the government has absolute advantages in information resources and management decisions, while enterprises are superior to the destination residents in capital, technology, market experience and other aspects, objectively making the participation of community residents gradually marginalized. In the early stage of tourism development, it often appeared that "who invests, who benefits". For residents who can only earn meager profits by working in scenic spots or selling small goods, the distribution of interests among the government, enterprises and community residents is extremely uneven, and the wealth gained from tourism is concentrated in the hands of a few people. In addition, when the interests of community residents conflict with the government or developers, the former is sometimes sacrificed, so as to safeguard the later, and the subject status of community residents is weakened again. Even though the local young people participated in tourism development in their hometown at the beginning, after a few years, they gave up returning to their hometown to start a business and turned to migrant workers, because most families faced closure due to various problems such as poor management and poor business, as well as lack of income and confidence for reasons such as business monopoly, resulting in the loss of talents in the tourism destination community.

3) Low Level of Residents' Participation

In the development of community tourism, the goal level of residents' participation in community activities is low. Residents mostly participate in the operation of specific affairs, especially temporary problems and cultural entertainment activities in the community, but rarely participate in decision-making and management. In some cases, residents passively participate in the formed decisions under the mobilization and persuasion of the community committee and the staff, or passively implement the decisions after the formation of the residents, the individual residents lack the obvious initiative. In addition, in tourism development, administrative departments and developers sometimes pay more attention to the opinions of tourism experts, but ignore the voices of aboriginal people.

2.2.3 Countermeasures to Promote Effective Community Participation

According to the practical problems of community participation in tourism destinations, in order to make the community play a real role in tourism development and promote sustainable development of tourism, it is necessary to cultivate residents' awareness of participation, strive to broaden the way of community residents' participation, establish a reasonable benefit distribution mechanism and an effective community participation decision-making mechanism.

1) Improve Residents' Awareness of Community Participation

First of all, through publicity, education and training, residents can change their ideas, eliminate their inner sense of community indifference, and stimulate their internal awareness of active participation and the behavior of understanding and supporting community construction, such as publicizing the positive significance of community participation, the construction of the community, the content of activities, so as to let them know that the interests of the community, the government, the collective, the enterprise and the individual are complementary, interrelated and mutually reinforcing. They also need to realize that tourism development is an effective way for them to get rich quickly, not only stimulating residents' enthusiasm for participation from the perspective of practical interests, but also letting residents recognize community development tourism from the heart, spontaneously creating an atmosphere of public opinion conducive to community participation, and enhancing the sense of responsibility and participation in community construction.

In addition, in order to make residents have a strong sense of participation in the sustainable development of tourism, it is necessary to carry out large-scale and vigorous tourism publicity and education activities, which must be national and regular. The idea of sustainable development of tourism should not only become a compulsory course in vocational and skill education and training of tourism communities, but also be integrated into mass media such as TV, radio, newspaper and Internet, so as to arouse the daily attention of all members of the community to the sustainable development of community tourism. Then, the government and its managers should make clear their own positioning, focus on planning, organization and coordination, policy support and financial guidance, and gradually cultivate residents' ability to organize themselves. Social committees should be grassroots self-governing organizations for residents to manage, educate and serve themselves. They should properly handle the relationship with the government, residents and various community organizations, fully protect the legitimate rights and interests of residents, and actively seek the combination of the work of social committees and the needs of residents. In the process of work, they should listen to the aspirations of residents, understand and try their best to meet their reasonable needs, so as to enhance the sense of identity of residents.

2) Expand the Channels for Residents to Participate in the Community

At present, due to the separation of ownership and management rights in many tourism destinations, a large amount of capital investment required for tourism development is generally introduced through investment promotion, as well as advanced technology and management, which is easier to achieve the rapid development of local tourism. However, due to the wide gap in economic strength, the main affairs of tourist attractions are often controlled by nonlocal enterprises, and the local residents have weak rights. Most of them participate in the economic activities of tourism in the way of individual operation, and the degree and level of participation are low, which is not very attractive to residents. In order to promote community participation in tourism activities, it is necessary to improve residents' participation ability and quality, and try to broaden the ways of community residents' participation.

In terms of participation ability, residents can only simply participate in the economic activities of tourism development, partly because of their own lack of culture, skills, quality and other aspects. Therefore, in order for community residents to fully and extensively participate in the development of community tourism, it is necessary to carry out tourism education and related skills training, such as the implementation of professional knowledge of tour guides, hotel reception etiquette training, and the popularization of tourism industry knowledge. It is also important to train them in foreign language, model of operation, hotel service, commodity development and other knowledge training, to improve the quality of community residents, so that they can better participate in tourism development. At the same time, it is necessary to strengthen the popularization of legal and environment protection knowledge, which helps residents deepen their understanding of the development of community tourism, and consciously maintain the tourism image and ecological environment. In practice, it can establish long-term cooperative relations with local colleges and vocational colleges or entrust tourism administrative departments and tourism enterprises to provide training activities for residents, adhering to the combination of long-term education and short-term training. On the basis of the improvement of residents' ability, the quality of community participation will definitely improve. Moreover, residents can be encouraged to establish joint-stock cooperative enterprises through the form of equity participation, and collectively participate in the development and the management of tourism. In this way, it can not only transform the operation model of "each fighting for its own" into joint-stock cooperation and group management, but also guide residents to take the initiative to participate in community tourism activities and the protection of natural resources and cultural heritage, and promote the high-quality and sustainable development of community tourism.

3) Establish a Standard Community Participation Benefit Distribution Mechanism

Residents have the closest relationship with local natural and cultural resources, and are the core stakeholders of tourism destination development and the key subject of community construction. One of the purposes of developing community tourism is to benefit local residents, and a reasonable benefit distribution mechanism is the fundamental guarantee of community participation in sustainable development of tourism. However, in some scenic spots, the form of community residents' participation is single, and they benefit little from tourism activities; in turn, the income of community residents in tourism development determines their recognition of community participation. Therefore, in the planning, operation and management of tourism destination, the interests of communities should be fully taken into account so that community residents can truly gain benefits from tourism development.

On the one hand, a diversified profit distribution mechanism should be established. Residents can participate in the distribution and operation by means of compensation in kind, monetary compensation, policy compensation, shares and dividends. On the other hand, local governments and management departments should create conditions to encourage and guide community residents to directly engage in tourist business activities such as guesthouse, restaurants, agriculture and retail, and gain profits from them. In addition, tourism service employment limited employment of community residents under the same conditions. It can also provide distribution channels for farmers' native products by integrating resources. For example, China National Building Materials Group has created a "Hebaodian" e-commerce platform, which provides a convenient and professional sales channel for farmers with the model of "Internet+Company+Cooperative+Farmers", but in practice, local community farmers do not know enough about this platform, and it is necessary to further expand publicity, integrate resources and give full play to its functions. In short, on the basis of giving consideration to the interests of local governments, tourism enterprises and community residents, it is necessary to let community residents get the most practical and full benefits, embody the principle of giving consideration to efficiency and fairness in the distribution of interests in tourism development, so as to improve the quality of life and maintain long-term enthusiasm for participation.

4) Establish a Decision-making Mechanism for Community Participation

In exercising its functions, the government should adapt to the reality and future trend of social development and change the inherent decision-making mechanism. Through the establishment of coordination and management institutions composed of stakeholders including local government, tourism enterprises, community residents and so on, the community residents can effectively guarantee the right of participation, discourse and decision-making in the development of tourism resources. The government shall, on the basis of respecting public opinion, formulate tourism development plans and operation management schemes. Community residents shall also have the right to set up tourism associations and other non-governmental organizations to supervise the development of tourism resources and the operation of tourism enterprises within the community, and have the right to protest against unreasonable development and the destruction of the ecological environment.

For community residents, if they want to be the main body of tourism development and truly enter the decision-making and implementation system of major issues such as planning and exploitation, the first problem to be solved is to change the current vulnerable status. Community residents should form community tourism organizations through democratic election and voluntary combination, integrate the strength of community members, participate in the management of tourism destinations, and communicate with local government departments and tourism developers on an equal footing in the name of community organizations to protect the legitimate rights and interests of the community. The mass nature of community tourism organizations determines that it should take the requirements and wishes of activities as the starting point of all work and activities, and represent and express the wishes of the majority of community residents. Its primary function is to protect the interests of community residents, mainly including the sharing of tourism destination management power and economic rights; moreover, the education function includes the cultivation of community residents' awareness of participating in tourism development and the improvement of community residents' cultural quality and science and technology management quality; finally, the function of economic construction, community tourism organizations through the establishment and improvement of democratic management systems, actively carry out rationalization suggestions, summarize the opinions of organization members, and review the developers of the planning and decision-making programs. In addition, community tourism organizations can hire relevant experts and scholars as consultants to provide guidance for organizational work, so as to ensure the scientific and rational nature of community policies and behaviors.

Chapter 2 The Community Management of Tourism Destination

Chapter Summary

Based on the definition of tourism destination community, this chapter mainly introduces several typical models of tourism destination community management and summarizes the experience. Tourism destination community management is inseparable from the community participation of various stakeholders. Therefore, on the premise of being clear about the basic situation of the community participation, this chapter introduces the development present situation of the community participation tourism in our country, then puts forward targeted and constructive measures to promote effective community participation.

Issues for Review and Discussion

1. What other problems and conflicts do you know about tourism community participation and how they were resolved?

2. Three models of community management in tourism destinations, which one do you think is better? Why?

Case Study

Participate Together and Get Rid of Poverty

Case Analysis

Tips

Government Crowdsourcing: A New Trend of Public Participation in Social Governance

Exercises

Chapter 3
The Tourist Management of Tourism Destination

Knowledge Graph

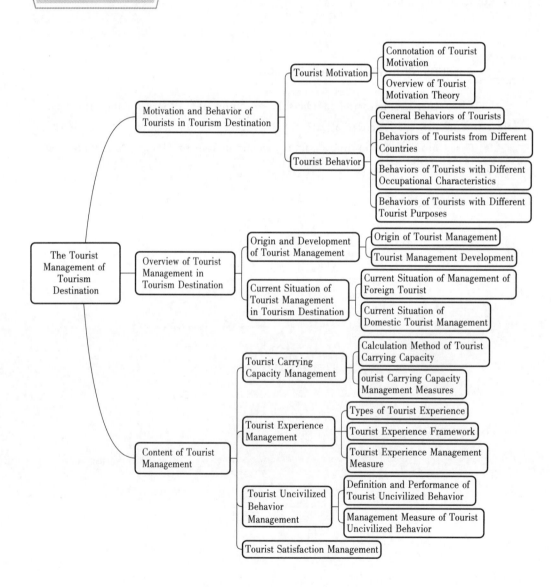

Chapter 3   The Tourist Management of Tourism Destination

Learning Objectives

(1) Master the connotation, general theory and psychological model of tourists' motivation.

(2) Understand the behavior of different types of tourists in the process of travel.

(3) Understand the origin and development of tourist management as well as the importantce of management at home and abroad.

(4) Master the specific content and measure of tourist management.

Technical Words

English Words	中文翻译
motivation of tourists	游客动机
behavior of tourists	游客行为
tourist management	游客管理
tourist carrying capacity management	游客承载量管理
tourist experience management	游客体验管理
tourist management of uncivilized behavior	游客不文明管理
tourist satisfaction management	游客满意度管理

Introduce Case

Intelligent Passengers Flow Management of Huangguoshu Scenic Spot in Anshun City

3.1 Motivation and Behavior of Tourists in Tourism Destination

Motivation is the cause of behavior and the internal psychological process that causes the behavior, it maintains the behavior and points the behavior to a goal in order to meet people's needs. Before deciding to travel, tourists must be motivated by a variety of motives, such as going out to relax, to explore wonders, to appreciate beauty. In order to better understand tourists' motivation and behavior, this section first proposes the connotation and relevant theories of tourists' motivation, the psychological model of tourists' motivation and the relationship between tourists' motivation and tourism operators'

behavior. Then on this basis, it introduces the general behavior of tourists, and distinguishes the special behavior of tourists from different countries, different occupational characteristics and different tourist purposes.

3.1.1 Tourist Motivation

Tourist motivation is one of the most important components of tourist behavior. Many scholars believe that tourist motivation is the decisive factor of tourist behavior, which directly affects tourists' choice of tourism destination.

1) The Connotation of Tourist Motivation

The purpose of studying tourist motivation is to explain tourists' various behaviors. Motivation is a kind of driving force. When there is a need, there will be a motivation to meet the demand. Everyone is trying to keep a balance of material, spiritual and social factors in their heart. When a need arises, this balance will be broken and must be restored by satisfying this need. Tourism marketers make tourists recognize the products and services they need through publicity and promotion, so as to meet the needs of tourists. Tourist motivation is complex and difficult to measure, but its study can answer many questions about the reasons for tourists' decisions and behaviors.

2) Overview of Tourist Motivation Theory

(1) Push and pull theory.

Most researchers believe that the motivation of tourists can be divided into push factor and pull factor. The push factor is the reason for tourists to travel, and the pull factor decides tourists to choose a specific destination. Gnoth (1997) thought that the pushing force is the internal power of tourists to meet their inner needs, and the pulling force is the cognition and preference of tourists to the tourism destination. In 1979, through in-depth interviews with several tourists, Crompton classified the social and psychological motivations of pleasant tourists into seven categories, including escaping from daily life, self-discovering, relaxing, showing status, returning to nature, improving family relations, and strengthening social interaction. At the same time, there are two cultural motivations: education and novelty seeking[①].

(2) Tourist motivation theory based on maslow's hierarchy of needs.

According to Maslow's hierarchy of needs (1954), human needs are completed in one level and one level needs to be satisfied before higher level needs can be generated. From low to high, needs can be divided into physiological needs, safety needs, belongingness needs, esteem needs and self-actualization needs. Based on Maslow's hierarchy of needs theory, Beard (1983) and Ragheb (1983) established the leisure motivation scale. Pearce

---

① https://wenku.baidu.com/view/a121e5f314fc700abb68a98271fe910ef02dae5c.html.

(1988) proposed the ladder of tourism motivation. He divided tourism motivation from low to high into five levels: relaxing, escaping or seeking stimulation (physiological needs), establishing connections with others (relationships), seeking status and achievement (self-respect and development) and self-realization.

(3) Social psychological model of tourist motivation.

The social psychological model of tourist motivation believes that the satisfaction brought by tourism can be the goal and reason of individual travel. This intrinsic reward can be classified as thrill seeking or escape from real life. Iso-Ahola argued that these two types of factors exist all the time and that at a certain stage one type of factor will be stronger than the other[1]. For example, a tourist may choose to ski in Colorado. The choice of vacation place indicates escape, but skiing also indicates motivation to seek fulfillment. Later, Iso-Ahola expanded the categories of tourists' motivation. Figure 3-1 shows how tourists escape from real life by abandoning personal worries and interpersonal barriers, and how they satisfy their self-reward by seeking stimulation through social interaction (challenge, learning and exploration) in tourism.

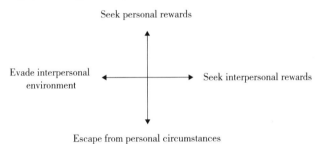

Figure 3-1　Types of escapism and thrill-seeking motivation in leisure tourism

(4) Tourist motivation and tourist operator behavior.

To meet the needs of tourists is the direction of action of tourism operators. In view of the motivation of tourists seeking novelty and diversity, tourism operators must strengthen the following three aspects.

① Highlight the uniqueness in tourism exploitation.

If a region wants to exploit tourism successfully, it must start with resources and products to explore its distinctive features, so as to attract tourists to seek new and different things. In the development of tourism, there are two points to pay attention to. First, we should try to maintain the original appearance, highlight the regional characteristics. For example, Tengwang Pavilion is one of the three famous buildings in the south of the Yangtze River, when exploited, it should highlight its characteristics different from the other two famous buildings. For instance, in the architectural design, it

---

[1] Iso-Ahola S E. Toward a Social Psychological Theory of Tourism Motivation: A Rejoinder[J]. Annals of Tourism Research, 1982, 9(2): 252-262.

should be restored as old, highlighting the characteristics of the only song and dance drama pavilion. Second, It should have the power of discovery and creativity in avoiding imitation and plagiarism by all means. In recent years, all parts of China have imitated the construction of various theme parks, resulting in the same theme park wtih the same modes and style, so failure is common.

② Highlight the novelty in tourism marketing.

Tourism marketing is a variety of efforts made by tourism operators in order to recommend tourism products to tourists and achieve exchange. To meet and guide the needs should be the core of tourism marketing. In today's tourism consumption concept, tourism market environment is changing, in order to meet the needs of tourists seeking new and different, tourism operators should try to highlight the novelty of tourism marketing. It includes two meanings: first, the new concept, which means tourism operators must constantly update the concept with science and technology marketing; second, the new method, tourism operators should take use of the advantages of traditional marketing methods. At the same time, constantly innovate marketing methods, and overcome the shortcomings of traditional marketing methods. For example, the traditional marketing of travel agencies is based on route marketing, due to the travel routes with no patentability, the rapid mutual simulation among travel agencies makes it difficult to highlight the novelty of travel agency marketing. Therefore, the new marketing method of travel agencies can be considered to do business marketing with appropriate route marketing in order to attract more tourists.

③ Highlight individuation in tourism service.

Standardization and individuation should be emphasized in tourism service. Standardization is the basis and individuation is the guarantee. Standardization emphasizes similarity, while individuation emphasizes difference. The motivation of seeking novelty, difference and individual differences of tourists determines that the tourism services provided by tourism operators must highlight individuation, and only by individuation can they attract tourists and provide them with quality service. Therefore, tourism operators must pay attention to two aspects: one is to provide different services for different tourists. For example, the travel services for business travelers mainly emphasize comfort and convenience, while the travel services for recreational travelers emphasize simplicity and economy; the other one is to provide different services to the same tourists at different times and on different occasions. For example, for a tourist who comes to the Forbidden City many times, the tour guide can consider providing services from different angles according to his/her mood and the "new and different" things he/she is interested in each time, so as to meet the needs of tourists.

3.1.2 Tourist Behavior

Tourist behavior is affected by a variety of psychological factors, which is not easy to give a clear explanation. However, all the tourist behaviors are completed under the control of their traveling consumption psychology and the influence of the traveling environment. Therefore, based on this common character, it can be seen that tourists' consumption psychology and tourism environment are the basic elements of tourist behaviors.

1) General Behaviors of Tourists

(1) Tourist behaviors from the perspective of tourist personality.

Psychologists in the study of personality make classification about the person's personality, one of the most famous and the most commonly used personality character is divided into introversion and extroversion. Few people have extreme personalities, most people are between these two extremes, one part of people are close to the introversion, another part are close to the extroversion, the rest are intermediate, and they are normally distributed. People with two personality tendencies have obvious different characteristics in tourism consumption behavior, as shown in Table 3-1.

Table 3-1　Tourist behavior of tourists with different personality tendencies

Introversion	Extroversion
Like familiar travel destinations	Like less traveled destinations
Like traditional travel activities	Enjoy new experiences and new pleasures
Enjoy fun and sports activities under the sun	Like new and unusual travel activities
Small amount of activity	A large amount of activity
Like traveling by car	Like traveling by airplane
Prefer fully equipped accommodation, such as family restaurants, tourist shops	Just general hotels, not necessarily big modern hotels and shops for tourists
All the schedules must be arranged in advance	Only basic arrangements are required, with greater autonomy and flexibility
Like familiar atmosphere, familiar entertainment projects, exotic mood to be less	Enjoy meeting and talking with people from different cultural backgrounds

(2) Tourist behaviors from the perspective of tourism process.

From the perspective of tourist, the tourism process includes the preparation stage before travel, the tourism stage at the tourism destination and the return stage after travel. From the point of view of tour guide service, tourists' travel process is only in the stage of tourist destination. This stage is the essential stage for tourists to travel abroad, and also the stage when tourists' tourism behavior is the most sufficient.

In the initial stage of arriving at the tourism destination, the tourists face with a completely unfamiliar environment, and they come into contact with people (including tour guides) and things for the first time in his life, so they feel that they have no relatives. They are not only the strangers in the evnironment but also do not understand the local conditions and customs. And there may be language difficulties (especially foreign tourists), climate, food discomfort and other problems. This situation, on the one hand, makes them feel curious, surprised and excited; on the other hand, there are some inexplicable unease. At this time, the behavior of tourists is complex with whispering, remaining silent, pointing, and even shouting. However, there is one thing in common, that is, they will place their eyes and hopes on the tour guide, hoping that the tour guide can understand their mood and can help them understand this strange environment, so that they can get a happy, smooth and safe travel life.

At this stage, as tourists gradually get familiar with the tour guide, get to know the destination situation and gradually adapt to the environment, tourists' uneasy mood begins to relax and their thoughts gradually become active. Their behaviors are mainly manifested in two aspects. First, they have a strong interest in traveling. They go to visit those beautiful, strange, ancient, magnificent natural landscapes, cultural relics, historic sites, modern architecture and folk customs. Second, the number of questions begins to increase, they eager to learn about the destinations, the local people and things they saw and heard, such as the Chinese population, birth policy, unemployment, transportation, environment, social insurance and so on.

As time passes by, tourists have a basic understanding of the destination situation and are more familiar with the tour guide. Tourists' psychological burden has been basically eliminated, and their initial sense of restraint, caution and strangeness no longer exists, which makes their personality more obvious. First, they pay more attention to the realization of their tourism goals, especially those tourists who hope to have a deeper understanding of a certain aspect through tourism. They will put forward deeper and broader problems, and will put forward a variety of reasonable and unreasonable requirements, hoping tour guides to help them achieve successfully. If they cannot achieve, they will express dissatisfaction. Second, they are more laissez-faire in words and deeds. Because tourists are more relaxed at this stage and tend to have a sense of mental paralysis, their memory and thinking ability will be dispersed or transferred intentionally or unintentionally. During the tour, they don't pay attention to the explanation of the tour guide as before, and some go their own way. People who are usually forgetful are more likely to lose things, and people who are usually loose are more likely to lack the concept of time, people who are usually lively become more casual and free.

Before the end of the tour at the destination, the psychological activities of tourists begin to become complicated again, and they will have a sense of urgency and anxiety similar to but different from the initial stage of arriving at the destination, so their behaviors are also diverse. Some people are eager to ask the tour guide to help them with unmet requirements; some people are homesick and look forward to reuniting with their families as soon as possible; some people are eager to go to the store shopping to buy some gifts to relatives and friends; some people worry about overweight luggage; some people are busy sending messages to relatives and friends, making phone calls, reporting the return date of travel and so on. In short, at this stage, the mind of the tourists is extremely scattered, busy with personal matters.

2) Behaviors of Tourists from Different Countries

Tourists from different countries, regions and ethnic groups are influenced by the traditional culture, customs and lifestyle for a long time. Therefore, when they travel to a foreign country, they cannot behave without the cultural characteristics of their own countries, regions and ethnic groups. For a certain same question, easterners and westerners not only differ in the way of inquiry or treatment, but also may involve taboos. Therefore, the book enumerates the habitual behavior of tourists in several popular tourism destinations in specific tourism activities, from which some differences can be glimpsed.

(1) American tourists.

Generally speaking, they are more cheerful, they have generous manners, they are fond of novels, they pay attention to practical benefits, they love to talk, and they have casual behaviors. In travel, they often start from personal preferences, regardless of others, think what they say, ask questions, make more requirements, regardless of the impact.

(2) British tourists.

Generally speaking, they are more reserved and calm, they have few words. In tourism activities, they see more, listen more and speak less. They do not take the initiative to express their opinions, but they are more punctual, disciplined and follow the arrangement of activities.

(3) French tourists.

Generally speaking, they are enthusiastic and informal, they like to talk with people, they are more optimistic, they love life and value freedom. In tourism activities, they are more active, and have unrestrained behavior, like free activities.

(4) German tourists.

Generally, they are more diligent, energetic, disciplined and clean, and they love music. In tourism activities, they pay attention to the contract and are particular about the quality of products and services.

(5) Korean tourists.

Generally, they have strong self-esteem and they usually pay attention to etiquette. During travel activities, they talk to each other with respect to avoid damaging their self-esteem.

(6) Japanese tourists.

Generally, they are studious and competitive. They pay attention to reality and advocate etiquette. For example, they have a strong collective concept and time concept; after the schedule is determined, it shall not be changed. Even if the time is very tight, they shall take a cursory look according to the schedule. They also love shopping, and are easily influenced by peers. However, their safety awareness is poor, tour guides need to repeatedly remind them to pay attention to personal and property safety.

3) Behaviors of Tourists with Different Occupational Characteristics

Tourists with different occupational characteristics have different travel needs and motivations, as shown in Table 3-2.

Table 3-2 Behaviors of tourists with different occupational characteristics

Occupational characteristics of tourists	Behaviors
Businessmen, financiers, senior professionals, etc.	Do not pursue fashion, like buying antiques, the demand for service accounted for a large proportion and high requirements
Nouveau riche, senior executives, founders of large enterprises, etc.	Pursuing luxury tourism consumption
Intermediate entrepreneurs, intermediate administrative personnel	Laying emphasis on the taste and style of tourism products
Non-managerial employees, blue-collar families, small business owners	Paying attention to the quality of tourism products for "value for money"
Ordinary worker	Focusing on instant gratification and pleasure
Unemployed and underdeveloped minorities	Little demand for tourism

4) Behaviors of Tourists with Different Tourist Purposes

People travel under the impetus of certain tourism motivation. Tourism motivation is reflected as a tourism purpose, and it is the pursuit result of motivation stimulating behaviors. Purposes play a direct role in restricting tourists' travel behaviors, so that people's behaviors in the process of travel revolve around the realization of tourism purposes. According to the classification of the World Tourism Organization, the purposes of tourism can be divided into six categories: sightseeing and entertainment for vacation, business or professional visit, visiting relatives and friends, religion or worship, medical treatment and health care and others. Within each category there are several species. Table 3-3 presents several different tourist behaviors for different tourist purposes.

Table 3-3 Behaviors of tourists with different tourist purposes

Tourism purposes	Behaviors
Learning tourism	Dedicated to professional learning, in-depth investigation of local society, visiting scenic spots, taking photos and buying souvenirs
Incentive tourism	Investigating the business of local peers, living a comfortable life, visiting scenic spots, taking photos and buying souvenirs
Special tourism	Investigating the business of local counterparts, conducting extensive exchanges with local counterparts, visiting scenic spots, taking photos and buying souvenirs
Health tourism	Treatment or convalescence of diseases, communication with doctors and fellow patients, purchasing medicines and health care equipment, sometimes visiting scenic spots, activities are light
Sports tourism	Participating in sports or fitness activities, visiting scenic spots, explorinng the meaning of life, taking photos, buying souvenirs

3.2 Overview of Tourist Management in Tourism Destination

With the rapid development of China's economy, society, culture, science, technology and the continuous improvement of people's living standards, tourism has been transformed from a "luxury" to an "ordinary commodity". In this era of national tourism, the management of tourists in tourism destination is a concrete measure to govern tourism according to law and promote the healthy development of tourism, an effective means to eliminate or reduce tourism accidents and ensure the safety of tourists, as well as an objective requirement to protect resources and environment and achieve sustainable development. Therefore, this section first reviews the origin and development process of tourist management, and then analyzes the current situation of tourist management at home and abroad from ancient times to the present. It can be found that compared with the mature theories and methods of foreign countries, there are still great deficiencies in tourist management in China. It is very necessary to develop and perfect our tourist management system on the basis of learning lessons from foreign advanced theories and combining with our specific national conditions.

3.2.1 Origin and Development of Tourist Management

Tourist management means that the operators and managers of scenic spots take tourists as the management objects, and use scientific management methods and techniques to guide, organize, restrain and manage the whole process of tourists' activities in the scenic area on the basis of fully understanding the behavioral characteristics of tourists in the scenic area, so as to realize the high-quality tourism experience of the tourists and the sustainable utilization of tourism resources in the scenic area.

1) Origin of Tourist Management

The research and practice of tourist management originated from the management of public parks in western countries due to the increase of visitors in these parks. In the early 20th century, a massive increase in the availability of cheap energy led to a boom in social prosperity and a huge increase in personal travel, which in turn increased the number of park visits. In the 1960s, public parks in the United States began to be overused, and concerns about their negative effects increased. In order to ensure that these resources are still available to the next generation, tourist management is becoming increasingly important. Therefore, it can be said that environment protection is the direct motivation of tourist management research and practice, and leads to the formation of "environment-oriented" tourist management model. With the popularity of mass tourism and the intensification of tourism competition, the quality of tourist experience is gradually being valued, and tourist management is an important means to improve the quality of tourist experience and increase tourist satisfaction. The satisfaction of tourist has thus become another important motive of modern tourist management.

2) Tourist Management Development

For more than half a century, tourist management has been emphasized and developed in many national parks in Europe and North America, and expanded to some common tourism attractions and tourism destinations in developing countries. People's understanding of tourist management has also experienced a process from the capacity of tourist environment to the number and intensity of tourist utilization to the control of tourist activities and tourist influence, and gradually formed a relatively standard tourist management framework at last. Tourism destinations with forestry background, such as nature reserves and forest parks, are the first to generate tourist management consciousness in China, and then affect other tourism destinations. Unfortunately, it has not been paid enough attention.

3.2.2 Current Situation of Tourist Management in Tourism Destination

It can be seen that tourist management originated and developed in the West and received great attention. As for China, due to the influence of national conditions, history and other reasons, there is still a certain gap with western countries. Today, with the vigorous development of tourism, we can promote the tourist management of touristm destination in China through a comparative analysis of the current situation of tourist management between China and the West.

1) Current Situation of Management of Foreign Tourist

As a management concept, tourist management has been widely used by tourism destination in developed countries. Since the 1960s, through theoretical research and practical exploration, a series of tourist management theories have been formed in western countries, such as recreational carrying capacity (RCC), recreational opportunity sequence (ROS), limit of acceptable change (LAC), visitor experience and resource protection (VERP), visitor risk management (VRM). In addition, some visitor management methods and models from the United States, Canada, Australia and other countries, such as visitor impact management (VIM), visitor activity management program (VAMP), optimized tourism management model (OTMM), are still guiding the tourist management of many similar tourism destination in the world[①]. They have established an indicator system reflecting the quality of visitor experience and resource condition, and established minimum acceptable standard, as well as management measure and monitoring technique to ensure that the state of the corresponding area meets the above standards.

2) Current Situation of Domestic Tourist Management

The theoretical research and practical operation of tourist management in China are relatively lagging behind, resulting in invalid or inefficient tourist management, which is extremely disproportionate to the rapid development of tourism in China. The current situation of tourist management in China is mainly reflected in the following aspects.

(1) Pay attention to economic benefit and ignore tourist management.

Tourism destination managers focus on how to attract tourists and promote consumption, but they do not take into account the negative impact brought by large numbers of tourists, and forward-looking sustainable development strategy. Some tourism destinations are driven by economic interests. In order to make tourists spend as much as possible, they ignore education of tourists' environmental awareness and civilized tourism,

---

①曹霞,吴承照.国外旅游目的地游客管理研究进展[J].人文地理,2006(2):17-23.

and even turn a blind eye to the uncivilized behavior of some tourists. In the absence of unified planning and sanitation facility, some tourism destinations are blindly developed in order to generate economic scale. Although managers of some tourism destinations have realized the importance of paying equal attention to both protection and development, they lack proper knowledge and operable measures and means in specific operation mechanism and management technology, especially in tourist management.

(2) Training management is not in place, lack of management awareness and methods.

Tourism practitioners are not stable, the quality of grassroots management personnel is not high and the training and management are not in place, so that the awareness and methods of tourist management are weak. Tourists take photos, play on cultural relics, or throw garbage in the scenic spot at will, but the some scenic spot management personnel are "accustomed" or "turn a blind eye" to such uncivilized behaviors, and rarely come forward to persuade and stop the situation. Travel agencies seldom publicize and prompt the outbound tour groups about the necessary cross-cultural differences and appropriate behaviors, and tour guides or team leaders do not take on the responsibility of reminding and supervising them during the tour. Some tour guides even publicize superstition and mislead tourists to touch cultural relics in order to bring good luck.

(3) Service facilities are not perfect, lack of scientific plannings.

Scientific and reasonable plannings directly affect tourists' behaviors and tourism activities. The uncivilized or destructive behaviors of tourists are partly caused by the lack of scientific plannings and imperfect service facilities. The location of the parking lot, the design of the travel path, the choice of the way of recreation and the guidance of the signage system are all closely related to the crowding of tourists and the impact on the environment. Unreasonable functional zoning will lead to negative impacts of tourist activities on the environment; the unreasonable number, location, distribution and opening of garbage cans, the insufficient number of toilets and rest facilities will lead to the increase of uncivilized behaviors.

(4) The management of scenic spots is chaotic and the relevant service system is absent.

If the management of scenic spots is chaotic, it cannot manage tourists. The chaotic management of the scenic spots is manifested in the lack of unified planning and management of vendors' stalls which may regardless of the cleaning of environmental hygiene. There is no requirement for food and drink consumption, and the commodity price in the scenic spot is higher than the market price, so many tourists bring their own food and drink and rest everywhere to eat. Vendors chase tourists to sell goods, occupy the land at will and charge for photos, and tourists are "ripped off" from time to time. The scenic spots charge is unreasonable, the situation of repeated charge is serious, cleaning personnel are not in place, garbage is overflowing everywhere, transport is not timely. Especially during "the Golden Week", many scenic spots are overcrowded, in the overload reception state, related services cannot keep up, resulting in a variety of inconvenience and dissatisfaction of tourists, uncivilized behaviors occurr frequently.

3.3 Content of Tourist Management

After understanding the basic theories, development, status quo and other relevant contents of tourist management, how to carry out tourist management has become an urgent problem to be solved. Therefore, this section proposes that tourist management includes but is not limited to the following aspects: tourist carrying capacity, tourist experience management, tourist uncivilized behavior and tourist satisfaction management, and puts forward specific measures for each aspect of management.

3.3.1 Tourist Carrying Capacity Management

Carrying capacity management of tourist is an important part of tourist management, which is a tool to ensure the personal safety of tourist, improve tourist satisfaction, promote the sustainable use of tourism resources and improve the service and management level of scenic spot.

1) Calculation Method of Tourist Carrying Capacity

(1) Instantaneous carrying capacity.

It refers to the maximum number of tourists that the scenic spot can accommodate at a certain point under the premise of ensuring the safety of tourists in each scenic spot and the safety of tourism resources and environment. The calculation formula of instantaneous carrying capacity C_1 is:

$$C_1 = \frac{\sum X_i}{Y_i}$$

X_i—the effective tourist area of the i scenic spot.

Y_i—the tourist area per unit of the i scenic spot, namely the basic space bearing standard.

Taking the Wulingyuan core scenic spot in Zhangjiajie as an example(as shown in

Table 3-4), according to the formula, the instantaneous carrying capacity of the Wulingyuan core scenic spot is 61,733 people.

Table 3-4　Effective sightseeing area and instantaneous carrying capacity of the Wulingyuan core scenic spot

Measuring the project	Area (m²)	Measure indicators (m²/ person)	Instantaneous environmental capacity (person)
Grade one walkway	56,227	2	28,113
Grade two walkway	52,020	3.5	14,862
Grade three walkway	41,900	5	8,380
Square	15,185	2	7,592
Viewing platform	5,573	2	2,786
Total	61,733 people		

(2) Daily carrying capacity.

It refers to the carrying capacity of daily space, which is the maximum number of tourists that can be accommodated by the scenic spot under the premise of ensuring the safety of tourists and tourism resources and environment in each scenic spot during the opening time of the scenic spot. The formula of daily carrying capacity C_2 is:

$$C_2 = \frac{\sum X_i}{Y_i} \times (T/t) = C_1 \times Z$$

T—the effective opening time of the scenic spot every day.

t—the average time spent by each tourist in the scenic spot.

Z—the average daily turnover rate of the whole scenic spot.

According to the survey and research, the average tourist time of the Wulingyuan core scenic spot is about 5.8 hours, so the turnover rate and maximum carrying capacity of the Wulingyuan core scenic spot are calculated as follows.

Summer: the opening time of the scenic spot is 11.5 hours, velocity rate=T/t=11.5/5.8≈1.98.

Therefore, the maximum carrying capacity=instantaneous carrying capacity×turnover = 61,733×1.98≈122,231person-times/day.

Winter: operation time of scenic spot is 9.5 hours, turnover rate=T/t=9.5/5.8≈1.64.

Therefore, the maximum carrying capacity=instantaneous carrying capacity×turnover=61,733×1.64≈101,242person-times/day.

Chapter 3 The Tourist Management of Tourism Destination

(3) Ecological carrying capacity.

It refers to the maximum number of tourists that can be accommodated in a certain period of time under the premise that the ecological environment will not deteriorate. Taking tourist routes as an example, the ecological carrying capacity assessment method is based on the entrance of scenic spots as the starting point, and the intersection of main tourist routes as the ending point. According to the field observation, the ecological environment destruction (conflict) of the main scenic spots in the tourist routes should be recorded(as shown in Table 3-5).

Table 3-5 Comparison table of ecological carrying capacity levels

Total carrying capacity level	Significant conflicts of concern (unit)	The degree of concern
Below standard	0	No more attention needed
Close to the standard	1-2	Need to increase low level concern
Standard	3	Need to increase medium level of concern
Higher than the standard	>3	Need to increase high level of attention

(4) Social carrying capacity.

It means that under certain time conditions, the public facilities around the scenic spots can meet the needs of tourists and community residents at the same time, and the impact of tourism activities on the cultural environment of the tourism destination is within an acceptable range. There are many indicators to reflect the social carrying capacity of a tourist area. From the perspective of service facilities, the accommodation reception capacity is the most basic index to reflect the social carrying capacity of the tourist area.

According to *the 2016 Statistical Bulletin of National Economic and Social Development of Zhangjiajie City*, the city has 3,199 hotels with 113,000 beds. With the improvement of social living standards, tourists will increase their requirements for choosing accommodation, and the acceptable reception elasticity coefficient is 1.5. Therefore, the amount of available accommodation is similar to the social carrying capacity, which is estimated as follows.

Social carrying capacity (accommodation reception capacity) =total number of accommodation beds (person-times/day×reception elasticity coefficient=113,000 person-times/day×1.5=169,500 person-times/day.

Carrying capacity can also be assessed in terms of visitors' perceptions of public facilities, service consumption, ecological impacts and cultural impacts. It can also be measured from the social benefits, economic benefits, ecological benefits, cultural heritage, interpersonal relationships, overall happiness and other aspects of tourism brought by residents.

(5) Psychological carrying capacity.

It refers to the maximum number of tourists that can be accommodated in a scenic spot under the premise that tourists have no adverse feelings and are satisfied with their psychological emotions during tourism activities in a certain period of time(as shown in Table 3-6).

Table 3-6 Evaluation index, mean and weight of tourist psychological carrying capacity

First-level index	Second-level index	Third-level index	Item average	Dimension average	Weighted value
Psychological indicators of tourists	Evaluation of social development	The traffic inside the scenic spot is very convenient	3.8	3.8	0.11
		The tourism supporting facilities are complete and convenient for rest	3.6		
		Scenic area public security is very good, no petty theft or arbitrary violence phenomenon	4.2		
		The scenic spot parking space is abundant and not crowded	3.6		
	Evaluation of economic development	Travel accommodation is convenient, sanitary condition is good	3.6	3.5	0.55
		The scenic spot is convenient and cost-effective	3.0		
		Local scenic area staff service attitude is good, do not cheat customers	3.9		
		Local tourism private personnel service attitude is good, do not cheat customers	3.7		
		All kinds of consumption price are reasonable	3.2		
	Environmental impact assessment	The scenic spot is picturesque	4.4	4.2	0.17
		Fresh air in scenic area	4.5		
		Scenic rivers and streams are clear and have good water quality	4.3		

continue

First-level index	Second-level index	Third-level index	Item average	Dimension average	Weighted value
Psychological indicators of tourists	Environmental impact assessment	The scenic area is quiet and peaceful with low noise	4.0	4.2	0.17
		The scenic spot maintains good environmental hygiene, and there is no garbage piling up	3.9		
	Cultural impact assessment	The local culture is distinctive and attractive	4.1	4.0	0.17
		Distinctive cultural resources have been effectively protected	4.1		
		Traditional culture has been inherited and carried forward	4.1		
		The local people are mostly civilized	4.0		
		Most of the local people speak Mandarin	3.9		

By investigating tourists in the Wulingyuan core scenic spot, calculating the mean values of each item and dimension, and referring to experts' evaluation weights of social development evaluation, economic development evaluation, environmental impact assessment and cultural impact assessment of tourists' perception, we calculated the psychological carrying capacity of tourists C_3 is as follows:

$$C_3 = 0.11 \times 3.8 + 0.55 \times 3.5 + 0.17 \times 4.2 + 0.17 \times 4.0 \approx 3.7$$

According to the standard of tourists' psychological carrying capacity, those with a score of 0-60 belongs to the state of overload and needs compulsory management; 61-80 points belongs to the acceptable range and needs auxiliary management; 81-100 indicates that tourists have strong bearing capacity and do not need too much management but need to maintain monitoring. According to the calculation, the psychological carrying capacity of tourists is about 3.7, equivalent to 74.5 points of the percentile system, which belongs to the acceptable range, indicating that the congestion of the Wulingyuan core scenic spot does not cause serious psychological pressure to tourists, and the development of tourism reception facilities is relatively perfect and mature.

2) Tourist Carrying Capacity Management Measures

(1) Peripheral diversion.

Peripheral diversion is to guide tourists to divert tourists before entering the tourism destination, using a variety of methods to control the time of tourists entering the park, so as to achieve the purpose of regulating the flow of tourists(as shown in Table 3-7).

Table 3-7　Peripheral diversion measures and purposes

Methods	Measures	Purposes
Tickets are reserved for limited time periods	Limited and time-by-period reservation management of tickets on the Internet	Predict the number of visitors and disperse the flow
Time-sharing adjustment of ticket price	Introduce ticket discount policy during off-peak hours in off-peak season and peak season	Release tourism demand and ease the pressure of reception during peak season
Develop secondary scenic spots	Develop new secondary scenic areas around it	Relieve pressure on core scenic spots
Issue forecast and early warning information	Release early warning information on the number of tourists to the public	Guide tourists to arrange tourist routes reasonably
Visit the scenic spot at different times	Through the booking and coordination mechanism of travel agencies, tourists are guided to visit different scenic spots at different times	Prevent excessive concentration of tourists and ease crowding
Scenic spots rotation vacation system	Implement rotation management for different scenic spots	Avoid overuse of resources

(2) Internal regulation and control.

Internal regulation and control refer to the maintenance of the internal order of scenic spot by improving the rationality of the use of the internal space of the scenic spot, so as to alleviate the crowding degree of the key nodes and avoid accidents(as shown in Table 3-8).

Table 3-8　Internal control measures and purposes

Methods	Measures	Purposes
Improve infrastructure	Improve the slippery and narrow roads in scenic spots	Ensure that roads are unobstructed and safe
	Improve trash bin design and layout	Alleviate the problem of garbage accumulation in scenic spots
	Expand the rest area, improve the outdoor rental facilities; provide sunshades, fans, etc., to improve the environment of the rest area	Improve the effective utilization rate of facility resources
Optimize the tour route	Make a reasonable combination of different sightseeing routes and core sightseeing spots	Prevent tourists from centering too much on the core tourist spots

Chapter 3 The Tourist Management of Tourism Destination

continue

Methods	Measures	Purposes
Optimize the tour route	Coordinate group tourist routes and alternate routes to visit various scenic spots	Avoid excessive concentration of group tourists at the same time and reduce the degree of crowding
Promote civilized tourism	Through tickets, brochures, radio and other forms to remind tourists to orderly tour	Reduce conflicts between tourists in line and waiting
	Increase professional guidance personnel	Regulate the behavior of tourists and ease the crowding of tourists
Area car guide	Open the interregional bus inside the tourism destination to realize the orderly diversion and route distribution of scenic spots	Use transportation to guide visitors to different routes

(3) Tourist guidance.

Tourist guidance refers to the regulation and methods to guide tourists' behavior and reduce negative emotions of tourists through public information and reasonable queuing methods(as shown in Table 3-9).

Table 3-9 Tourist guidance measures and purposes

Methods	Measures	Purposes
Publish real-time data	Release information on the number of tourists in each scenic spot inside and outside the scenic spot through display screens, broadcasts, display boards, etc.	Pass on the congestion of scenic spots and guide tourists to arrange the tour route reasonably
	Publish congestion information in congested areas	Let tourists understand the reason of congestion, reduce the anxiety and confusion of tourists
	Update scenic map and road sign	Ensure the accuracy of tourists' information and make tourists plan their routes reasonably and accurately
	Set up notices in advance at bayonets with special requirements, such as security checks, to remind tourists of specific requirements	Improve bayonet pass efficiency, reduce unnecessary waiting and potential conflict
Strengthen queue management	Arrange the staff to dredge and standardize the team of tourists	Maintain site order and ensure queuing efficiency

continue

Methods	Measures	Purposes
Strengthen queue management	Entertainment is provided in the queuing area	Relieve tourists' impatience in queuing
	Update ticket checking equipment and simplify procedures	Improve the efficiency of ticket checking and avoid congestion
Limited stay during rush hour	Limit the time visitors can stay on steep and dangerous trails during peak hours	Avoid tourists from huddling together and causing danger
Stop selling tickets and extend the validity period of tickets	When the number of tourists reaches the upper limit on one day, ticket sales and entry will be stopped immediately	Control the number of tourists and reduce ecological conflicts; improve the tourist experience

3.3.2 Tourist Experience Management

Tourist experience is a process in which tourists change and adjust their psychological structure by contacting the outside world. It is a sequential process realized by means of sightseeing, communication, imitation and consumption in tourism. The process of tourist experience is a continuous system, which is composed of a series of situations with unique and special meanings, forming a different behavior environment from people's daily life. Tourist expectation is the yardstick of tourist experience quality in the process of tourist experience. In addition to entertainment, education, escape, aesthetics, and empathy, the types of tourist experience are different. In order to create a comfortable and unique tourism experience for tourists, tourism products should be shaped according to the principles of difference, participation, authenticity and challenge.

1) Types of Tourist Experience

Tourist experience is divided into five categories, referred to as "5E", namely entertainment, education, escape, estheticism (aesthetic), empathy.

(1) Entertainment experience.

According to the different degree of participation, entertainment experience can be divided into three categories: ornamental entertainment, participatory entertainment, ornamental participation.

(2) Education experience.

It is a way of experience for the purpose of acquiring knowledge and technology, which is integrated into the whole process of tourism through learning.

(3) Escape experience.

According to the different reasons for tourists to escape from reality, they can be divided into three types of escape experience, that is, escaping from the familiar life style, getting rid of work pressure, and escaping from complex interpersonal relationship.

(4) Estheticism or aesthetic experience.

Beautiful things can make people feel good and happy. Although tourists have little active participation, they have a lot of individual feelings because they are deeply involved in the situation. According to the different aesthetic objects, tourists' aesthetic experience can be divided into three categories: natural aesthetic, social aesthetic and artistic aesthetic.

(5) Empathy experience.

It refers to that tourists externalize or transfer some of their inner emotions to others or other objects, and experience the happiness of tourism in the process of empathy. Tourists act as "another self", pursue the "ideal of self" and escape from the "reality of self" in a strange tourism environment.

2) Tourist Experience Framework

The tourist experience is the synthesis of all goods, services, and environments purchased or experienced. The visitor experience is a multidimensional structure whose core lies in the interaction between visitors and destinations or between community residents and other visitors. When creating the experience environment and situation, the tourism destination can produce the tourism experience only by putting the tourists in themselves and letting them actively participate in the experience production process.

As shown in Figure 3-2, the framework of tourist experience describes the composition of tourist experience in the context of tourism destination marketing, including two core axes of ordinary and extraordinary, cognitive and emotional, and four influencing factors: interpersonal interaction factors, physical environment experience factors, situational factors and individual characteristics.

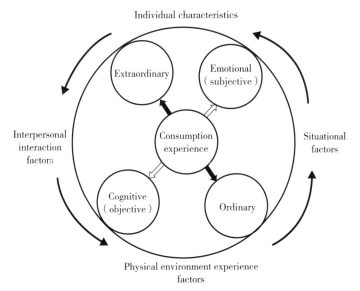

Figure 3-2 Framework of tourist experience

Different tourists are affected differently by these factors, so the experiences they get are also different. The conceptual framework is a multidimensional structure composed of internal and external factors, and combines the experience viewpoints of tourism enterprises and tourism consumers, which will jointly shape and influence the formation of tourist experience.

(1) Ordinary and extraordinary experience.

The first axis represents a continuum of tourist experience ranging from "ordinary" to "extraordinary". Peak (extraordinary) experience occurs when the travel experience reaches the highest position. Ordinary experience is routine experience in daily life and in normal environment and event, while extraordinary experience is completely immersive experience.

(2) Cognitive and emotional experience.

The second axis is the internal response of tourist experience, that is, the scope of experience changing from cognitive (objective) experience to emotional (subjective) experience. In every consumption experience, experience is an activity involving both cognitive and emotional processes. Tourists can construct their own travel experience in some ways. After understanding and evaluating the experience factors accepted, it is found that different people have different degrees of acceptance and absorption of consumption experience, which will induce different experience results.

(3) Physical environment experience and interpersonal interaction.

Tourist experience is the spontaneous interaction between physical environment and human. These factors can be controlled by tourism enterprises, through processing and improvement to meet marketing goals, attracting tourists physical environment, interpersonal interaction element and the sensory information to fully mobilize tourists senses (sight, smell, touch, taste, hearing), so as to effectively improve tourist consumption experience.

(4) Individual characteristics and situational factors.

Individual characteristics and situational factors are often out of the control of tourism enterprises. The creation and implementation of products and services in the same tourism destination are not always the same, and the tourist experience is not limited to the products and services themselves, but will be affected by the type and stage of consumption situation and individual characteristics. Situational factors related to the travel process, such as travel partners and destination characteristics, affect the acceptance and satisfaction of tourists to these experience elements. Every consumer will decide his/her willingness and ability to experience according to the situation and personal characteristics.

3) Tourist Experience Management Measure

(1) Create environment for interpersonal interaction.

Interpersonal interaction is an important source of tourist experience, and the significance of the connection between tourists and destinations often comes from the interaction between tourists and community residents, especially when these interactions produce interpersonal meaning, the experience is more profound. Tourism destination managers should actively plan and create opportunities and scenes for tourists to meet with other tourists and community residents, and promote the generation of positive emotions through creative images and promotional videos.

Managers can also create a social atmosphere for specific customer segments to enhance the tourist experience by having employees wear special uniforms, maintaining good body posture, making eye contact and smiling at customers.

(2) Create a multi-sensory atmosphere environment.

The integration of tourists in the physical environment with a variety of perceptual (vision, smell, touch, taste, hearing) information can effectively promote tourist experience. In tourism destination management, we should try our best to create a good atmosphere, including clean and tidy streets, fresh hotel environment, happy color scheme, and a well-designed, practical and visually attractive environment, which are all important ways to effectively enhance the experience of tourists.

(3) Create an emotional atmosphere.

Cognitive - emotional experience is the peak experience of tourists. Tourism destination managers should create all kinds of atmosphere to promote the generation of emotion for tourists, such as arranging some exciting nodes in the tour route, arranging some unexpected surprises for tourists in festival activities, and arranging some moving details in the service reception.

3.3.3 Tourist Uncivilized Behavior Management

Because of the temporary and remote nature of tourism, some tourists may bring their bad behavior to the tourism destination. In view of the uncivilized behavior of different tourists, managers should quickly make effective management measures to keep pace with the times, which can ensure that tourism destination resources are not damaged and safeguard the image of tourism destinations as well as the rights and interests of residents.

1) Definition and Performance of Tourist Uncivilized Behavior

The uncivilized behavior of tourist means that the behavior of tourist in the course of visiting does not conform to social morality, relevant law and regulation and damage the resources and environment of tourism destination. It will even cause adverse effect or irreparable loss. Its essence is a kind of behavior that violates morality or law, which will have a negative impact on tourism destination, society, and even the image of the country.

2) Management Measure of Tourist Uncivilized Behavior

(1) Strengthen the supervision and punishment of tourist uncivilized behavior.

Tourism destination should strengthen the construction of monitoring equipment in key areas, establish law enforcement teams in scenic spots in accordance with the law, jointly punish uncivilized behavior in accordance with the law, establish a blacklist system for uncivilized tourists, and increase the illegal cost of uncivilized behavior.

(2) Restrict the activity area and content.

Fixed-point protection measures should be taken to restrict the entry and use of tourists by means of nets, ropes, coverage, separation and copying in places where resources are fragile and uncivilized behaviors are easily triggered.

(3) Scientific layout of tourism facilities to create a high-quality tourism environment.

Tourism destination managers and government departments should restrict or guide tourists through reasonable planning of routes and layout of tourism facilities so as to provide them with a clean, hygienic, well-equipped and well-served tourism environment.

(4) Create civilized tourism atmosphere.

Tourism destination managers and government departments should strengthen social propaganda and education through new media technology to improve public awareness of civilized tourism, advocate civilized tourism behavior, and create a good civilized tourism atmosphere.

(5) Formulate management rules for uncivilized behavior.

According to relevant laws and regulations, scenic spots should formulate special uncivilized behavior management regulations according to the characteristics of resources, guide tourists to make correct tourism behavior through public announcements, education and explanation, and make tourists aware of the possible negative impact of uncivilized tourism behavior.

3.3.4 Tourist Satisfaction Management

Satisfaction is a kind of psychological state, which refers to a person's subjective evaluation of the quality of a relationship. It is the pleasure after the customer's needs are met, and it is the relative relationship between the customer's expectation of the product or service in advance and the actual feeling after the actual use of the product or service. Tourist satisfaction is the comprehensive score of tourists on travel itinerary, scenic spots, accommodation, catering, shopping, time arrangement, tour guide explanation, travel car and so on. Whether tourists are satisfied with a tourism destination or not affects the reputation, image, development prospects and tourists' willingness to revisit and recommend the destination.

Nowadays, tourism destination uses customer management information system to improve customer satisfaction and strive to remain invincible in the fierce competition. Disney, for example, uses modern digital technology to perfect its customer management system. Disney's customer management system consists of two parts: Pal Mickey and the customer information database. Pal Mickey is a toy doll equipped with a powerful infrared sensor in its nose, which can provide tourists with the shortest travel route tips and information of various entertainment activities, and is convenient for customers to make decisions in the process of playing. Moreover, Disney has also established a huge customer information database, which can be updated at any time. Disney staff can know the source of tourists and the specific situation of their visits at any time, and provide personalized services according to the specific situation. The Disney company has implemented the concept of "putting the customer first" very well in the Disney University training program. When they train employees, they start from the details to teach employees how to smile to tourists, how to greet tourists, and more importantly, to teach employees how to treat guests in a polite way and communicate with tourists happily and how to help solve the problems of tourists. Disney not only goes out of its way to help customers, but also listens to them. Disney treats tourists without distinction; it only cares about making every visitor happy and satisfied.

In a favourable environment where the industry system works well, French tour providers offer unique quality services to both domestic and international tourists. According to the the international tourist satisfaction survey, most of respondents are satisfied with their visit to France. In the planning and management of scenic spots, France does not sacrifice its precious cultural heritage for economic interests. On the contrary, through the development of tourism, its value can better serve the public, including local people, and at the same time strengthen the protection of historical and natural heritage. A tour of the Seine River, one of the most visited parts of Paris, offers a glimpse of France's creativity in conquering the world's tourists. In addition, French tourism practitioners also pay great attention to the application of high and new technology, and walk in the forefront of the electronic age. In the museums of all sizes, visitors can usually see the humanized application of new technology, which makes people's visits more interesting. Finally, well-organized cultural festivals also make France more attractive, and high-level local festivals can be said to blossom everywhere, such as the Cannes International Film Festival in the south, the Nice Carnival and the Avignon Festival, these events attract many tourists from all over the world every year.

Chapter Summary

To manage tourists in tourism destinations, the first step is to master the psychological motivation of tourists and understand the possible behaviors of different tourists in the process of tourism. Therefore, this chapter firstly defines the connotation of tourist motivation, makes a brief analysis of tourist psychology, and summarizes the behavior of different types of tourists. Then it traces back the origin and historical development of tourist management, and introduces the current situation of domestic and foreign tourist management. Finally, it summarizes and refines the specific content of tourist management and corresponding management measures.

Issues for Review and Discussion

1. What should we do when tourists do not obey the management of the scenic spot?

2. Talk about your behavior in the process of traveling in combination with your personality, occupation, tourism purpose, etc.

Chapter 4
Service Management of Tourism Destination

Knowledge Graph

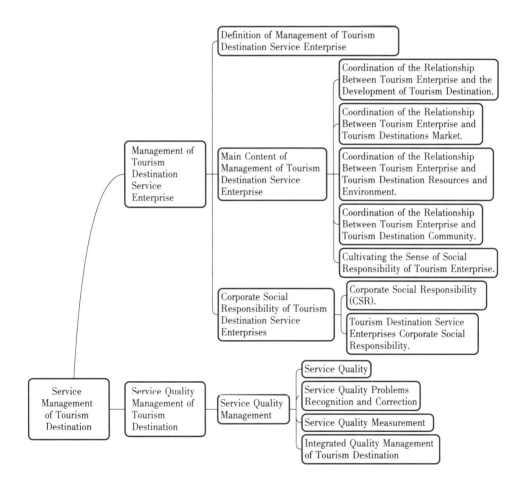

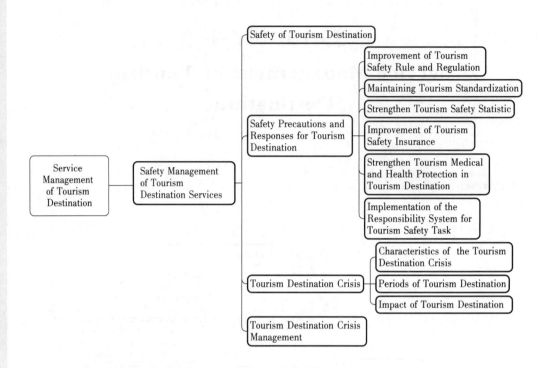

Learning Objectives

(1) Understand the basic concept of service management of tourism destination.
(2) Figure out the importance of crisis management of tourism destination.
(3) Cultivate the ability for excellent service for future career.

Introduce Case

Comprehensive Relationship Flow Management in the Phoenix Ancient City

Technical Words

English Words	中文翻译
motivation of tourists	游客动机
behavior of tourists	游客行为
visitor management	游客管理
tourist carrying capacity management	游客承载量管理
visitor experience management	游客体验管理
visitor management of uncivilized behavior	游客不文明管理
tourist satisfaction management	游客满意度管理

4.1 Management of Tourism Destination Service Enterprise

4.1.1 Definition of Management of Tourism Destination Service Enterprise

When tourism needs developed to a certain extent, organizations that provide tourists with related products and services to obtain social and economic benefits emerged. In the context of market economy, the types of organizations specializing in the provision of tourism products and services mainly exist in the form of a business, which is so called tourism enterprises. Hence tourism enterprises refer to those economic organizations that mainly aim at providing tourists with various products and services that meet their needs.

Compared with other types of enterprises, tourism enterprises are more resource-dependent, entrepreneur-led (small and medium-sized enterprises are more easily influenced by entrepreneurs) and are affected by market volatility.

Tourism destination service enterprises refer to local tourism destination enterprises which are regulated and coordinated by administrative, legal and economic means in order to achieve better economic, social and environmental benefits of the destination.

4.1.2 Main Content of Management of Tourism Destination Service Enterprise

1) The Coordination of the Relationship Between Tourism Enterprise and the Development of Tourism Destination

The development of tourism enterprises does not necessarily mean that it should bring the overall development of the tourism destination. Uncontrolled tourism development and tourism operation are highly likely to cause instability, recession and other negative phenomena in tourism destinations. Hence tourism destination administrations should play their role as planners, supervisors and coordinators. They should coordinate the relationship between tourism enterprises and the development of tourism destinations.

Firstly, tourism destination administrations should develop explicit and reality-dependent goals, and then make appropriate planning and institutional arrangements. Secondly, tourism destination administrations should clearly define tourism market access standards and operating norms. Thirdly, tourism destination administrations should carry out investment promotion, resource development and management of operation power, tourism projects approval, supervision and regulation of tourism enterprises market behaviors in accordance with corresponding plans and standards. Meanwhile, tourism destination administrations should supervise and urge the development model of tourism enterprises to innovate and reform in order to meet the requirements of changes in the market environment, and urge tourism enterprises management to proceed from the needs of the public. With such management measures, it ensures that the development of tourism enterprises is consistent with the development direction of tourism destinations and avoids blind and unnecessary development.

2) Coordination of the Relationship Between Tourism Enterprise and Tourism Destinations Market

Tourism is a highly competitive industry. In the market environment, tourism enterprises may appear short-sighted in pursuit of economic interests. Some tourism enterprises may take advantage of incomplete and asymmetric tourists information, and adopt unfair competition methods to attract tourists with inferior tourism products and low-cost consumption, which leads to the loss of tourism enterprises that provide high-quality products in the competition, resulting in "bad money drives out good" phenomenon.

Therefore, an important content of tourism destination enterprise management is to coordinate the relationship between enterprises and market. The specific performance is that, under the premise of abiding by the laws of the market, tourism destination administrations create a series of systems and norms to constrain tourism enterprises market behaviors. Through the creation of a series of systems and norms, tourism destination administrations regulate and stabilize the market, guide the healthy development of the market, create a fair, healthy and orderly tourism market.

3) Coordination of the Relationship Between Tourism Enterprise and Tourism Destination Resources and Environment

Tourism enterprises are closely related to tourism destination resources and environment. In the market mechanism, the blind pursuit of economic interests by tourism enterprises may have various negative impacts on tourism destination resources and environment, such as destructive consumption of resources and environmental pollution, which in turn affects the sustainable development of tourism destination.

Hence, a vital aspect of tourism destination enterprises management is to coordinate the relationship between tourism destination enterprises and tourism destination resources and environment. Tourism destination administrations need to actively adopt measures such as construction system norms, supervision and monitoring, publicity and education, punishment or compensation to urge tourism companies to abide by corporate ethics, adhering to the principle of minimizing environmental impact, and properly handling the relationship between tourism revenue and environmental protection compensation.

4) Coordination of the Relationship Between Tourism Enterprise and Tourism Destination Community

Tourism Enterprises are closely related to tourism destination communities. The excessive pursuit of economic interests by tourism enterprises may also have various negative impacts on the tourism destination communities, such as unfair distribution of income, rising price, traffic congestion, and noise disturbance. Hence tourism destination administrations should take measures such as institutional guarantee, information release, publicity and education to make tourism destination enterprises realize the importance of social responsibility, help enterprises understand the needs of the communities for corporate social responsibility, and jointly determine community improvement projects with enterprises. Tourism destination administrations also should promote enterprises to develop and participate in public welfare undertakings to alleviate social conflicts.

5) Cultivating the Sense of Social Responsibility of Tourism Enterprise

The key to coordinating above-mentioned relationships between tourism enterprises and the development of tourism destinations lies in cultivating the enterprises themselves. Moreover, it should help tourism enterprises take the initiative to assume the social responsibility related to tourism destinations, and promote tourism enterprises to take actions such as caring for resources and environment, and supporting local communities to alleviate the contradiction between the development of enterprises and tourism destinations. We will discuss more on cooperatate social responsibility in the followings.

4.1.3 Corporate Social Responsibility of Tourism Destination Service Enterprise

1) Corporate Social Responsibility (CSR)

Corporate social responsibility is a controversial but vital concept. The scope of the modern concept of corporate social responsibility actually encompasses everything from voluntary practices based on corporate discretion to moral obligations and corresponding activities in response to social expectations.

The essence of corporate social responsibility is to deal with the relationship between enterprises and society, that is, the content and object of responsibility. In terms of responsibility, corporate social responsibility roughly includes economic responsibility, legal responsibility and charitable responsibility. Objectives of responsibilities include managers, shareholders, consumers, employees, non-governmental organizations (NGOs) and other stakeholders. The differences in positions and interest demands of different stakeholders will lead to different expectations for corporate social responsibility.

As for the measurement of corporate social responsibility, it normally involves three types, respectively reputation index, content analysis and questionnaire method. The reputation index method is a method that obtains the ranking result of corporate reputation after subjective evaluation of various aspects of corporate social responsibility by experts and scholars from relevant departments or institutions. The content analysis method refers to the analysis of the relevant information and data of various reports or documents (including annual reports, social responsibility reports, official website articles, and news reports) disclosed by enterprises. The questionnaire method generally evaluates corporate social responsibility by implementing a prepared corporate social responsibility scale and collecting respondents' scores on the scale items.

2) Tourism Destination Service Enterprises Corporate Social Responsibility

Tourism destination service enterprises CSR shares some specialties. Firstly, CSR shares the characteristics of industry. For other industries such as manufacturing, social responsibility and environmental responsibility are often complementary to their economic and legal responsibility. However, tourism destination service enterprises often rely heavily on local resources and environment. Meanwhile, behaviors of tourism destination service enterprises will directly affect the sustainable development of tourism destination. Therefore, the core of tourism destination service enterprises CSR is social and environmental responsibility.

Secondly, the scope of tourism destination service enterprises CSR is wider and deeper. Compared with the relationship between the manufacturing industry and its stakeholders, the relationship between tourism destination service enterprises and their shareholders, tourists, tourism destination communities, ecological environment, government departments, etc., is more complex and close. As for tourism destination development, it is necessary to balance the interests of all stakeholders, combine economic development, nature protection, cultural heritage and other issues, and actively undertake the social responsibility of stakeholders (such as corporate employees, communities, ecological environment). Differing from manufacturing, tourism destination service enterprises should take responsibility to fulfill more aspects such as environment protection, culture inheriting, and community development supporting.

Thirdly, stakeholders have stronger bargaining power with tourism destination service enterprises CSR decision-making. For manufactures, managers' decision-making is mainly based on the principle of profits that is responsible to shareholders, and other stakeholders lack influence. However, the stakeholders of tourism destination service enterprises are more extensive. They have strong bargaining power, and can significantly influence the business decision-making and strategic implementation, which increases the difficulty of CSR implementation.

As for the tourism destination service enterprises CSR measurement, content analysis method and questionnaire method are the most popular, and a few studies have begun to use the data provided by some CSR index databases for analysis. In terms of tourism destination service enterprises CSR dimension division, it is mainly determined based on specific situations of researches.

From the perspective of corporate stakeholders, the government, investors, consumers, NGOs, communities, media, the public, and other competitive or cooperative enterprises outside tourism destination service enterprises, as well as other stakeholders like entrepreneurs, management decision-makers, and employees within tourism destination service enterprises will have a binding or facilitation role in tourism destination service enterprises' fulfillment of CSR. It can be seen that the CSR performance of tourism destination service enterprises will be affected by both external and internal factors of tourism destination service enterprises.

External impact factors mainly involve policy and regulatory environment, government administration, demands of external stakeholders, external supervision, market competition intensity, industry CSR self-discipline mechanism, and industry enterprise demonstration effect. The internal impact factors mainly involve the enterprise internal interest needs, the enterprise's cognition and attitude to CSR, the ability of the enterprise to perform CSR, the nature of the enterprise, and the level of enterprise ethics.

The above impact factors not only play their roles independently, but also often have complex mutual influence and interactive effect between them. For example, the policy and regulatory environment can affect the demands of external stakeholders, external supervision, and industry CSR self-discipline mechanisms. They also affect the CSR cognition and attitude within the enterprise, and then affect the implementation of CSR. The different CSR performance capabilities of tourism destination service enterprises will also lead to different demands and expectations of external stakeholders and different supervision pressure.

4.2 Service Quality Management of Tourism Destination

4.2.1 Service Quality

The word "quality" has different meanings in different contexts. The existing definitions of quality are mostly based on the manufacturing industry with the full consideration of engineering and manufacturing practice. Generally, it refers to whether the quality of the product produced is within the tolerance level compared with the set standard (such as the size of the welding gap in the automobile manufacturing industry). In the service industry, the quality refers to an operationally driven quality. It mainly considers whether the product or service produced is in line with the set standard, and it is closely related to the goals of improving productivity and reducing costs. Researchers pointed out that the nature of service requires different methods to define and measure. Services are generally intangible and multi-facted. These characteristics make evaluation of the quality of service much more difficult than that of tangible product. Since customers are often involved in the production process of services, it is necessary to distinguish between the service delivery process (also known as functional quality) and the actual output or result of the service (also known as technical quality). Customers compare their perceived service delivery with actual results, the conclusion is often referred to as perceived service quality. Hence, researchers generally define service quality from the fact that the customer's actual perception is consistent with expectation or the actual perception exceeds expectation.

Service consumption involves three main phases respectively: pre-purchase stage, service encounter stage and post-encounter stage. For pre-purchase stage, it involves need awareness, information searching, optional schemes selection, decision-making etc. For service encounter stage, it involves service contact, service experience and service consumption. For post-encounter stage, it involves consumer service quality evaluation, which play a significant role on future repurchase behavior and recommendation.

4.2.2 Service Quality Problems Recognition and Correction

Figure 4-1 shows the gap model on potential gaps within the service organization which may influence consumer service quality perception. It helps managers to point out and correct service quality problems from the perspective of the overall firm. For gap 1, it is the knowledge gap, which stands for the difference between what senior management believes customers expect and what customers actually expect. And for gap 2, it is the policy gap, which stands for the difference between management's understanding of customers' expectations and the service standards they set for service delivery. The managers have set up a policy decision that they will not deliver what they think customers expect. The reasons for setting standards lower than customer expectations are often based on cost and feasibility considerations. The gap 3 is the delivery gap, which stands for the difference between specified service standards and the service delivery teams' actual performance on these standards. The gap 4 is the communication gap, which stands for the difference between what the company communicates, and what the customer understands and subsequently experiences. The communication gap is caused by two sub gaps, respectively the internal communication gap and the external communication gap.

The internal communication gap refers to the difference between what the company's sales personnel and publicity deliver such as the product's features, service quality level and performance, and what the products actually behave. And the external communication gap, which also can be regarded as the over-promise gap. This gap can be caused by the sales evaluation of promotion, publicity and sales personnel, which can lead to over-promise for generating sales. The gap 5 is the perception gap, which stands for the difference between what is actually delivered and what customers feel they have received. Since customers are unable to accurately judge service quality, it may exist the gap. The last gap is the service quality gap, which stands for the difference between what customers expect to receive and their actually perception of the received service. In conclusion, based on the gap model, the first, fifth and sixth gaps stand for external gaps between consumer and the organization. And the second, third and fourth gaps stand for the internal gaps between different functions and departments in the organization.

The gap is unavoidable. However, in the process of service design and delivery, any gap that arises has the potential to disrupt the relationship between consumers and the organizations. Since the service quality gap (referred as the gap 6 in the gap model) is the most significant one, the ultimate goal of improving service quality is to eliminate or narrow the service quality gap as much as possible. For achieving that goal, normally, the organizations work to close the other five gaps shown in the gap model. The organizations need to identify causes of each gap and develop targeted strategies to estimate the gap and improve service quality.

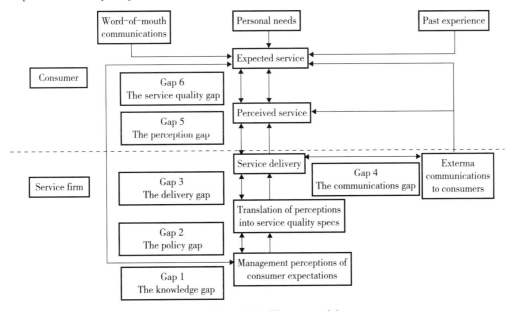

Figure 4-1 The gap model

4.2.3 Service Quality Measurement

Consumer central service quality standards and measurement methods can be divided into soft measure and hard measure. Managers need to determine whether improvement goals have been significantly improved after implementing changes. For soft measures, they don't mean simple observation, but they should be done through in-depth interviews with consumers. Soft standards provide the organization's employees with direction, guidance and feedback for meeting consumer satisfaction. It quantifies soft standards with the measurement of consumer perception and beliefs like service auality(SERVQUAL).

On the contrary, hard measures refer to features and activities that can be calculated, timed, and measured by inspection. These measures may involve waiting time for call centre or specific services, correction rates of orderings and payrolls and the efficiency of service failure recovery, etc. The development of corresponding standards often requires reference to the proportion of a particular measure achieved. The challenge for service providers is to ensure that operational measures of service quality reflect customer needs.

Excellence service organizations make uses of both soft and hard measures. These service organizations are good at listening to feedback and suggestions from consumers and frontline staffs (those who come into contact with consumers). The larger the service organization is, the more significant it is to create a formal feedback program using a variety of professionally designed and implemented customer feedback programs and research programs.

For soft measures, service organizations normally learn from consumer feedback. In the rivalry of marketing, the ultimate competitive advantage is learning and changing faster than the competitors, such as learning from consumers faster and turning knowledge into action faster than competitors. An effective consumer feedback system plays a vital role of fastening organization study. The goal of an effective consumer feedback system normally can be divided into three types: evaluation and benchmarking of service quality and performance, customer-driven learning and improvement, creation of a customer-oriented service culture.

The goal of evaluation and benchmarking of service quality and performance is to answer the following question "how satisfied are our customers", which involves knowing organization performance compared with competitors, whether special service investment has get return from consumer satisfaction, and where the organization should go in the next step. In general, the core of comparison with other organizations (like branches, teams, service offerings and competitors) is encouraging managers and service employees to improve their performance, especially in the situation of service consequences relevant with the compensation. Benchmarking on the other side doesn't mean simply to compare with organizations in the same industry, sometimes it should benchmark with companies from other industries providing similar services.

Customer-driven learning and improvement can answer the questions of "what makes consumer satisfied or unsatisfied", and "what advantages we need to remain and what disadvantages we need to redress". Hence, for guiding organization service improvement measurement, it needs more comprehensive and detailed process and product information, as well as to aim at higher service investment return.

The goals of creation of a customer-oriented service culture focus on consumer needs, satisfaction and the development of service quality culture. It contains a sustainable improving and changeable culture. For the above goals, organizations generally can achieve the first one well, but lose the chances of the rest.

Hard measures refer to the process and result of operation, such as normal operation time, service response time, service failure rate and delivery cost. In the process of complicated service operation, kinds of service quality measurements are used to record status of each service stage. Hard measures can show service performance with control charts. It is a simple way to measure long-term service performance against specific service standards with hard measures. Control charts can be used to monitor and present individual variables or overall indices. Control charts are visible and easy to identify the development tendency.

4.2.4 Integrated Quality Management of Tourism Destination

Tourism destination integrated quality management (IQM) is a model of destination management brought forward by European Union with considerations of related theories and thoughts of total quality control (TQC). IQM seeks to improve the continued satisfaction of tourists, the local economy, the environment and the quality of the local community life. The core guidance is consumer needs, and it aims to boost the quality and competitive advantages of tourism destination, gain comprehensive benefits of tourism and realize the sustainable development of tourism destination.

The characteristics of IQM are dynamic, comprehensive and proactive. Based on the Figure 4-2, tourism destination service quality management is constructed with five stages which respectively are identifying partners, deciding movements, executing actions, measuring effects, evaluation and adjustment. These five stages are equipped with dynamic management concept and are also dynamically changing in a continuous cycle.

For identifying partners, this stage requires a plan that lives up to its name and is supported by leadership authority. And leaders should also have appeals and influences to relevant collaborators and partners. For deciding movements, this stage requires to develop a necessary strategic direction according to the current situation. Meanwhile, the strategic direction should get supports from related collaborators and partners and should be under the supervision of leaders. As for executing actions, this stage provides several kinds of services for public and private organizations and implements all kinds of measures inside and outside system, which establishes the foundation. As for measuring effects, this stage mainly conducts satisfaction surveys on different target groups with a series of indicators and regularly measures the effect. For evaluation and adjustment, lessons are learned from the analysis results at this stage, and relevant recommendations are adopted and adjusted accordingly.

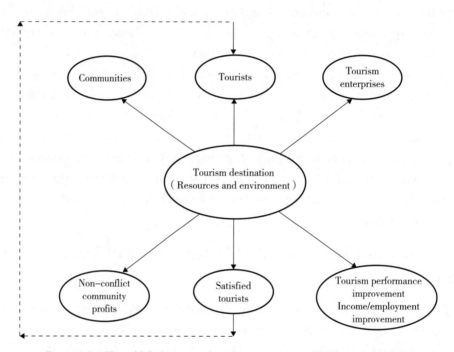

Figure 4-2　The model of integrated quality management (IQM) of tourism destination

The second characteristic of tourism destination service quality management is comprehensive. The tourism destination service quality management should contain four key factors which are tourist satisfaction, local tourism industry satisfaction, local residents' life quality and environment quality. The absence or weakness of any one key factor can arise a serious impact on the overall quality of a tourism destination. Hence, in evaluation dimension of service quality performance measurement, not only the quality of tourism products but also the comprehensive evaluation of tourism destination quality are considered. In terms of observation indicators, it includes not only quality perception indicators, but also quality management indicators and quality performance evaluation indicators.

By establishing service quality management benchmarks, each tourism destination can find its own shortcomings through comparison, learn lessons from the experience of service quality benchmarks, actively improve quality management levels, and improve tourist satisfaction.

Chapter 4 Service Management of Tourism Destination

The fundamental goal of integrated quality management is to enhance the competitiveness of tourism destination for achieving sustainable development. Therefore, policies and actions are needed to balance sustainable tourist needs, environmental needs, and the needs of present and future generations of local communities. For a tourism destination, many factors will have an impact on the tourist experience. It needs a "quality chain" with a series of links to ensure tourist final satisfaction. Hence, tourism destination managers need to consider the tourism destination from a systematic perspective, coordinate and manage the main stakeholders related to the tourism destination, such as tourism enterprises, tourism government departments, tourism and community organizations, residents, and these stakeholders should work together to achieve success.

The starting and ending points of achieving service quality management goals should be to meet tourists needs. The satisfaction and recognition of tourists are the keys to winning the market, creating value and realizing benefits in the long term. Quality only exists in tangible products and intangible services that meet the tourists needs and expectations. The service quality of tourism destination is not a rigid standard, but provides the products and services that tourists need. For this reason, it is necessary to carry out tourist market research, clarify the needs and evaluation of the existing tourist market, identify potential tourists' market needs, and provide tourists with services and products that meet the tourists needs rather than just meet the standards. In order to satisfy tourists, the various stakeholders who serve tourists must be satisfied. Only in this way can tourism practitioners, tourists, and community residents benefit from service quality management. The goals of integrated quality management are employees' satisfaction, tourists' satisfaction, positive social impact, and improved business performance. The concepts of integrated quality management contain full participation, whole process participation and all-round management. Full participation stands for that all those who provide direct services to tourists, as well as all personnel related to tourism, including tourism administrators, tourism enterprise personnel, related industry personnel, and local community residents. Whole process participation refers to the management of all factors affecting each link of the tourist experience. All-round management means that quality management is reflected in all aspects of tourism destination management, and the measures taken can be reflected in all activities of the tourism destination, including strategy formulation, marketing and promotion management, tourism destination information management, product development and improvement, creation and management of tourism destination atmosphere, etc. Meanwhile, quality management requires continuous improvement, which means that quality management has no end. It is not achieved overnight, but an uninterrupted, dynamic process of continuous improvement through innovation and learning.

4.3 Safety Management of Tourism Destination Services

4.3.1 Safety of Tourism Destination

According to Maslow's hierarchy of needs, safety needs are one of the most basic human needs, including the needs for personal safety, stability in life, and freedom from pain, threat, or disease. The safety of tourism destination refers to the personal, property and psychological safety of tourists during their activities in tourism destination. Tourists' perception of the safety of a tourism destination is a significant factor in decision-making. Establishing a safe tourism destination image and environment is crucial to tourism destination management.

For example, a man went "wild fishing" and died in the scenic spot, the travel company failed to fulfill its safety obligations, so it took responsibility for 30%[①]. In recent years, with the continuous occurrence of tourism safety accidents, the safety of tourism destination has begun to arise public attention. Government departments and relevant tourism managers pay more attention to the safety experience of tourists, and try to prevent and reduce safety incidents as much as possible.

Safety is the lifeline of tourism, the foundation and the basic element of tourism development in tourism destination. Paying attention to the safety and avoiding the occurrence of tourist safety accidents are of great significance to the normal development of tourist activities and the spread of tourism destination's reputation.

The major impact factors of safety concerned respectively are tourism environment, tourist behaviors and management failures. The development of tourism activities requires certain natural and social environment foundations. When there are unstable factors, the tourism environment will show an unsafe state. For environmental factors, natural disasters mainly include two categories: sudden natural disasters and long-term natural disasters. Sudden natural disasters include earthquakes, volcanic eruptions, subsidence, ground fissures, collapses, landslides, mudslides, storms, floods, tsunamis, sandstorms, toxic gas pollution and so on. Long-term natural disasters include drought, desertification, soil erosion, air pollution, plague, etc. For social environmental factors, the unsafe state of the social environment mainly comes from social and management disasters, including disasters or damages caused by wars, terrorist attacks, social unrest, criminal activities, fires, and mismanagement of tourist facilities.

---

① https://baijiahao.baidu.com/s?id=1732606985457309388&wfr=spider&for=pc.

As for tourist behaviors, some tourists deliberately pursue high-risk tourism behaviors including extreme sports, canyoning, adventure tourism, wilderness survival and other tourism projects which increase the possibility of accidents. In addition, tourists carried out some unsafe behaviors unconsciously leading to safety accidents, such as random throwing of cigarette butts, picnics in dry seasons, outdoor barbecues.

For management failures, on the one hand, the impact of management errors on the environment and behavior has aggravated the insecurity of the tourism environment. Large-scale tourism development has damaged the mountains, water bodies, atmosphere, animal and plant communities and other ecological environment of tourism destination to a certain extent, causing some natural disasters, such as landslides and rock collapses caused by construction excavation. On the other hand, management negligence and mistakes will also deteriorate the social environment and lead to various criminal activities, such as robbery, murder, extortion, burglary, fraud, pornographic services, gambling, etc. Based on the nature of the event, the security incidents in tourism destination can be divided into safe events and security events (as shown in Table 4-1). Safe events are unintended incidents that cause unintended harm to tourists, which may result from natural disasters, infrastructure problems, the environment of the tourism destination, and tourist behaviors and activities. For example, safe events may include floods, fires, infectious diseases, food poisoning, traffic accidents, and safety incidents related to visitor activities such as accidental slips, falls, cuts and burns, property damage. Security events mainly refer to incidents in which tourists suffer damage due to the intentional actions of others, such as terrorist attacks, wars, civil unrest or political unrest[1].

Table 4-1　Manifestation of tourism destination safety incidents

Category	Subcategory	Manifestation
Safe events	Natural disaster	Earthquakes, floods, hurricanes, volcanic eruptions
	Destination management related	Infrastructure issues (e.g. poor sanitation), safety standards for tourist facilities (e.g. fires, construction errors), traffic accidents (e.g. car accidents, air crashes), health problems (e.g. legionnaires' disease)
	Nature related	Hurricanes, typhoons, floods, extreme temperatures, etc.
	Tourists related	Extreme sports, hazardous leisure activities, failure to follow instructions, poor physical fitness, unfamiliarity with the task or environment
Security events	Crime	Robbery, assault, rape, kidnapping, murder, etc.
	Terrorism	September 11 attacks, London underground bombing, Kunming railway station terrorist attack

---

[1] Peattie S, Clarke P, Peattie K. Risk and Responsibility in Tourism: Promoting Sun-safety [J]. Tourism Management, 2005, 26(3): 399-408.

continue

Category	Subcategory	Manifestation
Security events	War	Syrian war, Russian-Ukrainian war
	Civil or political unrest	Thailand political turmoil

4.3.2 Safety Precautions and Responses for Tourism Destination

The core of safety management is prevention, which is mainly reflected in perfecting the legal system of tourism safety, establishing a perfect tourism safety education system and establishing a perfect preventive mechanism. Safety precautions require the protection of laws and regulations. On the premise of fully respecting the existing laws, it is the key to the safety management of tourism destination to formulate necessary safety precaution management rules. These rules should include preventive content, standards and procedures, as well as standards and procedures for monitoring and management. Corresponding regulations should be formulated to standardize the content and methods of tourism safety for tourists, tourism practitioners, community residents and tourism administrative departments. Tourism safety goes beyond the scope of traditional safety management. It is necessary to establish a multi-departmental safety prevention mechanism to ensure long-term and timely operation of safety work.

Tourism safety management and prevention play a macroscopic role in reducing or avoiding safety accidents. When tourism safety accidents occur, appropriate plans should be taken to actively deal with them. The basic tasks of safety management of tourism destination involve the following components.

1) Improvement of Tourism Safety Rule and Regulation

It is very necessary to stipulate the goals, contents and principles of tourism safety tasks based on the law, and to clarify the safety tasks responsibilities and authorities of various departments, positions and personnel, which can ensure that tourism safety tasks have laws and regulations to follow, establish a good order of tourism safety tasks, and constantly strengthen the management of tourism safety.

2) Maintaining Tourism Standardization

It stands for that tourism destination governments should strengthen the construction and implementation of various tourism safety standards, standardize tourism activities of tourists, standardize tourism services for tourism enterprises employees, and standardize the operation and management of tourism enterprises. The main purpose is to ensure the safety of tourist activities and to continuously improve the level of tourism management.

3) Strengthen Tourism Safety Statistic

First, it is necessary to strengthen the daily statistics of tourism safety and establish a database of tourism safety events in order to analyze and study tourism safety issues. Second, it requires to strengthen coordination and cooperation with public security, transportation, hospital, insurance and other departments to jointly establish a tourism safety information network. Third, it requires timely and appropriate disclosure of tourism safety statistics and information to the society, so as to attract tourists' attention and improve tourism safety awareness.

4) Improvement of Tourism Safety Insurance

Based on the relevant provisions of *Insurance Law of the People's Republic of China and Regulations on the Administration of Travel Agencies*, in 1997, the China National Tourism Administration (now renamed the Ministry of Culture and Tourism of the People's Republic of China) promulgated *the Interim Regulations on Travel Accident Insurance for Travel Agencies*. The regulation compels travel agencies to take out accident insurance for travel safety. Meanwhile, tourists should also improve their awareness of the prevention of travel safety issues. With considerations of the specific conditions of travel activities, tourists should purchase other travel insurance from insurance companies on a voluntary basis to reduce the harm and loss caused by travel safety accidents.

5) Strengthen Tourism Medical and Health Protection in Tourism Destination

In order to deal with the safety problems such as sudden diseases, epidemics, food poisoning, traffic accidents, and accidental injuries during the tourism process, it is an important part of the basic work of tourism safety to strengthen the medical and health protection in tourism destination.

6) Implementation of the Responsibility System for Tourism Safety Task

It requires improving the mechanism of the tourism safety management system, and clarifying the responsibilities, scope of work and corresponding rights of each department and unit of tourism safety management. It is necessary to ensure that all relevant departments assume the responsibility of the main body of supervision of tourism safety tasks, and implement various requirements of tourism safety tasks.

According to *the Implementation Rules for the Interim Measures for Tourism Safety Management*, tourism security accidents are mainly divided into the following different levels.

① A minor accident refers to an accident that causes minor injuries to tourists, or economic losses of less than 10,000 yuan.

② A general accident refers to an accident causing serious injury to a tourist, or economic loss of 10,000 yuan (including 10,000 yuan) to 100,000 yuan.

③ A major accident refers to an accident causing death or serious injury to a tourist, or an economic loss of 100,000 yuan (including 100,000 yuan) to 1,000,000 yuan.

④ A catastrophic accident refers to an accident that causes the death of many tourists, or the economic loss is more than 1,000,000 yuan, or is of particularly serious nature and has a major impact.

The general procedures for handling security accidents in tourism destinations need to follow the following steps.

① Report incidents in a timely manner. After a travel security accident occurs, tourists and tourism practitioners should immediately report to their travel agency and local travel administration. The local tourism administrative department shall report to the national tourism administrative department in a timely manner after receiving the report of general, major or catastrophic accident.

② Protect the scene and call for help. In the event of a travel security accident, the relevant personnel at the scene must cooperate with the public security organizations, strictly protect the scene of the accident, and immediately report to the relevant departments of tourism, public security, firefighting, maritime, medical, and emergency centers at the place where the accident occurred, requesting emergency rescue support.

③ Cooperative rescue and investigation. When a travel security accident occurs, local administrative departments, relevant business units and personnel must actively cooperate with public security, traffic and other departments to find out the cause of the accident. The organization should carry out emergency rescue for tourists and take effective measures to properly handle the aftermath.

④ On-site treatment. After a tourism security accident occurs, the responsible persons of the relevant tourism business units and the local tourism administrative department shall rush to the scene in time, organize and command and take appropriate measures in a timely manner. Major and catastrophic travel security accidents must be reported immediately, and efforts should be made to protect the accident scene.

It is well known that media can influence tourists' perceptions of tourism destination. Once a travel security accident occurs, mass media reports on the negative event will spread rapidly. The fear and anxiety of potential tourists increase, while the image and reputation of the tourism destination will be damaged. The frequency and depth of coverage of safety and security events will also diminish over time. However, once security accidents occur repeatedly, continuous media coverage and interpretation will further deepen and solidify the negative image of tourism destination. Therefore, tourism destination management organizations and the tourism industry should cooperate with the media to proactively convey more accurate and fair information to the outside world, cooperate with marketing methods, display the revitalized results of tourism destination, and try to balance and offset the negative image constructed by the media.

4.3.3 Tourism Destination Crisis

Crisis generally refers to those sudden events that are related to the life or death of an organization or individual. Scholars define "tourism crisis" as any event that poses a threat to the normal operation of the tourism industry and its related businesses, which can negatively affect the tourism industry's perception of a destination, and in turn can damage a destination's reputation for safety, attractiveness and comfort. The decline in the number of tourists and their tourism spending has led to a recession in local tourism and disrupted the continued operation of local tourism industry activities[①]. The United Nations World Tourism Organization (2003) defined a tourism crisis as an unanticipated event that affects tourist confidence in a tourism destination and disrupts normal operations. The Pacific Asia Travel Association (2003) defined a tourism crisis as a natural or man-made disaster with the potential to completely destroy tourism. In conclusion, tourism destination crisis can be defined as a sudden natural or man-made event that may threaten the normal operation of the tourism destination and the normal life of the local community, cause the tourism economy to fluctuate to a certain extent, cause tourists to have a negative impact on the confidence of the tourism destination, and have actual or potential impacts on the physical and mental health of tourists.

1) Characteristics of the Tourism Destination Crisis

Compared with the general crisis, the tourism destination crisis has the following characteristics.

(1) Sensitivity.

The tourism industry is highly dependent on the mobility of the population and the safety of the tourism destination. Any event that may have an impact on the movement of people and the safety of the people may form a tourism destination crisis. Therefore, the tourism destination crisis is in high sensitivity.

(2) Vulnerability.

Since tourism is a higher-level requirement of human beings, short-term travel restrictions do not directly affect the survival and development of human beings. When a

---

① Sonmez S F, Bachmann S J, Alien L R. Managing crises [M]. South Carolina: Clemson University, 1994.

crisis occurs, the first thing that people prohibit or give up is often tourism. It can be seen that the vulnerability of tourism destination in the face of crisis is obvious.

(3) Resilience.

Related to vulnerability, tourism is often a very resilient industry, and is one of the fastest industry to recover and it can even experience retaliatory growth after a crisis event. Therefore, tourism destinations are very resilient in the face of crises.

Based on the causes and impacts of crises, tourism destination crises can be divided into different types of tourism crises according to their causes, origins, evolution rate, market performance, duration and scope of influence, as shown in Table 4-2.

Table 4-2 Classification of tourism destination crisis

Dimension	Standardization	Classification of tourism crisis
Crisis formation	Causes	Natural crises, technological or man-made crises, health crises, conflict events crises
	Origins	Exogenous crises, endogenous crises, relational crises
Crisis impact	Evolution rate	Tornado crises, diarrhea crises, long projection crises, slow fire crises
	Market performance	Periodic crises, regular crises, sudden crises, operational crises of tourism destination
	Duration	One-time crises, recurring crises, persistent crises
	scope of influence	Destination-scale tourism crisis, regional-scale tourism crisis, national-scale tourism crisis, and international-scale tourism crisis

2) Periods of Tourism Destination

As an industry crisis, the development and evolution of the tourism destination crisis can be divided into five periods, as shown in Figure 4-3.

(1) Incubation period.

The incubation period of a tourism destination crisis is also known as the warning period. It is the brewing and forming period of the tourism destination crisis. The signs of the incubation period are usually insidious, not obvious, and not easy to detect. However, sometimes there are early warning signals shown during this period. If the crisis signs can be monitored and discovered in time, and timely actions can be taken, the occurrence of crises in tourism destinations can be effectively avoided or suppressed, and the losses caused by crises in tourism destinations can be greatly controlled.

(2) Outbreak period.

The outbreak period of tourism destination crisis refers to the period when the crisis changes from recessive to dominant, spreads rapidly, and causes harm to tourism and tourist destination. When the crisis is latent at a certain stage and the harmfulness is conceived to a certain extent, it will cause a crisis to erupt. The outbreak of the crisis is violent and the destructive effect is huge, which will bring large-scale damage to tourism organizations and individuals in a very short period of time. Meanwhile, this damage will rapidly deepen, accumulate and spread.

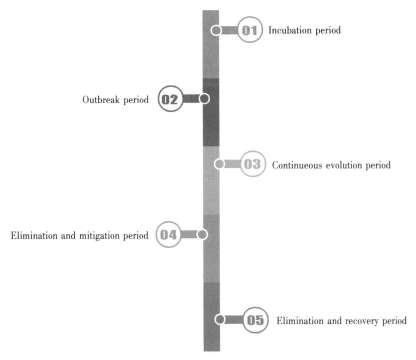

Figure 4-3　The development and evolution of the tourism destination crisis

(3) Continuous evolution period.

The continuous evolution period of the tourism destination crisis refers to the period when the crisis is still developing or worsening, but the speed of its evolution has slowed down and the degree of harm has gradually reached its peak. In this stage, compared with the outbreak period, the degree of harm of the crisis continues to deepen, the scope continues to expand, and the scope of coverage becomes even wider, posing a direct threat to the viability of tourism organizations and a comprehensive blow to the tourism system.

(4) Elimination and mitigation period.

The elimination and mitigation period of the tourism destination crisis refers to the period in which the degree of harm of the crisis has turned from the peak to the decline, the contradictions and conflicts are continuously weakened, the degree of harm and the scope of influence are continuously reduced, the crisis situation gradually slows down and can be effectively controlled, and the tourism system begins to fully recover.

(5) Elimination and recovery period.

The elimination and recovery period of the crisis in the tourism destination refers to the period when the factors causing the crisis have been lifted and the tourism system has been fully restored and entered the original or normal state.

3) The Impact of Tourism Destination

The impact of tourism destination crisis refers to the various consequences of crisis events on various tourism stakeholders in tourism destination. The impacts of the tourism destination crisis are multifaceted.

(1) The impact of tourism destination crisis on tourists.

Tourists are the subjects of tourism activities, and they are the most sensitive and direct response to the crisis of tourism destination. Crisis in tourist destination may cause tourists to suffer physical and mental harm or suffer property losses, and also affect tourists' confidence in tourism destination and tourism demand, which may also lead tourists to change their tourism behaviors, such as stopping or delaying tourism activities, seeking alternative tourism opportunities, etc.

(2) The impact of tourism destination crisis on tourism enterprises.

Tourism enterprises are providers of tourism products and services. When tourism demand is damaged in the crisis, the supply side will also be affected to a certain extent, such as performance decline or business termination, a large number of idle tourism facilities and supply capacity, and corporate funds. If the supply chain is broken and tourism resources are damaged, tourism enterprises will face greater operational difficulties or even bankruptcy. When the tourism destination crisis lasts for a long time and there is no supportive policy, tourism enterprises will face the survival crisis or even the possibility of reshuffling.

(3) The impact of tourism destination crisis on tourism industry.

Affected by the relevance of the tourism industry, the tourism destination crisis not only directly causes a serious decline in the tourism market, but also affects all links of the entire tourism industry chain, affecting the economic and social benefits of related industries, thereby affecting the tourism industry in a sustained stability and healthy development during the period.

(4) The impact of tourism destination crisis on tourism destination management organizations.

The impact of destination crises on destination management organizations often occurs indirectly. A crisis event in a tourism destination will negatively affect the image or reputation of the tourism destination, resulting in a decline in tourist attractions and tourist numbers, a weakening of competitiveness, and to a certain extent, affecting various aspects such as economy, society, and life.

4.3.4 Tourism Destination Crisis Management

Tourism destination crisis management is to avoid and mitigate the serious threats and losses caused by crisis events to the tourism industry, and restore tourism operations environment and consumer confidence by monitoring, early warning, controlling, preventing, emergency treating, evaluating, recovering and other measures of risk factors that may arise in the process of tourism development and operation, and conduct communication, publicity, security and market research and other aspects. It is a scientific management method and decision-making behavior for the sustainable, healthy and stable development of the tourism industry.

Tourism destination crisis is unpredictable and destructive. Effective monitoring and evaluation of crisis can play an early warning role in avoidable crisis. Meanwhile, the crisis that has occurred should be dealt with in a timely manner to reduce possible damages. Another purpose of tourism destination crisis management is to maintain normal tourist order, restore business environment and consumer confidence. Relevant plans for possible crisis should be made. Related stakeholders can handle it as quickly as possible, then restore market order, and stabilize consumer sentiment. Guaranteeing the normal tourism activities and tourists interests, and promoting the harmonious and healthy development of tourism destination are the goals of tourism destination crisis management. The key to tourism destination crisis management is to mitigate the negative impacts of tourism crisis, thereby protecting organizations and people from damage and disruption to the balance of tourism destination.

There are four main functions of crisis management, respectively preparedness, response, mitigation and recovery. For preparedness function, it refers to reducing disaster losses and strengthening disaster relief behaviors so that organizations and individuals can respond in a timely manner. The response function is designed to provide emergency assistance, reduce the probability of injury or loss, and restore operation quickly. The role of mitigation function may be manifested in emergency or before disasters, and the purpose is to eliminate or reduce the possibility of a crisis. It includes taking all appropriate measures to delay, eliminate or lessen the impact of the crisis. Relevant mitigation strategies include revising building codes, creating new or revised land-use regulations (such as flood zoning control), and launching public education programs (such as tsunami awareness campaign). The purpose of the recovery function is to help the system return to normal levels, and its strategies include damage assessment, crisis counseling, provision of temporary housing, etc.

Risk perception theory is one of the most popular theoretical foundations of tourism destination crisis management. Risk perception refers to the individual's perception and cognition of various objective risks existing in the outside world, and emphasizes the influence of the experience obtained by the individual through intuitive judgment and subjective feelings on cognition. When faced with the risk of sudden crisis events, both individuals and organizations have irrational behavioral choices, which seriously affects the effectiveness of risk response. Risk perception theory guides the construction of management strategies and crisis communication for emergencies by analyzing people's risk perception and behavioral responses in the face of emergencies, and provides theoretical support for a series of management issues under emergencies in tourism destination.

Risk perception often leads to adverse consequences after multiple amplification mechanisms of specific social amplification effects, causing the impact to exceed the direct impact of the disaster itself. Therefore, risk perception theory focuses on the measurement of different dimensions in the perception process. Psychological measurement of risk is mainly the measurement of subjective characteristics and subjective feelings of the source of risk. It believes that perceived risk can be quantified and predictable, and that risk has a unique meaning for everyone, which varies from person to person, that is, different tourists have different judgments on the crisis.

Risk perception theory uses a psychological paradigm to establish a disaster classification system, which can understand and predict the reaction of stakeholders in tourism destination when faced with risks, and quantitatively judge the current risks, expected risks and risk adjustment expectations of various disasters. Conceptual cognition of risk is mainly the measurement of subjective characteristics and subjective feelings of the source of risk. It believes that risk perception is a process of dynamic change. There are several different risk assessment standards in everyone's mind, and there are also a series of connections in people's deep cognitive structure and external event. The central process, the product of external observation, important thought and image information, surrounding environment and other factors will affect the perceived risk. It also proposes a conceptual social cognition of risk based on the individual's risk cognition process for emergencies in tourism destination.

Case Study

Guiding Opinions of the Ministry of Culture and Tourism on Strengthening Tourism Service Quality Supervision and Improving Tourism Service Quality

Exercises

Chapter Summary

The service management of tourism destination is a complex system and impacted by several factors, such as the level of socio-economic development, characteristics of tourism consumption demand, tourism industry structure, and stages of tourism development. The services of tourism destination are complex, detailed, human and experiential. In order to meet the public needs of tourists, the government and enterprises, social organizations, etc. conduct market actions through government actions or under government guidance. One of these actions is travel security, travel security has changed from traditional post-event compensation to all-round services before, during and after the event. With the rapid development of economy, tourists call for higher standards of service and safety. It calls for related departments and enterprises of tourism destinations preparing fully to meet what coming next.

Issues for Review and Discussion

1. What are stages of tourism destination service quality management?

2. What is the security and the safety of tourism destination?

3. Please describe the manifestations of tourism destinations safety incidents and list examples.

4. What are the basic tasks of safety management of tourism destinations?

Chapter 5
Tourism Destination Planning and Development Management

Knowledge Graph

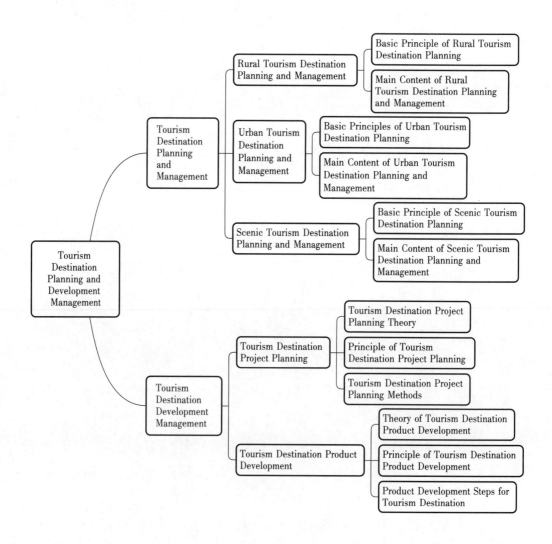

Chapter 5 Tourism Destination Planning and Development Management

Learning Objectives

(1) Understand and master the principles and contents of planning and management of the three types of tourism destination.

(2) Understand and master the relevant aspects of tourism destination project planning and product development.

(3) Be able to apply knowledge of destination planning and development management into practice.

Technical Words

English Words	中文翻译
urban tourism destination	城市型旅游目的地
rural tourism	乡村旅游
rural tourism destination	乡村型旅游目的地
tourism product	旅游产品
scenic tourism destination	景区型旅游目的地
tourism resource	旅游资源
tourism planning	旅游规划
tourism image	旅游形象
landscape heterogeneity	景观异质性
ecological sensitivity	生态敏感性

Introduce Case

The 14th Five-Year Plan for the Development of Culture and Tourism

5.1 Tourism Destination Planning and Management

5.1.1 Rural Tourism Destination Planning and Management

1) Basic Principles of Rural Tourism Destination Planning

(1) Natural ecology, harmonious development.

Rural tourism is closely linked to the natural environment, and similarly, rural poverty alleviation planning work needs to respect the natural ecological environment. Therefore, it is necessary to use the relevant principles of natural ecology to guide the development and construction of rural tourism poverty alleviation and emphasize the protection of the original natural environment. Ecology mainly includes two aspects of the meaning: the ecological balance and ecological aesthetic, that is, from the aesthetic point of view to reflect the characteristics of vitality and harmony. The implementation of poverty alleviation planning should ensure that the local rural tourism and natural ecological environment are integrated with each other to form a harmonious beauty. To make full use of the natural environment tourism resources, the theory of rural ecological balance system should be protected, and in the process of tourism poverty alleviation, the tourism resources should be moderately developed and utilized on the basis of maximizing the original local natural landscape characteristics, and efforts should be made to achieve the ecological harmonious development of the natural environment and tourism development.

(2) Rural characteristics, one village, one product.

The principle of one village with one product is one of the important principles for the countryside to carry out planning. As mentioned above, rusticity is an important feature of rural tourism, and likewise, the preservation of vernacular features should be the primary goal of rural tourism for poverty alleviation. In the planning process, we should pay attention to the protection of the local style and try to highlight the local characteristics. Through the excavation of the village's characteristic advantageous resources, the core tourism products are designed to support them and form the core attraction. At the same time, the village as the core tourism product is combined with the tourist consumption needs, and we need to develop and design a series of tourism services to go with it.

This will further enrich the structure of tourism products, expand the whole industry chain of rural tourism and realize industrial value-added. In addition, due to the different economic, cultural and social development of each region, different types of villages have different landscape characteristics. Therefore, planning rural tourism should be based on ensuring the benefits of poverty alleviation, and choose villages with unique appeal for tourism planning. "One village, one product" is the main issue that should be paid attention to in the tourism planning of poor villages, people should focus on the heterogeneity of regional tourism resources, to prevent the emergence of the same nature of the same model of tourism planning.

The characteristics of "one village, one product" can be highlighted through the design and development of different types of tourism products and tourism images, thus preventing homogeneous and vicious competition in the same area.

(3) Government-led, community participation.

Due to the special national conditions in China, rural tourism planning is mainly led by government departments. However, in the actual process, whether community residents can correctly recognize the importance of local traditional culture, and whether they can correctly inherit and protect local culture are the key issues in realizing rural tourism poverty alleviation work. Therefore, the principle of government‐led and community participation is an inherent requirement of rural leisure tourism planning. Community residents must penetrate into all levels of tourism poverty alleviation. On the one hand, local residents should participate in the whole process of tourism planning and supervise the implementation of various plans, emphasizing personal participation in the management of the links to achieve full participation of community residents; on the other hand, community residents should pay more attention to the protection of the ecological environment, as well as the protection and inheritance of traditional culture. At the same time, community residents are also important operators of tourism projects. For example, local residents can make and process traditional handicrafts and sell them to tourists, so that they can participate in the experience, which is important for inheriting and protecting local culture. An excellent rural tourism planning should be integrated with the ideas of local residents, meeting the needs of poor local residents, respecting the status of poor community residents, and fundamentally helping poor people to get out of poverty and become rich.

(4) Adapting to local condition and highlighting culture.

When carrying out tourism planning and construction, it should be combined with the actual development situation, specifically including the geographical location conditions, environmental resource analysis, tourism market analysis, market investment environment and other aspects of the actual analysis, according to local conditions, relying on the unique local natural geographical environment to explore the development direction unique to the village, to promote the planning as far as possible with the actual fit. It is important not to blindly follow the trend and copy without actual situation. For example, the infrastructure construction in rural areas is the basis for the survival of local residents, but these facilities are often influenced by the living habits of local residents and have great local customary characteristics. Therefore, the planning work should make full use of the local infrastructure that has been built, and if other tourism facilities need to be added, local construction materials should be used as much as possible in the construction, so that the new facilities and the local landscape can form a unified style. At the same time, rural folk culture display should also be extracted from traditional folk culture, so as to create the most pure and simple countryside that urban tourists desire.

2) Main Content of Rural Tourism Destination Planning and Management

(1) Strengthen resource survey and evaluation, and clarify development objective and positioning.

Before carrying out rural tourism destination planning, a reasonable assessment of local rural tourism resources should be made first. A comprehensive survey is conducted for local tourism resources, and based on relevant classification methods and evaluation systems, tourism resources are categorized and evaluated, and the planning content of rural tourism is clarified according to the actual distribution of tourism resources. Second, a comprehensive analysis of the market situation should be conducted. Through the basic information and data related to tourism destinations obtained from field research, the current development status of the tourism market should be comprehensively analyzed, and the future development direction of the tourism market should be predicted, and market segmentation and positioning should be carried out. Finally, we should comprehensively analyze the natural geographic profile, actual economic capacity, tourism market conditions and socio‐economic development of the tourism destination, and combine the previous resource analysis and market analysis to determine the advantages and opportunities of developing rural tourism in the tourism destination, while mapping out the disadvantages and difficulties faced therein.

In addition, it is necessary to clarify the development objectives, which can be subdivided into three categories: economic objectives, social objectives and environmental objectives. These three goals are not independent of each other, but a dialectical and unified relationship. Rural tourism destination planning should not only meet the needs of local residents to get rid of poverty and become rich, change the local socio‐economic development model, but also meet the actual needs of the tourist market, and at the same time ensure that the local ecological environment is not damaged, so as to achieve the sustainable development of the three goals of economy, society and environment.

(2) To promote the preparation and implementation of planning, clear implementation steps and priorities.

After the content of the plan is determined, it is necessary to organize relevant personnel to prepare a detailed implementation plan, clarify the steps and priorities of implementation, and promote the implementation of the plan preparation. The general work at this stage specifically includes: ①clarifying the basic scope of the plan; ②specifying the makers and executors of the plan; ③identifying the organizers and participants of the plan; ④establishing a coordination and guarantee mechanism for the planning process. After the preparation of the plan is completed, the results of the plan should be publicized, and the content of the plan will be more feasible and authoritative only after the results are fully understood by the public and considered by authoritative institutions.

After the plan is put into use, we should do a good job of timely tracking work, including the following three aspects: ①input and output ratio analysis: that is, statistical analysis of the benefits generated by the implementation of the plan, compared with the planning input; ②deviation evaluation and cause analysis: after the results of the analysis, compare with the expected target, such as most of the deviations, while analyzing the specific reasons for deviations; ③modification or re-planning of the plan: after finding out the actual reasons, if the deviation from the content of the previous plan is small, it can be adjusted by modifying and improving the planning scheme; if the deviation of the content is large and the planning scheme is obviously not in line with the actual local development, we should learn from the previous lessons and carry out re-planning. At the same time, in the process of feedback, we should pay attention to the change of villagers' attitude in order to ensure the villagers' enthusiasm.

(3) Establish Management and Supervision Mechanism, Clear Management and Supervision of the Subject.

No work is complete without a management and supervision mechanism, and a complete management and supervision mechanism can effectively ensure that the work is operating in the expected direction. Therefore, before the rural tourism destination planning, it is necessary to clarify the management and supervision subject, which can be the local government or tourism-related departments, or a special management and supervision team established. Moreover, the management supervision work is throughout the planning, such as before the planning, to manage and supervise the selection of the planning team; during the planning, to manage and supervise the relationship between planning and conservation; after the implementation of the planning, to supervise the operation of the planning, timely feedback, timely correction.

5.1.2 Urban Tourism Destination Planning and Management

1) Basic Principles of Urban Tourism Destination Planning.

(1) Scientific principle.

"Planning science" is the basic quality that planners must have. However, as a planning unit, although the general objectives and social requirements are generally consistent, in the specific measures and actions it often produces contradictions, especially in the environment, resources, land, cultural relics and other aspects of conservation and development. At this time, the planning unit must adhere to the truth, through extensive and in-depth communication to eliminate the gap in understanding, trying to convince the long-term development perspective to adhere to science and reduce losses.

(2) Political principle.

Maintaining unity with the local government on directional and fundamental issues is very important. Tourism has become the pillar industry of some cities, many city party committees and governments are very familiar with the city and love it, and strategic ideas are basically formed. Once the planning ideas do not match theirs, it will appear that planning is totally different from doing. Since this kind of planning does not have operability, it is a failure. Therefore, the planning preparation should be proposed through many exchanges, communication, argumentation.

2) Main Content of Urban Tourism Destination Planning and Management

(1) Define the city tourism development strategy.

The strategic focus and spatial steps of tourism development are clearly defined; the spatial structure of tourism development is clearly defined and land use is reasonably arranged; the destination marketing plan of tourism development is proposed through target market analysis; the framework of urban tourism construction is proposed in conjunction with urban planning, especially the arrangement of major infrastructure construction and priority development areas; the formulation of guarantee measures for the implementation of the plan are made, including tourism environmental protection and ecological construction, tourism management system, etc.

(2) Clear urban tourism planning, consider the individual needs of the city.

① Meet people's leisure needs.

With the continuous improvement of living standards, the demand for weekend vacations and sightseeing and leisure of urban residents has increased, and suburban tourism may become an important supplement to urban tourism and a new growth point of tourism economy. In order to ensure the healthy development of urban tourism, the tourism function of suburban areas must be included in the scope of urban tourism planning according to the scope and actual needs of suburban areas.

② Reasonable recreational facilities.

Reasonable recreational facilities have become a key element to be addressed in urban tourism planning, especially evening recreational activities which may be a key factor in a city's taste and core competitiveness in attracting tourists to stay, so that the planning of these elements which are not traditionally considered as urban tourism elements cannot be ignored.

③ Meeting individual demand for tourism products.

The city itself is a tourism product, and one of the measures for the city to become a tourism product is to renew and recreate public projects, and to transform public products directly into tourism products without affecting their original functions, such as characteristic streets, iconic architectural landscapes, bridges. Transforming public facilities such as city buildings, city square sub-centers, iconic city lots, city sculptures, and city greenery into tourism resources not only shares resources, saves capital investment, enhances the taste of the city, but also increases the length of stay of visitors.

(3) Pay attention to the cultural construction of the tourism city.

It is necessary to give constructive opinions on the style and pattern of the city. The city needs soul, and the soul is culture, which is regional and personalized. Architecture and roads are the main carriers of the city style, and architecture is the label of the city culture. The style of the city should be defined from the principle of the city as a tourism destination. For example, we can pay attention to the advice of geography or tourism scientists on the style and pattern of the city tourism planning. In addition, the city facilities and tourism facilities should reflect the cultural personality of this city to show the vitality of the city. The lobby and façade of the hotel, the architecture and decoration of the food and entertainment venues should be permeated with the cultural lineage of this city, both as a background to each other and each with its own characteristics. Urban tourism planning cannot ignore these background elements.

5.1.3 Scenic Tourism Destination Planning and Management

1) Basic Principles of Scenic Tourism Destination Planning

(1) The principle of wholeness.

When planning a scenic area, it is important to think about the tourist scenic area as a whole and to plan and design the tourist scenic area in a holistic way. The principle of wholeness needs to take the ecological wholeness and landscape heterogeneity into account. The content of ecological wholeness is that the landscape constitutes its own landscape elements, so that the landscape has its own uniqueness, while its ways of existence, goals and functions show a unified wholeness. Landscape heterogeneity refers to the variability that exists in a landscape system in terms of landscape element types, combinations and properties in space or time. The most important thing about heterogeneity is to carry out organic combination and protection of human landscape and natural landscape through the uneven distribution in landscape elements. To carry out comprehensive design according to the ecosystem, elements and functions of the scenic area, we should ensure the organic combination of ecological integrity and landscape heterogeneity of the tourism scenic area. As the landscape is constantly changing in form due to the development of time, this requires the tourism scenic area in the planning and design of the construction volume to be properly controlled, at the same time, requires proper limitation of the number of tourists in the tourism scenic area. The overall principle is the most important to ensure the stability and restoration of the landscape ecosystem.

(2) The principle of diversity.

The diversity of the landscape refers to the diversity of the structure and function of the landscape itself, with emphasis on achieving coherence among the elements within the landscape. The ecological environment of diversity should be closely combined with the heterogeneity of the landscape, so that it can play an important role in setting off the landscape pattern. Heterogeneity of the landscape pattern and the stability of the landscape pattern complement each other. The ideal planning and design of tourist attractions is to build a complex composed of various landscapes, which can improve the stability of the ecosystem and its natural resilience. The diversity of landscape mainly targets the connectivity structure of patches and landscapes, so the focus of the design is maintaining the diversity of landscape and creating diversity of tourism space.

(3) The principle of protection.

Tourism scenic spot in the design of the landscape is very different from the ordinary artificial landscape design, the use of artificial landscape design will not only make the original personality of the landscape disappeared, but also will bring serious damage to the natural ecological environment, and even will lead to part of the landscape be damaged and cannot be fully restored to its original state. Therefore, for important special tourism resources in tourism scenic area, such as important geomorphological landscape, biological landscape, human landscape (ruins, buildings and facilities) and other tourism resources, we should plan to take reasonable design means to protect.

(4) The principle of sustainable development.

Sustainable development is the base of the development of tourist attractions. Because the landscape is objectively irreducible, in the planning and design of the sustainability of the ecosystem of the development site, we should pay attention to the overall balance of the economic and social benefits of tourist attractions. Moreover, the scenic ecosystem has a certain degree of vulnerability, so in the planning and development of scenic areas, we should not only see the immediate benefits, but also pay attention to the long-term interests. We should always adhere to the development and protection of tourist attractions in parallel and pay attention to ecological and environmental construction and tourism attraction protection, so that the economy of tourist attractions can step into sustainable development.

2) Main Content of Scenic Tourism Destination Planning and Management

(1) Evaluation and analysis of scenic tourism resources.

The research of landscape resources is the first step in the development of scenic tourism destination planning, and it is also the preliminary work for the later evaluation and analysis of scenic tourism resources. A comprehensive evaluation and analysis of the current situation of scenic tourism resources can be carried out by conducting on-site investigation and data collection, including the characteristics of landscape resources within the scenic area, the affecting factors, the problems and challenges of planning and development, etc. By collecting these data and sorting out and summarizing them, it provides the right direction and reasonable basis for the scenic tourism destination planning. At the same time, in the background of the national full promotion of the main functional area planning, ecological sensitivity analysis of scenic spots is a strong support for the construction of the main functional area. Ecological sensitivity refers to the degree of influence of human activities and natural environmental changes on the ecosystem, and the level of ecological sensitivity is to determine the degree of damage to the ecological landscape in the case of external interference. The higher the ecological sensitivity is, the worse the ecological landscape stability of the scenic area will be; the lower the ecological sensitivity is, the better the ecological landscape stability of the scenic area will be.

(2) The construction of scenic landscape pattern.

Through the in-depth evaluation and analysis of the current resources, it is necessary to construct the landscape pattern for the whole scenic area. Scenic landscape pattern refers to the analysis and sorting out of the current resources of the scenic area, so that the primary and secondary structures of various elements of the scenic area can be derived and control methods can be proposed for the scenic landscape system as a whole. The main content of scenic landscape pattern construction is the target orientation and landscape zoning of the whole scenic area, and the scenic landscape pattern is controlled from the whole through the formulation of these two main contents. Based on the analysis of the characteristics of the scenic area and its own functions, the target system of the scenic area is established under the guidance of policies, and regulations and public participation, so as to clarify the target of the scenic landscape pattern planning. A scenic area will be divided into multiple functional areas by planning and design, and these divided areas need to reflect a unified cultural connotation or overall image appearance.

(3) Control of scenic landscape element.

Scenic landscape element, in fact, is a kind of expression of the traditional material form of the scenic area, and people, as the recipient of this form, have a self-cognition way of the composition of the scenic area. According to people's cognition of the objective world, scenic landscape elements can be divided into explicit and implicit scenic elements. Explicit scenic elements mainly refer to those concrete collections of scenic elements that tourists can see, touch and feel, such as natural landscape, space architecture; while implicit scenic elements refer to those abstract collections of scenic elements that tourists cannot obviously perceive, such as folk culture, tourist carrying capacity. Through reasonable planning and design, appropriate control of scenic landscape elements can make themselves converge with the aesthetic demand of tourists to the greatest extent, thus making the scenic spots more attractive and competitive.

5.2 Tourism Destination Development Management

5.2.1 Tourism Destination Project Planning

1) Tourism Destination Project Planning Theory

The direct foundation theory of tourism destination project planning is regional tourism development theory, among which, tourism destination development dynamic theory and sustainable development theory are the most significant guidance for tourism destination project planning.

(1) Theory of sustainable tourism.

Sustainable tourism is a theory of tourism development that was developed under the influence of sustainable development theory. Sustainable tourism has not yet formed a unified concept, but in 1990, at the Globe'90 International Conference in Vancouver, Canada, the tourism group action planning committee meeting resulted in a tourism sustainable development action strategy. It proposed that sustainable tourism should meet the following five objectives: ① to improve people's understanding of the environmental and economic effects of tourism and to strengthen their ecological awareness; ② to promote the equitable development of tourism; ③ to improve the quality of life in tourism host areas; ④ to provide tourists with a high-quality tourism experience; ⑤ to protect the quality of the environment on which future tourism development depends.

(2) Dynamic of tourism development.

Dynamic of Tourism development was introduced by laws in 1995, which argued that under the market-driven effect of the influx of tourists to a destination, local governments or investors should increase their investment in tourism facilities, infrastructure and hospitality industries in the destination to meet the consumption requirements of tourists and to reap the benefits of tourism. As the capacity of destination facilities and services increase, it is possible to accommodate more tourists, which requires destination marketing activities to aim at external target markets to win more tourists to visit. Driven by the economic benefits of tourism, investors and governments further invest in infrastructure, tourism facilities and hospitality services. The inculcation and promotion of tourism over a longer period of time have led to a series of changes in the social structure, economic pattern, landscape environment and even cultural quality of the destination.

2) Principles of Tourism Destination Project Planning

(1) Target market principle based on tourism resources.

Tourism resources of tourism destination are the fundamental factors on which tourism destinations rely to attract tourists, and are also the premise and material basis for the development of local tourism. In the socialist market economy, tourism destination development is an economic process, and the ultimate goal of tourism project planning is to make the destination find its target market successfully. An important part of tourism project planning is to conduct market research, and decide the configuration of tourism resources and the planning and construction of projects in combination with the local tourism resources of tourism destination. Without market research, tourism project, planning and development and construction are nothing and will fail.

(2) Principle of highlighting the theme image.

Regardless of the destination, in order to impress and appeal to the tourists when facing the target market, it is necessary to have a theme image that meets the consumer preferences of the tourists in the target market. A theme image is the soul of tourism project planning. Therefore, the principle of prominent theme image of tourism planning is the center of the whole project planning system. Without a prominent theme image, there is no tourism characteristics of the destination, and tourism destination will lose the attractiveness to the target market.

(3) Principle of characteristic innovation.

Features are the most important part of tourism destination project planning. The features planned for tourism projects vary according to the preferences of the target market demand. Therefore, tourism project planning itself requires innovation. Tourism is the activity of finding differences, and differences are fundamental to the attractiveness of tourism resources. Tourism project planning must be the creative new ideas and new concepts, it also should be changed with the specific situation and cannot be rigid. Even if others have successful models, we do not copy and apply, and we should make efforts to innovate, only then, the planning can be unique and have their own core competitiveness to achieve results.

(4) Principle of cultural connotation.

Culture is an intrinsic and essential attribute of tourism, and the occurrence of any tourism activity is dependent on the attraction generated by cultural differences. With the development of international tourism, more tourism projects have rich cultural connotation and the tourism market is more extensive. Tapping the cultural connotation is the key to enhance the taste of tourism projects and make them have a lasting vitality. Tourism project planning always targets consumer groups with specific cultural backgrounds in the target market that are basically the same in terms of language forms, thinking habits and values, so tourism project planning must be good at discovering and guiding the cultural motives behind tourism activities.

(5) Principle of feasibility.

Not all tourism destinations are ready for tourism project planning. That is to say, to carry out tourism project planning must meet or conform to some basic conditions, which is the basis and premise of project planning. Tourism destination location conditions, traffic conditions, resource conditions, environment conditions and economic conditions are the criteria to measure the feasibility of tourism destination project planning. Among them, economic investment feasibility is the focus of measurement. The investment in tourism project construction must have economic benefits and be conducive to improving the overall input-output efficiency of the regional tourism industry, in order to ensure that the investment project construction promotes the development of the regional tourism industry.

(6) Principle of system coordination.

In the tourism destination project planning, there are two systems of coordination. The first one is the tourism industry. It is a sub-system in the local economic system, and the multiplier effect of tourism development has obvious pulling effect on other sub-systems of the local economy, therefore, coordinating the relationship between tourism sub-system and other sub-systems can better develop the economy of the whole region. The second system is the tourism project planning itself, which consists of planning objectives, planning results, post-planning evaluation and other subsystems, and the reasonable and coordinated operation of each subsystem can finally complete the project planning. Therefore, the principle of system coordination is an important factor for the success of tourism planning, and it is necessary to use the ideas and theories of system theory to guide the project planning of tourism destination.

7) Principle of sustainable development.

Tourism sustainable development is proposed in the context of a series of crises and challenges facing the traditional tourism development approach. Because tourism resources are not infinite and the self-cleaning capacity of the environment is limited, in the modern society where the tourism economy is developing by leaps and bounds, it is more important to pay attention to the social and ecological benefits that tourism can bring. Therefore, the project planning of tourism destination must adhere to the principle of sustainable development, adopt a protective development approach, make the development of tourism resources compatible with the ecological environment, and carry out project planning for tourism destination on the basis of the permissible range of environmental carrying capacity and the right not to damage the fair use of tourism resources by future generations.

3) Tourism Destination Project Planning Methods

(1) On-spectrum analysis.

Tourism project planning is an innovative activity that requires the planner to have a wealth of knowledge and experience, a flexible mind and a sense of innovation. But this innovation is not the accidental idea of someone, there is a certain method. In tourism project planning, we can analyze from three aspects: resource, market and product. The resource aspect is mainly to evaluate the characteristics of tourism resources and to transform tourism products according to the investment capacity and market demand of the destination. The market aspect mainly analyzes the elasticity of tourism products and the product selection preferences of tourists. The product aspect mainly considers product innovation and spatial layout. Through the analysis of these three aspects, we can get the basis and inspiration for project planning from them.

(2) MIIR (market, project and resource).

This method is based on thought of the types of projects, according to the two major factors of market selection and resource constraints, gives the creative incentive(CI) method, also called the brain landscape method, which was first applied in a large number of foreign business management and achieved excellent results. The CI method is very simple and feasible, which is to use the power of the group, set up a creative group, strengthen the exchange and stimulation of knowledge, experience and inspiration among the group members, and collect their ideas to stimulate creativity.

(3) Project induction method.

It is actually one of the applications of the inductive way of thinking. It is a method of finding areas similar to tourism destinations in space and other tourism destinations at similar stages of development in time for project planning, and analyzing the degree of similarity and significance of these projects for this destination, so as to plan according to local resources, markets and other conditions.

5.2.2 Tourism Destination Product Development

1) Theory of Tourism Destination Product Development

(1) Tourism product life cycle theory.

Tourism product life cycle was first proposed by German scholar Walter Christaller in the study of tourism development in Europe. Canadian geographer Butler in 1980 elaborated on the theory of tourism product life cycle systematically which became a classic on this work. He believed that the tourism development of a place cannot be permanently at the same level, but evolves over time. This evolution generally passes through six stages: exploration period, participation period, development period, stable period, stagnation period and decline period or revival period. Butler stated that tourism attractions are not infinite and permanent, but should be viewed as limited and possibly non-renewable resources. Therefore, they need to be carefully protected and preserved. The development of a tourism area should be kept within the limits of a forecast-determined capacity, so that its potential competitiveness can be maintained for a longer period of time.

(2) Marketing theory.

The modern view of economics market is a network of buyers and sellers trading and disposing of a particular product. The tourism market is generally understood and defined from the seller's market, used in geographical terms to refer to the source of tourists, but can also go beyond geographical boundaries to refer exclusively to tourists of a particular type. Tourism market is the primary key issue to be solved in tourism product development and design. Tourism product development and design must study the selection of target market, tourism market forecast, marketing strategy, etc., divide the tourism place market into the first target market, the second target market, the opportunity market, etc., research the market to forecast the revenue, adapt to tourism demand, and produce marketable tourism products. At the same time, according to the market to develop tourism development strategy, it also needs to design tourism products, determine the grade and level of infrastructure and tourism facilities, determine the structure and quantity of tourism facilities, so that tourism products can be recognized by the market so as to produce economic and social benefits.

(3) Tourism products innovation theory.

Cui Fengjun put forward the tourism product innovation theory in 2002, whose basic ideas are as follow: the diversity and complexity of tourism product connotation and extension determine the multi-dimensionality of product innovation, which involves a variety of factors. It can be a kind of physical innovation that requires a lot of investment, or a spiritual creativity. The latter is undoubtedly more meaningful. It includes not only the optimization of tourism lines, tourism projects and product structures, but also the improvement of service quality, the increase of product types, the enhancement of product brands, the improvement of the general tourism environment, and the construction of tourism images. Dynamic process innovation adheres to the market-oriented without changing the product itself, re-understands and redesigns the process of product production to more effectively meet the needs of consumers as the starting point, constantly updates and regenerates its attractiveness factors and emphasizes the adaptability of the process to the market. Innovation of tourism products, that is, the creative development of products and competitive development, in essence, are to create demand and dig out the deeper potential of something. Innovation drives demand and guides consumer trend.

2) The Principles of Tourism Destination Product Development

In order to avoid the blindness and arbitrariness of tourism product design and development, tourism product design and development need some general principles. Only in this way can our development and design be holistic and forward-looking, and our tourism marketing can be recognized by the target market.

(1) Market-oriented principle.

Tourism product development and design must be market-oriented, with market demand as the starting point. It specifically contains two layers of meaning: one is the tourism market positioning, the second is the target market demand situation analysis. Firstly, the development of any tourism product cannot cater to the needs of all tourists, so it is very necessary for the designer of tourism product development to determine the main source market of the product by combining the local socio-economic development and the current development trend of tourism, so that the development and design of tourism products can have a strong target. Secondly, on the basis of the target market, the product developer also needs to further grasp the target market demand content, scale grade, level and development trend, so as to develop and design the right tourism products to achieve the expected economic benefits.

(2) Comprehensive benefit principle.

The development and design of tourism products require a large amount of capital investment, so it is always important to place a high priority on improving economic benefits in the development process. However, due to the cultural attributes of tourism products that differ from general material products, we need to not only ensure that tourism enterprises can obtain better economic benefits, but also emphasize the social and ecological benefits, and strive to improve the comprehensive benefits of the tourist site at the same time.

(3) Characteristic principle.

Tourism products, whether in the development of resources, facilities construction, or the provision of services, should have distinctive characteristics and personality to do "you do not have the same as mine, you are not as excellent as me, you become excellent then I get newer, you get new then I change something stranger". Distinctive characteristics and personality can often reduce the similarity and conflict with other tourism products, can make a deep and unforgettable impression on tourists, and therefore let the products have a stronger appeal. Highlighting the characteristics and the development of personality have become a modern tourism product competition to win the "magic weapon".

(4) Diversity principle.

The comprehensive nature of tourism products requires it to provide a variety of services to meet the full range and multi-level needs. Considering the different interests of tourists and different payment capacity, in addition to providing a wealth of individual products, each individual product should also have different grades and prices to attract different levels of tourists.

3) Product Development Steps for Tourism Destination

(1) Tourism resources survey and evaluation.

Products come from resources, and the census of tourism resources is the crucial first step in product design and development. In the survey of tourism resources, it is better to use the *Specification of China Tourism Resources Census (second revised draft)*, which is jointly formulated by the Institute of Geographic Sciences and Natural Resources Research and the Ministry of Culture and Tourism of the People's Republic of China. It is also advisable to make both total and mean value analyses for the evaluation of tourism resources, so that comparisons can be made on a national scale. At the same time, the survey of tourism resources also includes the survey and analysis of tourism development conditions.

(2) Market analysis and evaluation.

Market analysis and evaluation include two aspects. The first one is the quest market, and there are two specific ways: to conduct post-consumption reactive research in the tourist place, and to conduct intentional surveys of residents in the source market for a wide range of customers. This can be done through various market research methods. The second one is the supply market, mainly analyzing the nation and the province, especially the surrounding areas of the same type of tourism resources and development status, product composition, in order to form a reasonable division of labor and collaboration. It is necessary to determine the strength and weakness of local tourism resources and product development market feasibility to avoid the similarity of product themes, and duplication of development, and vicious competition of proximity tourism market.

(3) Product theme positioning and image design.

Theme positioning and image design are the important factors to determine the direction of product development on the characteristics of tourism resources essentially. Tourism product theme positioning and image design, first of all, can analyze the regional cultural lineage and resource characteristics comprehensively, can identify its cultural lineage and resources with outstanding local characteristics, comparative advantages or universal characteristics. Then through the coordination of cultural lineage, the breakthrough of cultural lineage or a combination of coordination and breakthrough, it establishes the theme of tourism products. The cultural lineage refers to the geographical background of the area where the tourism product is located, including geology, geomorphology, climate, soil, hydrology and other natural environmental features and historical, social, economic, cultural and other human geographic features. In harmony with the cultural lineage, tourism products logically have local characteristics; breaking through the cultural lineage is not obvious in the local characteristics but with a certain universality of tourism to form a surprising tourism product. Moreover, the theme and characteristics of tourism products are mainly reflected through the main scenery, landscape, therefore, we must grasp the "theme" and "main" with the coordination, avoiding the error of deviating from the two. At the same time, the configuration of tourism media should also be coordinated and consistent with the theme and characteristics of tourism products, in order to focus on reflecting or shaping the theme and characteristics. In addition, the theme of tourism products should also consider the needs of market demand and competition. At last, image positioning is the external packaging and abstract expression of tourism product theme, which needs to be designed by image design method for the conceptual image, visual image and behavioral image of product development, and the image design will be reflected in several designs later.

(4) Landscape design, activity design, route design.

The landscape design, activity design and route design are the creative play and concrete embodiment of the designer's artistic thinking, because the design itself is a kind of high state of art. Landscape design is the symbolic process of spatial information which is the design parameters for the experience of tourism consumers, that is, on the basis of full consideration of the technical feasibility of tangible objects to further strengthen or highlight the information contained in regional spatial resources as the function of the communication tower, making the information contained in the resources as clear and accurate as possible to the tourist, which includes the layout of space, facilities, the creation of mood. Activity design is actually to provide tourists with different ways to experience the content of the activities and all aspects of human daily life such as sightseeing, vacation, leisure, adventure, study and other activities, but for the function of the product, it is designed for different sensory participation; another is designed for the behavior characteristics of tourists, such as age, occupation and education level; route design is mainly from the combination of space and time. Among them, the spatial combination design is divided into thematic part and comprehensive part from the function, and the topological relationship is divided into radial part (small-scale), curvilinear part (medium-scale) and circular part (large-scale). According to the time limitation of the activity, the time combination is divided into weekend tour (small scale), holiday tour (medium scale), seasonal tour (large scale), etc. For example, the best time to view the sea of clouds in Mount Huangshan is autumn, winter and spring, and the jade band clouds in Cangshan are best to be seen in late summer and early autumn.

(5) The Overall Development of Tourism Destination Products.

Tourism destination product development as a whole mainly is the specific implementation of the above-mentioned design to determine the spatial and temporal development sequence, the type of product combination and the first development of the first product with its leading, driving and supporting role. The reason to choose the first product is that the city has a number of products with typical characteristics, for example, for Xishuangbanna, its first product is the tropical rainforest landscape and Dai customs, which can make the tourism industry in Xishuangbanna long-lasting. For a scenic spot, its first product is the its essence, which can reflect its theme part, for example, for a seaside resort, the first product is its beach and the surrounding recreational facilities. Tourism product development is actually the production process of the product, and it is more complex and specific after the product design, involving food, housing, travel, shopping, entertainment and other aspects, and is the design or planning from the blueprint into reality of the step.

(6) Marketing design of tourism product.

Nowadays, marketing is a necessary condition for tourism product to the market and product. Marketing and product design are two inseparable parts, especially for tourism product, marketing design needs to focus on the theme, characteristics and image of the product, and whether the essence of the tourism product can be expressed in various marketing methods and channels, which is related to the success or failure of marketing. Therefore, marketing design should also be an indispensable step in the design and development of tourism product.

(7) Travel market feedback.

Tourism product development does not mean the end of the design work, the success of the design and development of tourism product needs to be tested in the real market operation through the feedback of tourists to the product and the response of tourists to the product. The market response and sales volume are influenced by many factors, and the diagnosis of success and failure through market survey and analysis is important for further development, benefit improvement and sustainable development of the product.

(8) Improvement and optimization of tourism products.

Through the feedback of the tourism market, we should understand the strengths and weaknesses of the product and make timely improvement and optimization of the product. There may be problems in all aspects of the product from design to development, and the comprehensive and complex nature of tourism product make it difficult to transform the product as a whole, but even from a product life cycle perspective, many products also face the problems of transformation and optimization. Therefore, this step not only can be for the existing product local improvement, such as scenic environment improvement, route change, service and facility improvement, but also may be the overall product redesign and improvement. For a region, it may be the reselection of first product and the discovery of new product, for a scenic area, it may be the further development of project and activity within the area and the expansion of marketing.

Chapter 5 Tourism Destination Planning and Development Management

Chapter Summary

This chapter mainly introduces the relevant content of tourism destination planning and development management. In view of the planning and management of tourism destinations, this chapter makes in-depth discussions on three different types of rural tourism destinations, urban tourism destinations and scenic tourism destinations from two aspects of planning principles and the main contents of planning and management. For the development and management of tourism destinations, this chapter is mainly divided into two parts: tourism destination project planning and tourism destination product development, and introduces the relevant theories, basic principles, methods and steps of tourism destination project planning and product development.

Issues for Review and Discussion

1. What are the principles and content of planning and management of the three types of tourism destinations?
2. What are the principles of destination project planning?

Case Study

The Development of the Nanwan Monkey Island

Case Analysis

Exercises

Chapter 6
Tourism Destination Marketing Management

Knowledge Graph

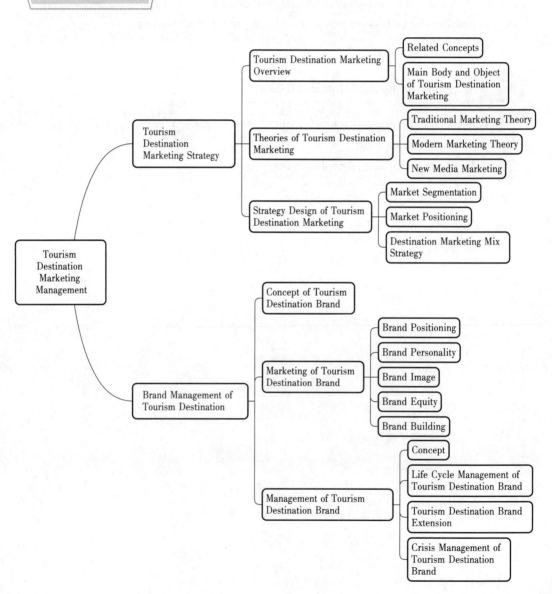

Chapter 6　Tourism Destination Marketing Management

Learning Objectives

(1) Understand the relevant concepts of tourism destination marketing and master the marketing theories of tourism destination.

(2) Learn how to design marketing strategies for tourism destination, make correct market segmentation, market positioning and choose appropriate marketing mix strategies.

(3) Understand the concept of tourism destination brand and the marketing strategy of tourism destination brand.

(4) Learn how to manage tourism destination brands, analyze the life cycle of tourism destination brands, master the content of tourism destination brand extension, and to learn how to manage the brand crisis of tourism destination.

Technical Words

English Words	中文翻译
tourism destination	旅游目的地
marketing theory	营销理论
marketing strategy	营销策略
brand marketing	品牌营销
brand management	品牌管理

Introduce Case

Brand Building

6.1 Tourism Destination Marketing Strategy

In the 1970s, the "Big Apple" was created as a tourism symbol for New York City in order to establish the image of the city as an important tourism destination in the United States. Since then, the marketing slogan "I LOVE NY" has become widely known. In 1998, the tourism circle of our country set off an upsurge to discuss the phenomenon of urban tourism. Shanghai discovered and combined tourism products under the theme of urban tourism, determined the tourist market, built and improved the urban conditions and focused the power of the related industry, with rich individual character of the whole image of urban tourism resort to attend to the domestic and international tourism market competition, reflected a kind of new tourism marketing concept—tourism destination marketing. And this marketing concept was a meaningful inspiration for the rest of our country from Shanghai urban tourism. Tourism destination marketing contributes to the sustainable development of tourism destinations in the future, ultimately achieves the unity of social, economic and environmental benefits, and promotes the development of tourism destination.

6.1.1 Tourism Destination Marketing Overview

1) Related Concepts

(1) Marketing.

Marketing refers to the process in which an enterprise discovers or excavates the needs of prospective consumers so that consumers can understand the product and then buy it. Marketing is an activity, process and system that bring economic value to customers, clients, partners and the whole society in the process of creating, communicating, disseminating and exchanging products. It mainly refers to the process of carrying out business activities and sales behaviors for the market at the same time of marketing, that is, the process of realizing the transformation of business sales.

(2) Marketing strategy.

Marketing strategy means that enterprises take customer needs as the starting point, obtain the information of customer demand and purchasing power according to experience and expectation of the business community, so as to organize various business activities in a planned way. It is a series of measurable and controllable activities aimed at improving sales and manufacturer's reputation for a certain target market. It is a combination of various marketing methods, such as product, price, channel, promotion and public relation strategy.

(3) Tourism destination marketing.

Lundberg (1990) believed that tourism destination marketing includes three aspects: providing tourism products and their overall image to the target market; determining the target market with travel intention and action; making the target market obtain trust and reaching the destination in the best way. Scholars at home and abroad have clearly defined the concept of tourism destination marketing, especially foreign scholars, their research in this aspect is far earlier than the domestic research. According to the literature research and review of *Research Progress and Evaluation of Tourism Destination Marketing in China and Abroad* by Zhang Pei (2015), *Research Progress and Enlightenment of Tourism Destination Marketing in China* by Li Xue (2011) and *the Current Situation and Prospect of Studies on Tourism Destination Marketing in China* by Gao Jing (2008), destination marketing strategy, organization and technology are the main contents of the research. Domestic research mainly involves the construction of destination image building and communication, product development and design, integrated marketing, network marketing and other marketing systems[①]. The target market of the tourism destination is to determine what the target of the tourism destination market is, so as to launch precision marketing. Researching on customer loyalty and specific marketing content of tourism destination can clarify the core needs of tourist customers in the precise market, and give specific marketing countermeasures for these core needs.

The marketing of domestic tourism destination started in 1998, and its concept first appeared in an article with the theme of *tourism destination marketing*. Although this article did not give a specific destination marketing concept, but it illustrated the core essence of tourism destination marketing, and powerfully promoted the future researchers to study the clear concept of tourism destination marketing. Due to the different understanding of tourism destination, domestic research on the concept of tourism destination marketing has different entry points. According to Wu Bihu (2001), from the perspective of market, besides primary marketing, secondary marketing and opportunity marketing, destination marketing should also include the establishment of the association system between destination products and these markets, so as to maintain and increase the market share of destinations. Zhao Xiping (2002), from the perspective of content, held that tourism destination marketing is to improve the value and image of tourism destination and make potential tourists fully aware of the distinctive advantages of this region. At the same time, tourism destination marketing should develop attractive tourism products, promote the products and services of the whole region, stimulate the consumption behavior of tourists, and improve their consumption amount in the region. Shu Boyang (2006) believed that as a project to attract tourists' attention, the basic idea of tourism destination marketing is to leap from product marketing to comprehensive image marketing, and promote the marketing operation mechanism from scattered individual marketing to integrated marketing communication.

Although many domestic scholars disagree about the concept of tourism destination marketing, in fact they all express the same connotation of the concept of tourism destination marketing. In the unified planning and determined tourism target market, by changing, strengthening and integrating all the key elements related to tourism in the target market, and then updating and changing the cognition of tourism consumers, we can effectively establish the brand image of tourism destination, constantly improve the satisfaction of tourism consumers, profoundly affect the behavior of tourism consumers, and finally achieve the whole tourism target market marketing strategy[②].

---

①张帅帅.宿州市旅游目的地营销策略研究[D].蚌埠:安徽财经大学,2016.
②贺甜甜.山东"山水圣人"旅游目的地营销策略研究[D].哈尔滨:东北农业大学,2020.

2) Main Body and Object of Tourism Destination Marketing

(1) Main body of tourism destination marketing.

① Destination marketing with tourism authorities as the main body.

The World Tourism Organization is promoting the concept of destination marketing system (DMS) to more destination marketing agencies. In China, it refers to the promotion of the concept and system by tourism authorities at all levels. According to the definition of Ministry of Culture and Tourism of the People's Republic of China, it is a complete solution for the construction of tourism destination city informationization. It realizes urban tourism informationization through a series of information technology products and corresponding support services, and on this basis, it utilizes national cross-media marketing resources to provide effective publicity and promotion for tourism in destination cities. In a word, the tourism destination marketing system with the tourism administrative department as the main body can not only effectively realize the information construction of destination cities and tourism enterprises, but also realize the integration of information technology and traditional tourism marketing, which is considered as a new tourism marketing model formed in the information age, and is bound to have a profound impact on Chinese tourism marketing.

② Destination marketing with tourism intermediaries as the main body.

Due to the non-storable and intangible nature of tourism marketing itself, the suppliers at the top of the tourism industry chain, such as airlines, tourist hotels and travel agencies, have to consider the fastest way to expand the market from the first day of business. However, due to the limitations of enterprises in capital, manpower and other aspects, it is not enough to develop direct marketing channel solely by themselves, so special tourism intermediaries are needed to complete "the last mile" of marketing channel. There are two common forms in tourism destination marketing with intermediaries as the main body. One is that destination tourism authorities or the combination of tourism enterprises and intermediaries carry out publicity campaigns to attract destination tourists with alternative relations to the local area. The other is that intermediaries treat all destinations differently according to their strategic layout in the country or region, and promote a few destinations with focus. The latter form is particularly noteworthy, because it avoids the interference from the destination itself and takes the intermediaries themselves as the main body of marketing, which is essentially different from the destination marketing of the tourism authorities. If the purpose of destination marketing carried out by tourism authorities is to attract tourists and promote the development of local tourism, then the purpose of destination marketing carried out by tourism intermediaries is to maximize the interests of their own enterprises. After entering the era of tourism e-commerce, due to the inherent advantages of e-commerce in the field of information processing, some large online booking companies and travel companies emerged. Different from the traditional travel agencies, the tourism intermediaries growing up in the field of e‑commerce have the following two characteristics: strong customer management ability and perfect information release network. Tourism enterprise can guide customers through technology and service means, thus it plays an increasingly important role in the field of tourism destination marketing.

③ Destination marketing with tourism suppliers as the main body.

Individual tourism suppliers basically do not have the ability of tourism destination marketing, but the combination of tourism suppliers in the form of tourism association has the ability to complete this work and has its unique advantages. Tourism association is a cooperative and loose organization formed by a certain form of combination of several tourism enterprises in a destination area. Common forms include hotels, travel agencies+scenic spots, hotels+scenic spots, airlines, travel agencies and so on. Of course, the competent government departments can also get involved. The original intention of forming a tourism association is mostly to integrate tourism resources, achieve complementary product advantages, make complementary division of labor, share customers, reduce communication costs, make the original single tourism enterprise together, and enhance the overall market competitiveness of the consortium member enterprises. Up to now, tourism association gradually plays an increasingly important role in destination marketing and becomes another force in destination marketing[①].

④ Marketing mechanisms of ternary main body.

Most of the tourism destination marketing activities in China are undertaken by the government or its functional departments, and the marketing subject is in a single form. The main body of tourism marketing should at least include government tourism organizations, tourism enterprises and local residents, that is, tourism destination marketing mechanisms of ternary main body.

a. Government tourism organizations.

The government‑led strategy has always been one of the strategies guiding the development of Chinese tourism industry. Government‑led has various forms of expression, among which the most important and intuitive expression is the construction of tourism infrastructure, the establishment and communication of tourism destination image and so on. As the main body of tourism marketing, government tourism organizations play an increasingly important and prominent role in the whole tourism economy. Tourism is a service industry, and tourism products have the characteristics of simultaneous production and consumption. Tourists cannot know the quality and performance of tourism products before they purchase tourism products. The same tourism product for different tourists or even for the same tourists in different time will

---

① 王桂霞,邱艳庭.国内旅游目的地营销主体模式——基于电子商务时代的探讨[J].市场周刊(研究版),2005(9):40-41,39.

appear great differences sometimes. The criteria for first-time tourists to make a choice can only be based on the image of the destination. The marketing of tourism destination is not only the marketing on the tourism product level, but also the marketing of the overall image of the destination. As the main body of tourism destination marketing, the primary task of government tourism organization is to establish, promote and spread the image of tourism destination and improve the accessibility of destination.

b. Tourism enterprises.

Tourism enterprises are the main body of market operation and market competition, the main providers of tourism products and services, and the direct beneficiary of tourism destination marketing. However, the utility of tourism enterprises and the publicity of tourism resources, tourism image and tourism infrastructure determine the responsibilities and functions of tourism enterprises in tourism destination marketing. Compared with government tourism organizations, marketing of tourism enterprises should be based on products and services. On the one hand, tourism enterprises should convey information coordinated with the overall tourism image of the destination to potential tourists in the stage of information collection of the destination through various communication channels, that is, to convey tourism elements such as unique food, comfortable accommodation, convenient transportation, fine scenic spot, personalized tourism experience and humanized tourism service of the destination. On the other hand, in the process of tourist activities, tourism enterprises should change their business ideas, establish CS(customer satisfaction) business strategy, implement emotional marketing, and provide humanized services. Under the service economy and experience economy, especially for tourism service industry, service can also attract tourists as the main resource element.

c. Local residents.

The appearance, dress, behavior and ideas of local residents constitute the core of the cultural environment of tourism destination. From the perspective of tourism resources or tourist attractions, the lifestyle, language, clothing and behavior of resident in tourism destination (some scholars call it "locality" or "nationality") become a part of tourism attractions in the eyes of tourists, and even have more significance for viewing and experiencing than scenic spots and other landscapes. Therefore, the cultural connotation of localism of tourism destinations should be fully explored in destination marketing. This requires destination residents, as the main body of tourism destination marketing, to get involved in the marketing with the attitude of masters and sincerely and kindly show their local or national character to tourists, rather than passively arranged by local tourism organizations or tourism enterprises as objects in tourism activities. Of course, this involves the distribution of interests of tourism destination, and the interests of local residents should be paid attention to during the development of tourism, or at least the vested interests of local residents should be respected without having a great impact on their lives. In the tourism marketing of destination, we should emphasize and publicize the cultural customs of destination and the friendly and hospitable image of tourism practitioners and local residents. Because the tourism destination marketing is to promote the tourism destination as a whole to the outside world, and the related infrastructure of the tourism destination and the construction of the macro environment of tourism have the nature of public goods, the main body of tourism destination marketing still takes government tourism organization as the core[①].

(2) Object of tourism destination marketing.

It is generally believed that the marketing object of tourism destination is tourism product. But the source of attraction for destinations goes far beyond the concept of tourism product. The marketing object of tourism destination should be the tourism destination itself (an overall product), which is comprehensive, including the overall image of tourism destination, tourism product and local cultural experience.

Frank Howie (2003) discussed systematically the question of whether place can be used as an object for marketing. One of Kotler's 10 marketing targets is location, he said that cities, states, regions and entire countries are actively striving to attract tourists, factories, corporate headquarters, and new residents. In the framework of Kotler's marketing concept, tourism destination marketing should belong to the category of place marketing, and the target of tourism destination marketing is the destination regarded as "product". The destination is the location of the facilities and attractions, as well as the "product" itself, with each tourist defining his own specific "product" according to his personal tastes and interests[②].

6.1.2 Theories of Tourism Destination Marketing

1) Traditional Marketing Theory

American Wendell R. Smith put forward the concept of market segmentation in 1956, which opened the prelude to the development of marketing theory. In 1964, Professor Neil Borden of Harvard University put forward the concept of marketing mix for the first time. In the same year, E. J. McCarthy, an American marketing expert, summarized marketing factors into the 4P theory based on product, price, place and promotion.

(1) STP theory.

American marketer Philip Kotler and others enriched and improved the concept of market segmentation based on Wendell R. Smith, and systematically developed it into

---

① 刘志红. 旅游目的地营销主体研究[J]. 现代经济信息, 2010(5):12-13.
② 王昕, 张海龙. 旅游目的地管理[M]. 北京:中国旅游出版社, 2019.

STP theory(as shown in Figure 6-1), which has become the core of modern marketing. "S" stands for market segmentation. It is a classification process in which the marketing subject, with the help of market research, divides the whole market of a certain product into several specific groups according to the differences in consumer needs and purchasing behaviors. "T" stands for target market selection, which is the precision of market segmentation and provides corresponding products and services to target consumer groups after segmentation. Target marketing requires clear customer classification and specific needs. "P" stands for market positioning. Based on the product's position in the market and consumers' attention to the product, the enterprise establishes a distinct product image and transmits it to consumers through effective means of information communication to establish the image of the product in the mind of target consumers and its position in the target market.

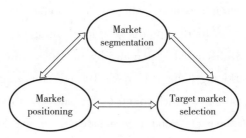

Figure 6-1   STP theory

(2) 4P marketing mix theory.

In the 1960s, E. J. McCarthy proposed the producer-oriented 4P marketing strategy combination, with product as the core marketing element. 4P marketing mix includes product, price, place and promotion. Product is tangible product that can meet the needs of tourists; price refers to the product pricing that meets customers' expectations and enables enterprises to make profits; place is to deliver the product to the target market in a certain way; the essence of promotion is to promote information transfer and feedback between product providers and buyers. The subsequent 6P, 10P and other marketing mix strategies are all based on the expansion of 4P, the core and basic framework have not changed.

2) Modern Marketing Theory

(1) 4C marketing theory.

In the early 1990s, American expert R. F. Lauterborn put forward the consumer-oriented 4C(customer, cost, convenience, communication) marketing mix theory. Customer refers to the tourists as the center to produce products that meet their needs. Cost is to study the purchase cost, energy cost and time cost that tourists are willing to pay for tourism demand. It can combine with the profit target to analyze and propose the optimal plan to retain customers and gain profits. Convenience refers to providing tourists with the convenience of purchase and use, and bringing tourists the greatest travel convenience. Communication is to create competitive advantages, understand the psychological trends of tourists, collect market information, conduct two‑way communication with tourists, and enhance the identity of tourists.

(2) 4R theory.

American scholar Don E. Schultz fully absorbed the essence of 4C marketing concept and innovated it. He proposed 4R(relevance, reaction, relationship and reward) marketing theory and pointed out that enterprises should combine the market development situation and build new initiatives with customers in a more effective way. Relevance emphasizes the close connection of the tourism market to achieve a high degree of fit between supply and demand; reaction requires timely and rapid response to changes in the tourism market and tourist needs; relationship refers to the establishment of a long term and stable good relationship with tourists; reward refers to a win-win situation for both tourists and tourism companies in the marketing process.

(3) 4V theory.

Wu Jinming (2001) and others comprehensively proposed the 4V(variation, versatility, value, vibration) theory. Variation means that in order to meet the diversified and personalized needs of tourists, marketing subjects need to carry out effective differentiated marketing by differentiating products, markets and images; versatility refers to providing a series of products with different functions (combinations) to facilitate the choice of tourism consumers and increase market opportunities; value means that tourism subjects should pay more attention to the added value of culture and brand created by products through technology, marketing and service innovation; vibration emphasizes on providing value innovation for tourism consumers, improving customer satisfaction and loyalty, and realizing the interaction and vibration between value provision and value pursuit with tourism consumers.

3) New Media Marketing

Based on the marketing theory, new media marketing uses the network and other new media platforms to realize the rapid transmission and timely feedback of marketing information. The role of new media such as Internet in tourism destination marketing is becoming increasingly prominent and has become the focus of research.

Gao Jing et al. (2007) believed that tourism official websites provide great convenience for destination marketing organization to carry out customer relationship management and multi-party cooperation, and they are the most convenient channels for destinations to display brand image and transmit tourism information. Chen Long (2013) studied the coordination mechanism of new media in tourism destination and proposed to change marketing ideas and exploit the tourism destination market by taking advantage of the rapid spread and wide range of new media. Fu Hongdan and Gao Wenyan (2015) analyzed and studied the characteristics of new media, such as convenience, rapid dissemination and strong interactivity, as well as the application principles and concretization in tourism destination marketing. Shu Boyang and Ma Xiongbo (2015) put forward the integrated marketing model of destination new media from the aspects of product content, marketing media, market platform, management technology and service relationship based on the analysis of the current situation and existing problems of tourism new media marketing[①].

6.1.3 Strategy Design of Tourism Destination Marketing

Because of the systematic, integrity and dynamic nature of tourism destination marketing, as well as the complexity of marketing process, tourism destinations must formulate effective marketing strategies. The destination also needs to define and describe itself in the competitive destination, which is a typical survey object of destination marketing. According to this area of research, the destination must behave the same as any company trying to sell a product. In other words, the marketing of a destination can be divided into a series of operations, including identifying its target market and positioning it relative to the competitive destination (Heath and Wall, 1992). A typical way to develop a marketing strategy is through destination branding (Morgan et al., 2004), which identifies and promotes the region by developing a strong brand. The brand also helps to identify the characteristics of the type of travel that a destination can experience.

1) Market Segmentation

The first reason for tourism market segmentation is that it can save promotional costs and improve efficiency. Imagine how expensive it would be to deliver a travel message to every consumer in the entire market. Secondly, even if the tourism destination can afford to pay such high fees, such promotion is still very inefficient, because the level of consumer needs varies greatly throughout the market. Therefore, different promotional information must be designed according to different types of consumer groups to encourage the purchase behavior of potential tourists.

(1) Definition of market segmentation.

Tourism destination market segmentation refers to the process of subdividing the whole potential tourism market into different groups according to one or several characteristics of tourists. Such segmentation can be based on the external characteristics of tourists, such as age, gender, income. It can also be based on the internal characteristics of tourists, such as psychological factors. In addition, the market can also be segmented according to the regional distribution of tourists and tourists' tourism

①张帅帅. 宿州市旅游目的地营销策略研究[D]. 蚌埠：安徽财经大学, 2016.

purpose.

(2) Market segmentation method.

① Subdivided by tourist demographic factor.

a. Age and sex.

One of the demographic factors that should be taken into account in market segmentation is age, as consumers of different age groups often have different requirements for tourism activities. Children's favorite activities are more romantic and childlike compared with teenagers. Similarly, young people can expect very different travel experiences from older people. Gender also becomes an important basis for tourism product segmentation. Different genders consider different factors and choose different tourism destinations and activities. Care must also be taken to avoid gender stereotypes that can lead to losing or offending potential tourists.

b. Race.

Another way to define potential tourist groups is subdivided according to race. The same races have common values, interests and ways of life. The theme of historical and cultural sites may be of interest to ethnic groups with a corresponding history. But just as gender is not the only means of market segmentation, race should also not be the only criterion of segmentation.

c. Income.

More consideration should be given to income in price-sensitive tourism markets. If the tourism destination product developed for a target market exceeds the tourists' ability to pay, the existence of the tourism product is meaningless. In fact, according to the ability of tourists to pay, tourism products with different prices can be designed to meet the needs of tourists with different income levels.

d. Family stage.

Tourists in different stages of family will show different needs in traveling. Destinations should design different tourism products for singles, couples or families with children. If destinations are thoughtful and provide products and services that meet the needs of different family types of tourists, they will attract more tourists.

② Subdivided by the psychological characteristics of tourists.

As psychological characteristics are the internal factors of tourists, it is more difficult to study and grasp than the external factors. Psychological characteristics can be studied from the aspects of tourists' lifestyle, value and social class.

a. VALS model.

The famous VALS model was proposed by Stanford Research Institute(SRI, 2005). VALS stands for value and lifestyle. Value is inner belief of how a person experiences life, and lifestyle refers to how a person lives. The VALS model proposed that consumers' consumption behavior has three motivations, namely, ideal fulfillment, fulfillment of a sense of accomplishment and self-expression fulfillment. If a consumer consumes to satisfy his/her ideal, the product must conform to his/her value and preference; if he/she wants to satisfy his/her sense of accomplishment, he/she will choose a product that shows his/her status; if he/she wants to satisfy self-expression, he/she is willing to buy social experience and sports product. The VALS model divides potential tourists into innovators, thinkers, achievers, experiencers, believers, strivers, makers, and survivors. The innovators have sufficient resources and high travel motivation, while the survivors have the least resources and lowest travel motivation.

b. Gallup tourism model.

The Gallup group has developed a model for segmentation of tourists, which divides them into five categories, each with its own characteristics. Adventurers are well-educated, have higher income, and enjoy culture and experience. They belong to the richest group of people in society, and they are willing to indulge and spoil themselves, and pay anything for it; travel is part of the routine for thrifty, older, mostly male, middle-income people; dreamers are older, mostly female, middle-income and educated people who value travel and prefer safe choices but also dream of adventure; worriers are people with lower levels of education and income who do not like to travel because they do not know the destination. Tourism destinations can design and promote their products according to the psychological characteristics of different types of tourists, so as to meet the needs of the target market.

c. Social class.

Social class is often used as demographic information because it is often linked to an individual's income and education level. Tourism market segmentation classifies social class according to psychological characteristics, because the higher the social class is, the more likely the potential tourists are to carry out tourism activities. The higher social classes are well educated, they like to seek novel experiences in travel, and their income level allows them to travel luxuriously or at least comfortably. The income level of the lower social class is not high, so the budget for tourism is limited. At the same time, the low educational background may make them less interested in tourism.

③ Subdivided by geographical factor.

Geographical segmentation refers to the division of the tourism market by the place of residence of tourists. Because there are different distances between the destination and the residence of potential tourists, they will consider the distance factor when choosing the destination. Usually, the farther away the tourist is from the destination, the longer and more expensive the trip will be in their plan. At the same time, the greater the geographical scope of the target market segmentation is, the greater the coverage and workload of the media publicity of tourism destinations are. Therefore, to attract long-distance tourists, there must be a very unique tourism destination core product. Conversely, if the destination has a unique tourism product enough to satisfy a certain type of tourism consumer group, it cannot consider the geographical factors too much.

④ Subdivided by tourism purpose.

According to the purpose of tourism, tourists can be divided into business tourists, tourists who visit relatives and friends, short-distance tourists and traditional vacationers.

The basic purpose of business tourists travel is work and business. Of course, business tourists should not be ignored. After coming to a destination, they also want to know the local characteristics and take part in some entertainment or tourism activities in their spare time. Some evening cultural performances or sports activities are good choices for them. If they have a good impression of the destination, they may also consider bringing their families on holidays in the future.

People who visit relatives and friends usually live in the homes of family or friends. They do not spend much on accommodation and food, but because their purpose is to visit relatives and friends, they have a lot of free time. As the family and friends of these tourists, they will recommend or accompany them to the local scenic spots or participate in various local activities. Therefore, tourism destinations can promote their tourism products to the family and friends of these tourists, that is, the local residents.

Short-distance tourists usually go away for just one weekend. The purpose of the trip may be to participate in cultural activities and sports, or to go shopping. Traditional vacationers typically spend their weekends or annual vacations in tourism destinations for varying lengths of time to relax and have fun. The tourism destination's promotion of various tourism products and various package promotions can make short-distance tourists more aware of what is worth doing in this tourism destination, so as to take this opportunity to participate in more activities[①].

2) Market Positioning

The concept of market positioning originally comes from the advertising strategy of marketing. The market positioning of tourism destination refers to the process of establishing and maintaining a unique position or a unique product in the tourism market.

Effective market positioning enables tourism destination to provide tourists with unique services and benefits different from other competitors. The key to market positioning of tourism destination is the brand image. However, it is far from enough to establish the brand image of tourism destination in the minds of tourists so as to distinguish themselves from other competitors. Market positioning requires tourists to feel the uniqueness of their products by comparing some specific product attributes of tourism destinations with competitors. The tourism destination market positioning should be considered more "different" rather than "better", and difference is crucial to the tourism destination market positioning. Nowadays, the effects of globalization have made most of the world's tourism destinations more and more similar. Standardized tourist facilities

---

① 王昕,张海龙. 旅游目的地管理[M]. 北京:中国旅游出版社,2019.

provide similar necessities for mass tourism, and this similarity has greatly damaged the opportunities for tourists to enjoy different tourism experiences. And the effective market positioning of tourism destination can make tourism destination products stand out in the huge competitive market. Successful destination market positioning can make the destination appear in the first place in the mind of target tourists. This awareness reflects the purchasing intention of tourists and their competitive advantages over other tourism destinations.

(1) Attribute selection of tourism destination market positioning.

In 2003, scholar Pike studied the images of 80 published tourism destinations and summarized the general decisive attributes of tourism destinations into 15 themes, as shown in Table 6-1①.

Table 6-1　The general decisive attributes of tourism destination

Attributes	Attributes
Nature/Scenery	Accommodation
Local culture	Sports activities
Cost/Value	Cafes/Restaurants
Good Weather	History/Historical sites
Infrastructure	Nightlife/Entertainment
Friendly locals	Getting there/Getting around
Safe and relaxing environment	Shopping
Lots to do	

This table covers most of the very important tourism destination attributes for the brand classification of tourism destination. Many competitive products will use these attributes, tourism destinations should combine their own situation, filter these attributes, and finally determine one or two tourism destination attributes in line with their own characteristics.

(2) Establish the market positioning of tourism destination.

① Steps of market positioning of tourism destination.

The market positioning of tourism destination consists of the following 7 steps.

a. Recognize the target market and tourism development environment of tourism destinations.

b. Recognize the competitive factors and development environment of tourism destinations in the target market.

c. Recognize the motivation and interest trend of tourists who patronize the

---

① Pike S. The Use of Repertory Grid Analysis to Elicit Salient Short-Break Holiday Destination Attributes in New Zealand[J]. Journal of Travel Research, 2003, 41(3): 315-319.

destination and those who do not.

d. Analyze the advantages and disadvantages of various competitive factors of tourism destinations in the target market.

e. Opportunity analysis of different positioning strategies.

f. Select and implement market positioning strategies.

g. Always monitor the implementation effect of market positioning strategies.

It is important to note that tourism destination must design their positioning strategies for only one or very few attributes. In the process of information transmission, the tourism destination should grasp a powerful attribute for publicity, too much attribute introduction can only cause tourists' confusion.

② Establish criteria for successful market positioning.

Successful tourism destination market positioning enables valuable promises to truly influence tourists' consumption decisions in terms of functional, emotional and self-expressed benefits. There are three criteria for establishing a successful market positioning.

a. Feasibility of market positioning. The local tourism industry and the destination should have the ability and willingness to implement the established destination market positioning.

b. Communication of market positioning. The tourism destination must establish a close, attractive and unique relationship with the tourism market, and strive to re-establish the characteristics of the tourism destination in the tourists' mind, or change the tourists' old views of the tourism destination.

c. Sustainability of market positioning. To maintain the position that a destination has established among the tourism markets over the long term, it needs to be able to cope with the competition anytime and anywhere.

(3) Three important factors for market positioning.

When the tourism destination has established its market positioning, it must choose the way to present its tourism destination brand to the public. For a tourism destination, the three most important elements of market positioning propaganda are the name, symbol and welcome word of the tourism destination.

① Name.

The core of tourism destination brand is the name of the destination. A good name can leave a deep first impression on tourists and become a good beginning of communication between tourism destination and tourists, thus providing conditions for conveying more information to tourists. However, due to political, economic and other practical reasons, very few tourism destinations can choose their own names, because the vast majority of tourism destinations have already had their own names due to historical reasons. Of course, there are some tourism destinations that change their names to promote their brand.

② Symbol.

The names of tourism destination are usually not set up for tourism promotion, and the symbols of tourism destinations are particularly important when promoting the characteristics and benefits of tourism destinations. Symbol can make it easy for tourists to recognize the tourism destination brand, usually symbol can reflect the personality of a tourism destination.

③ Welcome word.

For many tourism destinations, symbols alone are not enough. Welcome word can add more meanings to the destination names and symbols. Welcome word refers to short sentence that conveys descriptive or persuasive messages for a tourism destination brand. Some tourism destinations mobilize local people to formulate the welcome word of the tourism destination. Good welcome word must be short sentence, and can represent the tourism destination to attract tourists, and this attribute must be unique①.

3) Destination Marketing Mix Strategy

McCarthy's 4P strategy, namely product, price, place and promotion, is the four core factors of tourism destination marketing. Any form of destination marketing mix is proposed and improved based on it, which includes the core content of marketing. Therefore, the tourism destination marketing mix strategy should also be composed of the following four: product strategy, price strategy, place strategy and promotion strategy.

(1) Product strategy for tourism destination marketing.

The primary problem of tourism destination marketing mix is what kind of tourism products to meet the needs of the target market, therefore, product strategy should be regarded as the cornerstone of tourism destination marketing mix strategy, it directly determines the price strategy, sales channel strategy, promotion strategy of tourism destination marketing, and determines the success of the whole tourism marketing strategy.

① The meaning of tourism products.

Tourism products have different definitions. From the perspective of suppliers, the so-called tourism products refer to the services provided by tourism operators to meet the comprehensive needs of tourists in the process of tourism by virtue of certain tourism resources and tourism facilities. Through the production and sales of tourism products, tourism operators achieve the purpose of profit. From the demander's point of view, tourism products refer to the experience that tourists obtain by paying a certain amount of money, time and energy to satisfy their desire to travel. Through the purchase and consumption of tourism products, tourists get psychological and spiritual satisfaction. As a

①王昕,张海龙. 旅游目的地管理[M].北京:中国旅游出版社,2019.

combination of service products, tourism products have the characteristics of comprehensiveness, intangibility, immobility, non-storage and synchronicity of production and consumption which are different from concrete labor products in physical form.

Philip Kotler uses five levels to express the overall concept of the product (as shown in Figure 6-2).

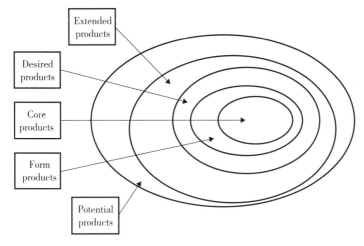

Figure 6-2 The overall concept of the product

a. Core products.

The core products are the basic utility and benefit of the product provided to tourists. Core products are what tourists really want to buy, so they are the most basic and important parts of the overall concept of tourism products.

b. Form products.

The form products, also known as tangible products, are the carrier of the core tourism products, the form in which the core products are realized or the specific form in which the target market meets a demand, and also are the appearance of the tourism products in the market. Form products generally have five characteristics, namely quality, style, characteristic, trademark and packing.

c. Desired products.

Desired products refer to a set of attributes and conditions closely related to the products that tourists expect to obtain when buying the tourism products.

d. Extended products.

Extended products, also known as additional products, refer to the sum of various benefits obtained by tourists when they purchase the form products and desired products. The extended parts of destination tourism products include security, information services, speed, accuracy and convenience. The extension can create customer loyalty by providing tourists with a variety of additional benefits.

e. Potential products.

Potential products refer to the degree and ability of the products to meet the potential desire of tourists. This is an effective way for tourism enterprise to seek to satisfy customers and differentiate themselves from their competitors.

② Marketing strategies in different life cycle stages of tourism product.

The life cycle of tourism product refers to the whole process of tourism product from being put on the market to being eliminated from the market after growth and maturity. Theoretically, the life cycle of tourism products can be divided into four periods: initiation period, growth period, maturity period, and recession period, as shown in Figure 6-3. In order to enhance the marketing effect and improve the economic benefits, tourism enterprise should be good at grasping the characteristics of product in different periods of the life cycle and adapting corresponding marketing strategies to meet the needs of guests and maximize their operating profits.

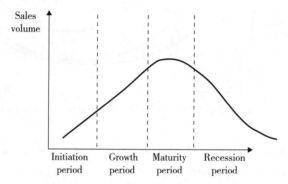

Figure 6-3 The life cycle of tourism products

a. Marketing strategies in the initiation period.

The initiation period mainly refers to that tourism products have just been put into the market, the corresponding scenic spots and infrastructure of tourism products are not yet complete, and the quality of various services still need to be improved. Tourists are not familiar with the products, the market sales are low, various costs are high, tourism enterprises have low profits, and the market competition is not fierce. The following marketing strategies can be adopted during the initiation period, as shown in Figure 6-4 below.

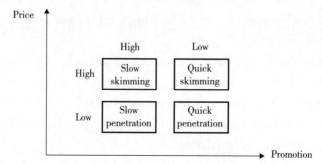

Figure 6-4 Marketing strategies in the initiation period

i . Quick skimming strategy.

That is to make the new tourism products enter the market quickly by means of high price and promotion cost. The following three conditions must be met to apply this strategy: firstly, the majority of tourism consumers in the potential market are not aware of the product; secondly, consumers who know about the tourism product are eager to get the product and have sufficient ability to pay; thirdly, tourism enterprises must face potential competition and cultivate "brand preference" as soon as possible.

ii . Slow skimming strategy.

That is to introduce new tourism products to the market with high price and low promotion cost. This strategy must meet the following four conditions: firstly, the market size is limited; secondly, most of the potential consumers in the market know the tourism product; thirdly, potential tourism consumers are willing to pay a premium; fourthly, the threat from potential competitors is weak.

iii . Quick penetration strategy.

It is the strategy of launching new tourism products with low price and high promotion cost. This strategy must meet the following four conditions: firstly, the market scale is large, and there are many potential tourism consumers; secondly, most of the tourism consumers are sensitive to prices; thirdly, consumers do not understand tourism products; fourthly, there is a strong threat of potential competition.

iv .Slow penetration strategy.

It is the strategy of launching new tourism products with low price and low promotion cost. This strategy must meet the following four conditions: firstly, the market is huge; secondly, tourism products are well-known; thirdly, the market price elasticity of the tourism product is large, and the market development space is large; fourthly, there are potential competitors.

b. Marketing strategies in the growth period.

During this period, new tourism products are gradually finalized and form certain characteristics, so they are increasingly accepted by consumers and have certain popularity. Product sale increases rapidly, advertising costs decrease, sale cost drops significantly and profit soars. However, due to the rapid growth of the market and profit, it is easy to attract more competitors, and the market competition is becoming increasingly fierce.

In the growth period, four strategies should be adopted: improve tourism product and improve product quality; develop and adopt new sales channel; explore new market; strengthen tourism promotion.

c. Marketing strategies in the maturity period.

At this point, the market growth trend slows down or reaches saturation, tourism products have been accepted by most potential buyers, and profits gradually decline after reaching the peak. At this time, the tourism market competition is fierce, products are imitated, substitutes constantly appear, and tourism enterprises need to invest a lot of marketing costs to maintain the product status.

The maturity period should generally adopt the following four strategies: market improvement strategy; product improvement strategy; marketing mix improvement strategy; research and development of new tourism products.

d. Marketing strategies in the recession period.

This is the stage when tourism products are aging and gradually eliminated by the market. On the one hand, new alternative tourism products appear, tourism consumer interests transfer and sales decline. On the other hand, sales promotion expenses increase, resulting in higher costs and lower profits. At the same time, many tourism enterprises are eliminated in the market competition and withdraw from the market, so the competition is diluted.

There are generally three strategies to choose in the recession period. The first is the strategy of giving up. The tourism products that have no future, cannot be saved, and cause losses to the enterprise shall be closed decisively and withdrawn from the market; for tourism products that still have a certain market, the strategy of gradually giving up can be adopted. While choosing the strategy of giving up, new products should be launched in time to enter a new round of cycle. The second is the strategy of concentration, which reduces promotion costs and channel costs. The third is the strategy of standing your ground, because even if competitors have withdrawn, there are still a number of nostalgic tourists in the market, and the enterprise can stick to a period of time and then quit, or wait for a new recovery.

Through the above analysis, tourism products have different characteristics in different periods of economic life cycle, and tourism enterprises can adopt corresponding marketing strategies according to different characteristics[①].

(2) Pricing strategy for tourism destination marketing.

Reasonable tourism price is an important means to enhance the competitiveness of tourism products and increase market share. Facing the increasingly fierce competition in the tourism market, each tourism destination and tourism enterprise are seeking various ways to improve their competitiveness. And one of the most basic and important means is to use tourism price. Only according to the characteristics and quality of their tourism products, combined with the situation of the tourism market, the destination can formulate reasonable tourism price, so as to make the tourism products more competitive.

① Three basic pricing methods.

In the process of tourism product pricing, tourism enterprises generally follow the following principles: cost is the bottom line of price, competitors and alternative products are the starting point of pricing, and customers' unique evaluation of tourism products is

①邹统钎,陈芸.旅游目的地营销[M].北京:经济管理出版社,2012.

the top line of price. Therefore, there are three basic pricing methods: cost‑oriented, demand‑oriented and competition‑oriented.

a. Cost-oriented pricing.

This pricing method is based on the cost of tourism products plus a certain percentage of profits and taxes to determine the price of the products, sometimes called "accounting pricing method", is the most basic and common pricing method for domestic and foreign tourism enterprises. Due to the different cost forms, the pricing methods mainly include cost plus pricing, marginal contribution pricing and investment recovery pricing.

ⅰ.Cost plus pricing.

This pricing method is based on the cost of the tourism product, plus a certain percentage of the expected profit. That is to say, the variable cost of the products is calculated, the corresponding fixed cost is allocated reasonably, and the price is determined according to a certain target profit. The calculation formula of this pricing method is as follow.

$$\text{Unit product price} = \text{unit product cost} \times (1 + \text{cost margin})$$

This pricing method is beneficial for tourism enterprises to maintain simple reproduction and economic accounting, but this pricing method ignores market demand, competition, tourism consumer psychology and other factors, so it has conservative and passive limitations.

ⅱ.Marginal contribution pricing.

This pricing method only calculates variable costs, and compensates fixed costs with the expected marginal contribution and makes profit. The marginal contribution is the difference between product sales revenue and variable cost. If the marginal contribution is greater than the fixed cost, the enterprise will have a surplus; otherwise, it will lose money. If the marginal contribution is equal to the fixed cost, the enterprise breaks even. The calculation formula of marginal contribution pricing method is as follow.

$$\text{Unit product price} = \text{unit variable cost} + \text{unit marginal contribution}$$

The core of this pricing method is that if the price of unit product is higher than the variable cost and the marginal contribution is greater than zero, the enterprise can consider production; unit product price is equal to unit variable cost, or the marginal contribution is equal to zero, which is the limit of pricing, because if the marginal contribution is less than zero, not only fixed costs cannot be compensated, but also variable costs cannot be compensated, and it is not worth producing products or providing services.

ⅲ.Investment recovery pricing.

This method, also known as targeted revenue pricing, determines price based on a company's total cost or investment, expected sale, and targeted revenue. Its basic formula is as follow.

$$\text{Unit product price} = (\text{total cost} + \text{target revenue}) / \text{expected sales volume}$$

The advantage of this pricing method is that it can guarantee the recovery of all costs and achieve the established target profit under certain sales conditions. However, this method ignores the decision and influence of price on sales volume by calculating unit price based on estimated sales volume. The price calculated by this method is difficult to ensure the realization of sales volume, especially when the price elasticity of product demand is large, this problem is more prominent. Therefore, only dealing in monopolistic products or having a high market share can enterprises rely on monopoly power to set prices in this way.

b. Demand-oriented pricing.

This demand-oriented pricing is to take customer demand into full consideration, take customer satisfaction as the center, and set the price on the basis of market demand status, product utility or product value concept that tourists can understand, so that tourists can feel that buying this product can obtain more value than buying other products. It is divided into the following methods.

ⅰ.Customary pricing.

For some products, because there are many similar products and the cost is relatively stable, the price has been maintained at a certain level for a long time, and supply and demand have reached a relative balance, thus there should be a certain degree of price fixity, that is, customary price. As long as the basic functions and uses of tourism products remain unchanged, tourism consumers are often willing to buy products at customary prices. Customary pricing is a typical demand-oriented pricing and a strategy often adopted by many enterprises after the products enter the maturity stage. In this case, tourism products cannot easily change the price, but price increase will affect sales, resulting in consumer dissatisfaction, price reduction will cause consumers doubt about product quality.

ⅱ.Perceived-value pricing.

This pricing method believes that the performance, quality, service, brand and package price of a certain tourism product have a certain understanding and evaluation in the mind of tourism consumers. Consumers often consider whether to accept the price of a commodity according to the level of value they know, feel or understand.

ⅲ. Demand price elasticity pricing.

Demand price elasticity refers to the sensitive degree of demand to price changes, that is, the degree of quantity demanded changes caused by price changes. This pricing method is to use the price elasticity coefficient of demand to judge the rationality of product pricing, which provides the basis for tourism to raise or lower the price. The price elasticity coefficient E of demand can be expressed by the following mathematical formula:

$$E = \frac{\Delta Q}{Q} / \frac{\Delta p}{p} = \frac{(Q_2 - Q_1)/Q_1}{(p_2 - P_1)/P_1}$$

"Q" represents the quantity demanded, "P" represents the price, "Q_1" and "Q_2"

represent the quantity demanded before and after price changes, and "P_1" and "P_2" represent the price before and after demand changes.

If $E > 1$, it indicates that the product is elastic, that is, the demand fluctuation is greater than the price fluctuation, and the price reduction can greatly increase the sales volume. If $E=1$, then the percentage change of price elasticity of demand is the same or close to the percentage change of price. Price reduction or price increase will increase or decrease sales volume, but have little impact on sales volume. If $E < 1$, it indicates that the product is inelastic. When the price is raised, the sales volume of the product will decrease, but the decrease is small, and the sales revenue will increase.

c. Competition-oriented pricing.

Competition-oriented pricing refers to the pricing method based on the market supply competition of similar products or services and the price of competitors. Adopting this pricing method requires tourism enterprises to combine their own strength, development strategy and other factors while competing. In practice, it is mainly manifested as the lead pricing method, going-rate pricing method and seal-bid pricing method.

② Other pricing methods.

a. Lead pricing.

This pricing method means that tourism enterprises adopt the attitude of taking the lead in pricing, work out the price in line with market demand, and can obtain good economic benefits in the fierce competition. Tourism enterprises that adopt this pricing method generally have a strong scale and strength in a certain region and are in an active position in the competition, which can become a model for local tourism enterprises.

b. Going-rate pricing.

This pricing method is based on the average market price of the same industry to formulate the marketable price of the products of the enterprises. The advantages of this method are as follows: average price is considered as "reasonable price" in people's concept and is easy to be accepted; it can avoid competition and enable enterprises to obtain stable market share. Practice shows that the price of similar products tends to follow the going-rate price regardless of perfect competition market or oligopoly market.

c. Seal-bid pricing.

This pricing method is mainly used in bidding transactions. In general, among similar products, the product with a relatively low price is more competitive. In the tourism marketing activities, the bidding competition process is often the price competition process, the competition results in the actual transaction price.

(3) Place strategy of tourism destination marketing.

Place is a bridge connecting tourism product producers and target customers, it is the key link for tourism enterprises to develop tourism market, achieve product sales and profit.

Place strategy of tourism product refers to the channels through which tourism product transfers from the production field to the consumption field. Place strategy is generally measured by two indicators, length and width. The length of place strategy of tourism product refers to the number of circulation links experienced in the circulation process from the producer to the consumer, which is actually the intermediary. The width of the place strategy refers to the number of similar intermediaries used in these links.

Generally speaking, the sales of tourism products are mainly accomplished through the following different types of place strategy.

① Direct sales channel.

It is a kind of sales channel in the early stage of commodity producers. The commodities produced by producers do not go through any intermediate links and directly meet with consumers, namely: producer → consumer.

Direct sales are convenient for tourists and can save tourists' time, but for tourism enterprises, the cost of direct sales is high. If there is no sufficient source of tourists, they will have to bear considerable risks. In the modern tourism market, the sales of large tourism enterprises, especially the international tourism market, are mainly not carried out through direct sales channel.

② Indirect sales channel.

With the development of market economy, sales channel is becoming more and more complicated. For the increasingly globalized tourism market, simple and direct sales are far from satisfying the market demand. In order to speed up the sales of tourism products, tourism enterprises must establish and have a smooth and effective sales network. In the modern tourism market, big tourism companies are trying every means to mass-produce tourism commodities and use modern science and technology to sell to all parts of the world. Tourism wholesalers, retailers, agents and other sales organizations and individuals together constitute a variety of channels for selling tourism goods, which can be summarized into four types:

Producer→retailer→consumer

Producer→wholesaler→retailer→consumer

Producer→agent→retailer→consumer

Producer→agent→wholesaler→retailer→consumer[①]

(4) Promotion strategy of tourism destination marketing.

Promotion is an important factor in tourism destination marketing mix. Promotion is the external manifestation of marketing communication, and the essence of promotion is the effective communication of information.

① 孙乃娟.黑龙江省旅游目的地营销策略研究[D].哈尔滨:黑龙江大学,2007.

① The Concept of tourism destination promotion.

Tourism destination promotion means that operators of tourism destinations transmit information about tourism enterprises, destinations and tourism products to potential buyers of tourism products through various promotion, attraction and persuasion methods, so as to promote their understanding, trust and purchase of their own tourism products to expand sales.

② Types of promotional mix for tourism destination.

Tourism destination is in a complex market information system, and promotion is the coordination of all sales efforts to establish information channels for selling products and services or promoting certain ideas. Tourism promotion mix is composed of advertising, public relation, business promotion and personnel promotion. Different promotion means have their own characteristics, and different enterprise products in different time and space circumstances should choose the promotion strategy and means suitable for their own needs.

a. Tourism advertising strategy.

Tourism advertising strategy is a kind of paid and impersonal display and promotion of tourism products initiated by tourism enterprises for existing tourists and potential tourists. Tourism advertising mainly focuses on tourism products, or tourists, or tourism industry. The goal of tourism advertising is to improve the awareness (popularity) of the destination of the target market, improve the image of the destination, encourage new tourists to visit the destination area, remind tourists of their past memories and encourage them to return to their old places and introduce information about changes in the destination's tourism products.

b. Tourism business promotion strategy.

Tourism business promotion strategy, also known as sales promotion, is a promotion method that stimulates consumers to make purchases in the short term and improves the performance of dealers and sales teams mainly through temporary rewards or displays. Tourism business promotion decisions are generally divided into six stages: firstly, calculate the target sales volume and sales model expected to be achieved through business promotion activities during the specified promotion period; secondly, calculate the possible revenue after the target sales volume is fully realized; thirdly, clearly explain the consumer situation in the target market segments of sales promotion; fourthly, choose the incentive means that are most attractive to the target market segment; fifthly, formulate and implement business promotion programs; sixthly, monitor and evaluate the results achieved.

c. Tourism public relation strategy.

Tourism public relation strategy is an activity in which tourism enterprises use various communication means to communicate and coordinate with all aspects of the public, including consumers, intermediaries, community residents, government agencies and news media, so as to establish a good social image and marketing environment. It has the characteristics of high reliability, wide range of action and strong propagation power. For example, a tourism intermediary can be invited to visit the destination for free, which can improve the impression of the destination, and make use of their sales channels and market development ability to recommend the region more to potential tourists and increase the number of reservations.

d. Personnel marketing strategy.

Personnel marketing strategy is a form of face-to-face communication with tourists and tourism intermediaries, mainly in the form of exhibitions, sales meetings, telephone sales, samples and so on. The personnel marketing method is flexible and targeted, and it is also easy to strengthen the purchase motivation, prompt transaction, and timely feedback market information, which helps to improve the level of marketing decision-making of tourism organizations. However, the spread is often small and the effect on mass tourists is limited.

The combination of these four strategies is called tourism destination marketing mix strategy. The basic idea of tourism destination marketing mix strategy is to formulate the tourism destination product strategy, and at the same time formulate the price, promotion and sales channel strategy, combined into the overall tourism destination marketing strategy, to achieve the purpose of delivering products to tourism consumers with appropriate commodities, prices, and promotion methods. The success or failure of tourism enterprises largely depends on the choice of these combined strategies and their comprehensive application effects[①].

6.2 Brand Management of Tourism Destination

6.2.1 Concept of Tourism Destination Brand

The concept of brand has been deeply discussed in general marketing, but at present, the Chinese and foreign academic circles have not reached a consensus on the concept of tourism destination brand. Zhang Wenjuan (2010) believed that tourism destination brand refers to tourists' association and perception of the overall image of tourism destination through brand name and logo, which represents the quality and beauty of tourism destination. Liang Mingzhu (2006) believed that tourism destination brand contains at least three meanings: firstly, tourism destination brand is a symbol; secondly, the tourism destination brand is the sum of the emotions, ideas and feelings aroused in the hearts of

---

① 邹统钎,陈芸.旅游目的地营销[M].北京:经济管理出版社,2012.

tourists; thirdly, tourism destination brand is a contract between tourism destination and tourists, a long-term commitment to emotion, taste and quality. Soyoung Boo and Busser (2009) believed that a tourism destination brand is a collection of differentiated features that distinguish it from competitors[①].

Tourism destination branding is more complex than other products and corporate brands because it involves many stakeholders. Domestic researchers define it more from two aspects of tourist perception and element composition. Feng Bin (2010), from the comprehensive perspective of tourism enterprises and tourists, believed that tourism destination brand is tourists' perception of the value provided by destination and the relationship between the two, and creates a good perception complex based on tourism resources and tourists' needs with the help of marketing means. In terms of element composition, Chen Hang and Wang Yuewei (2018) believed that tourism brand elements such as infrastructure, services and products embody the unique culture, core value and charm of destinations, which are displayed to tourists in the form of visual elements and language vocabulary. Liang Mingzhu (2004) regarded destination as a regional system, and the brand of this system should include six basic elements, such as advertisement, quality, culture, service, management and image, in addition to place names, patterns and signs. In order to adapt to the rapid changes in the tourism market, destinations gradually tend to build differentiated images with the help of brands to distinguish relevant competitors[②].

The so-called tourism destination brand refers to a comprehensive experience and cognition formed in the mind of consumers by name, term, sign, symbol, graph or their combination in order to facilitate consumers' identification of their own products or services, realize differentiation and establish comparative advantages in competition. The essence of tourism destination brand is relationship, which is the sum of all kinds of relationship among tourism destination and its name and consumers. First of all, it is the symbol of the tourism destination. Secondly, it is the experience and feeling of tourists' consumption in the tourism destination. The ultimate form of tourism destination brand is the comprehensive competitiveness of tourism destination.

6.2.2 Marketing of Tourism Destination Brand

1) Brand Positioning

The positioning of tourism destination brand is very important and is regarded as the essence of destination marketing. With different audiences and different life cycle stages of brands, tourists will have different understandings of tourism products in the same

---

① 张维亮,朱孔山.近十年中外旅游目的地品牌研究述评[J].中国管理信息化,2018,21(17):128-132.
② 刘辉,由亚男.旅游目的地品牌:国内研究进展与启示[J].湖北文理学院学报,2021,42(2):81-88.

destination based on different positioning strategies. In brand positioning, no matter what characteristics of the destination are chosen as its competitive advantage, it should have the property of dynamic change. It is important to identify a specific quality of the destination that will enable it to establish a unique emotional connection with consumers not only now but also in the future, and to build and position the brand based on that.

(1) Identify competitive advantages of the destination.

In the initial stage of the positioning of tourism destination brand, it is necessary to systematically design, collect and analyze reports through all research means to answer three questions. How is the competitor's tourism brand positioning? What are the needs and satisfaction degree of tourism consumers in the target market? What should be done locally to address competitors' brand positioning and potential consumers' real needs? The competitive advantage of the tourism destination is found from the answers to the questions.

(2) Accurately choose relative competitive advantage.

Through a complete index system, the advantages and disadvantages of tourism destinations are analyzed. Generally, this index system mainly involves the following aspects: tourism resources, tourism market demand, tourism product development, brand marketing, comprehensive benefits and so on. Based on the analysis of comparative advantages, combined with the current situation and trend of tourism consumption, we should choose the most suitable products for tourism destination.

(3) Show unique competitive advantage.

The difference of tourism destination brand is a relative concept. The existence of competitive brands is the basis of brand positioning, and tourism destinations need to demonstrate differentiation by reasonable and effective means, including tangible products, tourism service quality, brand experience, brand identification system, etc.

(4) Adjust the positioning of tourism destination brand.

The positioning of tourism destination brand is not static. When the following situations occur, the tourism destination managers must timely adjust the brand positioning: the original positioning is inappropriate, vague or too narrow, competing brands imitate each other and brand strategy is transferred. Managers must pay close attention to the changes of tourism market, competitors, consumers and enterprises themselves, and timely and actively complete the adjustment of the positioning of tourism destination brand[①].

2) Brand Personality

Brand personality is "a series of personality traits related to brands". Strong brands often have distinct brand personality, and unique brand personality will make consumers have more favorable association with brands. Aaker (1997) designed the brand personality

---

① 王昕,张海龙. 旅游目的地管理[M].北京:中国旅游出版社,2019.

scale (BPS) based on personality trait theory. Five dimensions of brand personality are summed up namely as sincerity, excitement, competence, sophistication and ruggedness, which provides reliable and effective measurement scales for studying brand personality. Considering the cross-cultural brand applicability of brand personality scale, Chinese scholars Huang Shengbing and Lu Taihong (2003) constructed a localized brand personality scale with five dimensions including benevolence, wisdom, bravery, happiness and elegance by investigating Chinese consumers, thus expanding the research direction of destination brands in the future.

Brand personality has both top-layer and middle-layer meanings. The top layer is the logical brand feature, the middle layer is the emotional interest and emotional connection, brand attribute and connotation are based on the top and middle layer. The top layer expresses the rational value of the brand, and the middle layer shows the emotional value and emotional connection. The brand interest pyramid sums up the relationship between customers and brands, which is often established in the process of customer research. In this research process, customers are often asked to describe the characteristics of the destination and answer what the destination means to them. When conducting research, customers should be asked directly to answer the questions in the interest pyramid (as shown in Figure 6-5[①]).

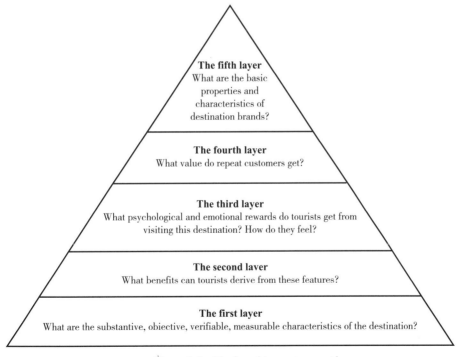

Figure 6-5 The brand interest pyramid

---

① Morgan N, Pritchard A, Pride R. Destination Branding: Creating the Unique Destination Proposition[M]. Oxford:Buttter-Heinemann,2004.

3) Brand Image

The research on the brand image of tourism destination has received wide attention. Brand image is a concept corresponding to brand ontology. It is the cognition and impression of a brand formed from the perspective of consumers. It is often confused with tourism image and tourism destination image. At present, the domestic research on the brand image of tourism destination mainly focuses on its constituent elements, classification of elements and characteristics of elements. Ma Dongyue (2011) summarized the brand image elements of tourism destinations into three parts: brand name, brand logo and brand logo language. Lu Peng (2015) believed that the image of an excellent tourism destination brand is not only reflected in the uniqueness of composition and color and the regional characteristics showed in the design of logo fonts, but also should meet the principles of moderate information and reflect tourists' demand, innovation, artistry and emotion. Qi Weiqi (2011) analyzed the brand image of urban tourism and believed that the brand image of urban tourism includes two parts: visual symbol system and landscape system. Taking waterfront tourism destinations as an example, Gao Jing (2015) proposed that the brand image of tourism destinations has five dimensions: sensory attraction, modern flavor, lifestyle, spiritual interest and cultural charm. Foreign academic circles have basically reached a consensus on the two aspects of brand image including cognitive dimension and emotional dimension. In different tourist stages, different dimensions have different impacts on the overall brand image of tourism destinations, among which cognitive image has the strongest influence, followed by unique image, while emotional image has the weakest influence[①].

4) Brand Equity

In the 1980s, foreign marketing scholars put forward the concept of brand equity to measure brand performance. There are different opinions on the concept of brand equity, such as the concept of consumer-based brand equity, the concept of business-based brand equity and the concept of financial brand equity. Aaker (1992) and Keller (1993) respectively defined brand equity from the perspective of consumers. Aaker (1992) believed that brand equity refers to a series of assets, including "brand loyalty, brand awareness, brand association, perceived quality and other proprietary brand" assets. Keller (1993) defined brand equity as "customers" differentiated responses to brand marketing activities due to brand cognition. Although the brand is essential for a destination to attract potential tourists, destination brand managers must evaluate the brand equity of the destination to determine the effectiveness of brand marketing campaigns. Scholars' definition of the brand equity of tourism destination is almost the

---

① 张维亮,朱孔山.近十年中外旅游目的地品牌研究述评[J].中国管理信息化,2018,21(17):128-132.

same as Aaker and Keller's consumer-based concept of brand equity, which lacks the characteristics of tourism destination brand equity. Scholars have realized this problem now. Liu Lijuan and Lu Xingyang (2016) proposed that the brand equity of tourism destinations is essentially a kind of relationship asset. Through brand marketing, potential tourists can form unique attitudes, emotions and behaviors towards the tourism destination, thus bringing value to stakeholders of the tourism destination. This concept emphasizes the interactive relationship between tourists and tourism destination brands, which has a certain novelty[1].

5) Brand Building

Marketing activities of tourism destination brand can bridge the gap between the destination's own advantages and the perception of potential tourists. Recognizing that brand building is a process of two-way interaction between destination and tourists, Weinreich (1999) proposed that destination marketers must consider the S-shaped curve of the whole process from brand emergence, development, maturity, decline and extinction (of course, the time limit is flexible, which can be weeks or centuries), rather than from the traditional product or brand life cycle point of view. Destination managers should regard it as several stages of the relationship between brand and tourists, rather than as S-shaped changes in tourist reception at different stages, which reveal the differences in brand communication requirements at different stages. Nigel Morgan and Annette Pritchard (2004) further proposed the concept of destination brand popularity curve, and believed that the popularity of tourism destination brand consists of five stages: fashionable, famous, familiar, tired and updated. Graham Brown et al.(2004) noted the role of events in brand marketing of tourism destinations and emphasized the importance of media relations in brand image creation and brand marketing opportunities generated by focal events. They believed that special events would superposition the image of tourism destinations to strengthen or change the brand of them. Xing Xiaoyan and Laurence Chalip (2006) conducted an empirical study on the impact of sports events on destination branding[2].

Brand pyramid, brand equity template and brand wheel are widely used in brand building. The three models each have their own advantages and disadvantages. The brand round is more comprehensive including products and experiences, but contains too much information, which is not conducive to targeted application by stakeholders. The brand pyramid and the brand equity template provide relatively simple information. It cannot provide a complete picture, but it is more operable on the application level, which needs to be screened and flexibly applied according to the actual situation.

---

[1] 韦瑾.基于游客的民族旅游目的地品牌资产形成机理——以西江苗寨为例[J].江苏商论,2021(6):56-60.
[2] 邹统钎.旅游目的地开发与管理[M].天津:南开大学出版社,2015.

(1) Brand pyramid.

The brand pyramid is a simple and practical analysis model that analyzes a destination's major assets to the essence of the brand at all levels, usually divided into five stages(as shown in Figure 6-6).

The first is rational characteristics, which are the main assets of the destination, which can be obtained by SWOT analysis. The second is emotional characteristics, focusing on the emotional output of tourists, that is, how they view and perceive this tourism destination, which can be obtained through qualitative tourist survey. Thirdly, brand characteristics are analyzed by competitors to extract the main characteristics that distinguish the destination from other destinations. This is a pithy summary that reflects how the destination will be perceived by key tourists. Fourthly, position description is distinguished from the tagline directly facing tourists. It is a strategic tone statement about marketing communication and can guide other relevant marketing activities. It contains keywords and key factors. Lastly, brand essence includes the DNA of the destination, that is, what the fundamental nature and characteristics are. It is usually a description of a core word, such as quiet and dynamic.

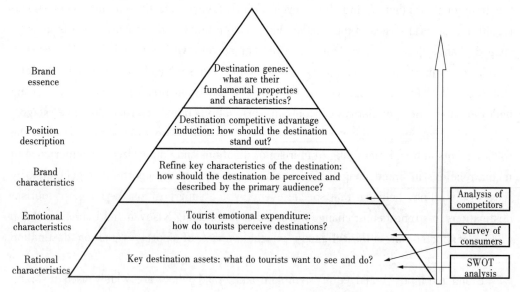

Figure 6-6 The brand pyramid

(2) Brand equity template.

For stakeholders, the brand equity template model can effectively apply the destination's brand equity to their own marketing activities, and can help each stakeholder to determine which products and experiences reflect the core value of which brand. Table 6-2 reflects three core brand values for active, young and adventurous segments, such as a stay in a secluded eco-lodge that can be a natural and spiritual satisfaction, or a hike on rough mountain roads that can be a natural and energetic experience.

Table 6-2　The brand equity template model

Product and Experience	Brand Value		
	Natural	Soulful	Vivid
Product			
Spa resort			
Secluded ecological lodge			
Experience			
Candlelight dinner on a desert island			
Hiking on rough mountain roads			
Kite and surf			

(3) Brand wheel.

The brand wheel is a comprehensive brand building model, absorbing the characteristics of the brand pyramid and brand equity template, containing all the core information in one chart, and illustrating the relationships at all levels[①].

6.2.3 Management of Tourism Destination Brand

1) Concept

There are many related researches on the management of tourism destination brand. Chinese and foreign scholars have analyzed and discussed the principles, characteristics, challenges, processes and influential factors of successful brand management of tourism destination, and reached consensus in some aspects. However, due to the different institutional basis and development potential of each tourism destination, the academic circle has not formed a recognized framework system for the successful management of tourism destination brand. Through the analysis, it is found that almost all tourism researchers believe that the realization of tourism destination branding is a long and arduous process. Tourism destination marketing organizations are faced with many pressures in brand management of tourism destinations, including numerous stakeholders, complex product composition, small marketing budget, weak ability to control the environment, political influence in the decision-making process, difficult to measure brand performance and sensitivity to external environmental changes.

Hankinson (2009) conducted in-depth interviews with the main managers of 20 tourism destination marketing organizations and found that the successful management of tourism destination brand needs to include five key factors, namely brand leadership, stakeholder cooperation, departmental cooperation, brand communication and brand culture. It also involves two intermediate elements, namely brand structure and brand authenticity.

---

① 邹统钎,陈芸.旅游目的地营销[M].北京:经济管理出版社,2012.

In terms of the subject research of the management of tourism destination brand, Zhou Xiaozhen (2013) believed that due to the unique "publicity" of tourism destination brands, the government, as the marketing subject of tourism destination, should be duty-bound to undertake brand marketing and provide policy support and monitoring for marketing. Feng Bin (2010), on the basis of analyzing the stakeholders of tourism destination brands with the modern experiential marketing theory, proposed to build a brand management organization to carry out strategic cooperation with tourism enterprises and effective communication with local residents. From the perspective of diversification, Gao Jing (2007) proposed that diversified marketing subjects should be formed, and tourism enterprises, tourism industry organizations and specialized tourism marketing agencies should be included in the scope of brand management subjects. Hu Jiajing (2014) proposed the brand value orientation based on stakeholder coordinated management.

At present, stakeholders are a major aspect and a difficulty in the research on brand management of tourism destinations. Due to the complex and changeable situation of tourism destinations, no consensus has been reached on how to achieve effective management of stakeholders. Tourism destination brand management needs to overcome the interest competition among stakeholders. Hankinson (2009) found that senior managers of different stakeholder organizations can be gathered together to jointly formulate tourism destination brand planning, so as to seek cooperation with some broader and smaller stakeholders under a normative framework and establish a long-term cooperative relationship. Marzano G. (2009) conducted a systematic study on the branding process of Australia's Gold Coast, and the results showed that although there are many stakeholders in tourism destinations, only a few of them control the main power. In addition, organizations or individuals with dominant power can exclude other stakeholders from the outside through power operation to strengthen their own control power[①].

Tourism destination brand is an associative support for consumers formed by destination managers through creating and maintaining work. It forms valuable propositions in function, emotion and self-expression, so as to establish the relationship between destination brand and tourists. It helps consumers to recognize the commitment made by the destination and is an important area of destination competition. The main contents of the tourism destination brand include the core value of the brand, the meaning represented by the brand, the brand personality, the brand appeal, and so on[②].

2) The Life Cycle Management of Tourism Destination Brand

The development of tourism destination brand is closely related to the development of tourism destination. Tourism area life cycle theory (TALC) discusses that tourism destination brand also goes through a development stage similar to the product life cycle,

①张维亮,朱孔山.近十年中外旅游目的地品牌研究述评[J].中国管理信息化,2018,21(17):128-132.
②王昕,张海龙.旅游目的地管理[M].北京:中国旅游出版社,2019.

as shown in Figure 6-7①.

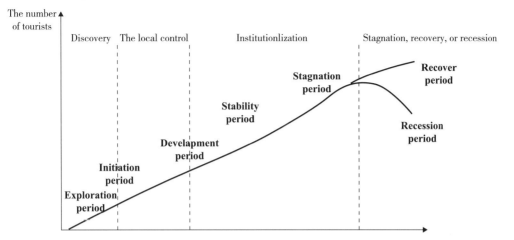

Figure 6-7　Tourism destination brand life cycle

As can be seen from Figure 6-7, the brand development of tourism destinations also has corresponding development cycles, and the characteristics of each development stage are different. Therefore, in the process of brand operation and management, the first thing is to design corresponding brand operation strategies according to the characteristics of each development stage of tourism destination brands, so as to ensure the sustainable development of brands.

(1) Exploration period.

The main characteristics of this period are the small number of tourists, very imperfect transportation and other tourist facilities, but the tourism sites are well preserved. Therefore, in the exploration period, tourism destinations should make full use of the uniqueness and ecology of natural resources, cultural resources and other tourism resources to prepare for the development of tourism brands.

(2) Initiation period.

This period is characterized by an increase in the number of tourists, mostly regular tourists. There was a publicity campaign, infrastructure has been built and improved and the government became involved in management and control. This period requires the establishment of appropriate tourism organization and decision-making procedures. At this period, tourism destination should decide the limit of tourism capacity with an eye to sustainable development. At the same time, in order to increase the effect of publicity, tourism destination should start to position their brands.

(3) Development period.

The main feature of this period is the surge of tourists, the number of tourists in the peak period is equal to or much more than the reception capacity; the infrastructure is improving day by day; and the original appearance of the tourism destination is affected. In

---

① 冯云.旅游目的地品牌营销研究[D].武汉:武汉大学,2005.

this period, tourism destinations are not only required to constantly establish and improve tourism service facilities, but also to strengthen the protective management of scenic spots due to the increasing pressure on the environment. Finally, it is necessary to maintain its own brand image as a tourism destination to avoid falling into vicious competition.

(4) Stability period.

The main feature of this period is that the total number of tourists increased but the growth rate starts to slow down. At the same time, the driving effect of tourism destination begins to appear. In this period, tourism destination should do their best to maintain the image of tourism destinations and strengthen the cultivation of tourists' brand loyalty.

(5) Stagnation period.

This period is characterized by the peak number of tourists, most of whom are conservative repeat tourists; some environmental, social and economic problems appear in tourism destinations and the tourism market is becoming increasingly competitive. At this period, the tourism destination should seek to make extensive commercial use of the facilities of the tourism destination, and carry out a large number of promotion and development activities to maintain the number of tourists.

(6) Recession period.

This period is characterized by a decrease in tourists. At this period, the tourism destination is required to extend the brand of the tourism destination by developing new tourism resources and elements on the basis of the original brand positioning, so as to inject new vitality into the original brand image and promote more tourists to visit.

(7) Recovery period.

Through the adjustment and extension of brand positioning, the development of tourism destination brand has entered the recovery period. At this period, the destination can be rehabilitated or revitalized by developing new markets or new products[①].

3) Tourism Destination Brand Extension

Brand extension is a kind of development strategy that an enterprise uses its existing brand to apply to new products or services in order to maintain or expand its market share. Foreign scholars Sheinin and Schmitt (1994) believed that brand extension includes two aspects: one is product category extension, the extended products have similar characteristics with existing products; the other is the extension of the concept of new product, which is defined as the development of competitive new product in the original product category. Brand extension can help existing consumers accept new product more quickly, reduce the uncertainty of consumers, and meet different needs of consumers. At the same time, enterprises can reduce marketing costs and improve the utilization rate of

---

① 李岚林. 旅游目的地品牌营销研究——以湘西地区为例[D]. 吉首:吉首大学,2012.

funds, so it is widely used in advertising, brand promotion and product development.

The biggest effect of a brand on a tourism destination is that as long as the value of a destination brand can be continued through careful brand accumulation and communication, the tourism destination brand is a resource that can be enjoyed continuously. Tourism destination conveys information about tourism resources and products to tourism consumers through brand construction and management. As tourism consumers become more and more familiar with the brand of tourism destination, they will pursue more and more detailed information. At this appropriate stage of development, tourism destination needs to expand their original tourism destination brand through brand extension strategies to strengthen their own brand extension capabilities. The extension ability of tourism destination brand is also the brand influence and radiation, which is the ability to break into related fields, develop extended brand and promote the product development of extended brand quickly and effectively with the help of original brand. With the continuous development of tourism brand theory and practice, tourism destination brand extension is also used by more and more mature tourism destinations and provides theoretical basis and practical experience for the brand management of their tourism products and tourism resources.

(1) Destination brand structure.

Destination brand structure refers to the composition of various tourism product brands of a tourism destination. Different tourism destination brands construct their brands differently, so they also have different brand structures. Some destinations have rich tourism resources and various tourism products, so the brand structure is more complex. However, some destinations have relatively single tourism resources and fewer types of tourism products and services, so the brand structure is relatively simple. In the tourism industry, a common brand structure is a national regional brand constructed by the national region or city brand, which is a sub-brand under the whole national brand. Each sub-brand has its own brand positioning, target market, competitive advantages and communication channels. At the same time, the development of sub-brand will enhance the brand value of the national brand.

(2) Decisive elements of destination brand extension.

The strategy of tourism destination brand extension has helped many destinations successfully save the time and financial resources of tourism product development and promotion, but destination brand extension is a double-edged sword, if not properly used, it will also bring tragic failures and lessons to tourism destinations. Therefore, only under certain conditions, a reasonable and rational extension of tourism destinations can ensure the success of brand expansion. On the contrary, if the original tourism destination brand is extended indiscreetly or excessively at will, it may blur consumers' image cognition of the original tourism destination, and even lose their goodwill and trust in the tourism destination. Tourism destination should pay attention to the following factors in brand extension.

① The popularity and reputation of tourism destination parent brand.

The popularity of tourism destination parent brand refers to the degree of familiarity with the destination among tourism consumers, while reputation refers to the degree of appreciation of tourism consumers to the destination brand. Both are measures of brand strength at a destination. Research shows that a strong brand can improve the brand awareness of extended products and promote the formation of favorable associations more than the general brand. Since the basic premise of tourism destination brand extension is that the original brand already exists, the destination extension brand launched in order to expand the market share and social influence of the host brand for tourism purposes has the brand advantage to support its expansion only when the original brand has certain market recognition and feasibility and belongs to the tourism destination favored by tourists. When choosing a tourism destination, tourism consumers often decide their itinerary according to their own judgment on the popularity and reputation of the destination, and will also map this judgment to the tourism products and service providers of extended brands. Tourism destination products with high popularity and reputation are safer for tourism consumers and have greater extension potential, which is conducive to the diversified development of destinations and enhance consumers' intention to choose destination extension brand products.

② The quality of tourism destination parent brand and extended product.

Tourism destination brand quality is an abstract feeling, and also a manifestation of destination brand association. The study found that high quality destination brand is very important for its brand extension. And the brand quality of the extension brand itself also affects the final success of the destination brand. If the brand quality of the destination extension brand does not conform to the expectations of the tourism consumers, for example, there is a huge gap between the desire to obtain mental and physical relaxation and pleasure and satisfy the curiosity of tourism resources in the extended brand of the tourism destination and the actual tourism products and services provided by the tourism destination, then even if the parent brand of the destination is very strong and has high quality reputation, the success of destination brand extension cannot be achieved. Also, the core value and brand image of the destination should be consistent with the core value and brand image of the original destination. Otherwise, it will bring confusion to the consumers and damage the original brand value and market value. In addition, there is a close correlation between destination extension brand and original destination brand, and they influence each other, that is, the brand value of original destination brand affects destination extension brand. The image of destination extension brand also works against the original destination brand. The core value of tourism destination brand limits the scope of brand extension in connotation, and the image of new brand must be contained in the original destination brand association.

③ The promotion environment and communication means of tourism destination brand extension.

The promotion environment and communication means of the brand extension strategy adopted by the tourism destination are also one of the important factors that determine the success or failure. The promotion environment of destination brand extension includes the tourism consumer market and the competitive environment of the tourism market, both of which have great influence on the success of destination brand extension. If the market capacity of tourism consumption is expanding in a rising trend, the newly launched destination brand will receive a good market response; on the contrary, the new brand promoted in the declining tourism consumer market not only cannot generate enough market feedback, but also may bring down the whole tourism destination due to the lack of funds and return benefits. The competitive environment of the tourism market refers to the challenges faced by other tourism destination brands in this market. Any tourism destination hopes to become bigger and stronger, so it will launch its extension brand or constantly reinforce and extend the connotation of the original brand. If compared with the extended brand or original brand of other tourism destinations, the tourism destination lacks competitive ability and comparative advantage, it is difficult to achieve the success of brand extension; on the contrary, if the tourism destination can seize the market gap and start at the time when the competition is relatively relaxed, it will bring unexpected harvest.

4) Crisis Management of Tourism Destination Brand

The crisis management of tourism destination brand is a series of management activities for tourism departments to prevent, deal with and make use of the crisis, and to establish a set of systematic communication, prevention, treatment, resolution and other daily management programs. The sources of brand crisis that tourism destination faces include human factors and natural factors. The effective brand crisis management mechanism must be established before the crisis occurs, we should also establish the brand crisis awareness, face up to the crisis sincerely after the crisis occurs.

As the well known saying in brand management circles, "brand crisis is the whetstone of brand achievement". A successful tourism destination brand is a model that survives various brand crises and accumulates experience and lessons so as to build and maintain the brand in a better and longer time. In essence, the crisis management of tourism destination brand is also the management of the overall value of tourism destination brand. From creation, construction to management, tourism destination brand is continuously accumulating the value of tourism destination brand equity. With the change of the market and other non-human factors, tourism destination managers need to deal with various factors, and constantly reduce the loss of brand equity value caused by internal and external reasons and try to recover and make up for it, so as to continue the accumulation of destination brand equity.

(1) Establish crisis monitoring and early warning system.

Destination brand crisis is unexpected and urgent. This means that the crisis management of tourism destination brand is often uncertain and emergent. Although the destination brand crisis is sometimes unpredictable, there are ways for tourism destinations to monitor and warn. Destination brands need to make periodic diagnosis of possible crises in order to find and deal with the problems timely, so as to ensure the healthy and stable development of destination brands. In order to monitor the destination brand crisis and the effect of destination brand management activities, the tourism destination management department needs to establish a destination brand crisis monitoring system to manage the destination brand completely and scientifically. Through systematic collection of information on the formation factors of destination brand crisis and a series of rigorous investigation and analysis process, the tourism destination can quickly and accurately grasp the development trend of the formation factors, judge the current stage and development direction of destination brand, and timely adjust the destination brand crisis management strategy so as to make adequate preparations to monitor the destination brand crisis. Tourism destinations can establish full-time departments and personnel for the brand crisis of tourism destinations, like the position of chief risk officer can be established. Professional brand consulting management agencies and experts can also be invited to assist in formulating early warning mechanisms and emergency plans for the possible brand crisis of destinations according to the experience and lessons of other similar tourism destinations. The tourism destination personnel should also know what the most basic means and measures should be taken in the event of a crisis, so as to avoid the long-term and profound impact of the crisis on the destination brand management.

(2) Establish the awareness of destination brand crisis.

Different tourism destination brands will encounter different crises in different periods of brand construction, but there is no denying that crises are everywhere and cannot be prevented. The brand of tourism destination is jointly built by many departments and organizations over a long period of time. Any negligence of a member may bring losses caused by improper handling of the destination brand crisis. Therefore, not only the operators and managers of tourism destination but also all relevant personnel of tourism destination should have the awareness of brand crisis. In the daily maintenance and operation work of destination brand, the mistakes and loopholes caused by management negligence should be reduced as far as possible, and the human factors should be reduced to the minimum, and the probability of crisis should be reduced. The makers and maintainers of tourism destination brands should understand that it is dangerous and fragile to rely solely on the rigid crisis system such as the tourism destination brand monitoring and early warning system. Only the comprehensive and advanced brand crisis awareness can form the golden defense line in the crisis management of destination brands, and it is possible to create an impregnable destination brand.

(3) Face the crisis honestly.

When the tourism destination brand crisis occurs, tourism destination may face pressure from the government, the media and the public. After the crisis, the public is in a period of high attention and sensitivity to the destination. If the tourism destination tries to cover up and conceal the truth with a fluke mentality, it will not only feel ashamed after the truth is exposed, but also cause hatred and contempt from the public and the media. The destination brand may collapse overnight and there is no room for recovery. Due to the unequal information among the public, media and tourism destinations or tourism agencies, the public's understanding of crisis events in destinations is often passive and delayed. Before exposing the truth to the outside world, tourism destinations can do a good job of communication with the media, and obtain the trust and support of the media. In order to shorten the crisis handling time and improve the efficiency of crisis management, tourism destinations should let the media get the latest news and sufficient information in the first time, and use various media communication platforms to answer the questions of the outside world candidly. Just as the meaning of the word "crisis", the burst of crisis also contains the germination of opportunities. If tourism destinations handle brand crisis properly, they can further deepen the positive image and association of the brand in consumers' mind by taking advantage of a potential success opportunity, and at the same time improve their own crisis management experience and practice to resist the possible brand crisis in the future, and keep moving forward in the crisis①.

Chapter Summary

Developing marketing strategy that can meet the needs of tourists is the key to successful destination marketing, and branding is also an important means to avoid destination marketing convergence. Learning a series of theories of tourism destination marketing enables tourism destinations to obtain sustainable competitive advantages.

Issues for Review and Discussion

1. What are the relevant concepts of tourism destination marketing?
2. How to design marketing strategies for tourism destinations?

Case Study 6-2

Shaoxing: Enter the "Chao" Amusement Park of the Song Dynasty

Case Analysis 6-2

Exercises

---

① 唐瑷琼. 旅游目的地品牌建设研究[D]. 上海:复旦大学,2008.

Chapter 7
Intelligent Management of Tourism Destination

Knowledge Graph

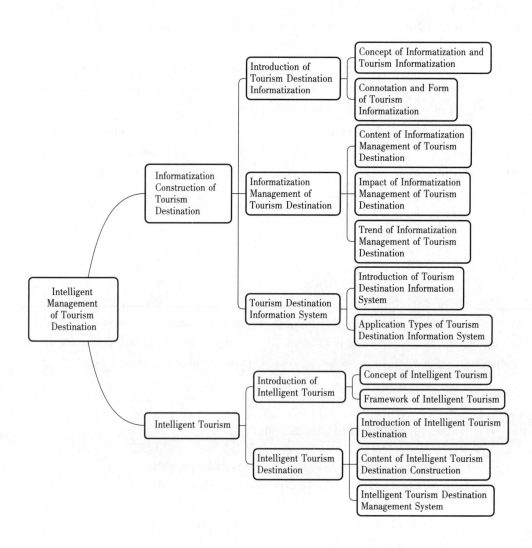

Chapter 7 Intelligent Management of Tourism Destination

Learning Objectives

(1) Understand the basic concepts and current trends of intelligent management of tourism destination.

(2) Cultivate fundamental thoughts about changes of intelligent technologies and utilities happened in recent years.

(3) Cultivate the abilities of taking advantages of IT for future tourism destination management.

Technical Words

English Words	中文翻译
tourism destination informatization	旅游目的地信息化
informatization management	信息化管理
public service management	公共服务管理
marketing management	销售管理
system standardization	系统标准化
subject diversification	主题多样化

Introduce Case

Digital Technology Helps Tourism Industry Accelerate the Recovery of Internet+, Bringing New Travel Experience

7.1 Informatization Construction of Tourism Destination

7.1.1 Introduction of Tourism Destination Informatization

1) Concept of Informatization and Tourism Informatization

There are many definitions related to informatization, but it is generally agreed that informatization refers to the process of using information communication technology (ICT) to transform traditional economy and social structures based on the development of ICT industry and the spread of ICT in various social and economic sectors. It also refers to the historical process of making full use of information technology, developing and utilizing information resources, promoting information exchange and knowledge sharing, improving the quality of economic growth, and promoting economic and social development and transformation. Informatization is not only a process but also a result. And when informatization is regarded as a comprehensive system, it can include both the process meaning of "informatization" and the result meaning of "informatization". However, in practice, due to the continuous innovation and development of information technology, informatization often focuses on expressing a process that continues with the development of information technology, and is a comprehensive system that is constantly being constructed and developed.

The narrow definition of tourism informatization mainly revolves around the integration and utilization of tourism information resources. Its representative point of view pointed out that tourism informatization refers to the process of integrating tourism-related information such as tourist attractions, scenic spots, tourist hotels, travel agencies, tourist transportation, shopping environment, etc., and through information technology or information systems, business managers and tourists can easily and conveniently obtain this information.

The broad definition of tourism informatization mainly revolves around the application of information technology, the relationship between tourism industry resources and tourism industry development. This view holds that tourism informatization refers to the full use of information technology, database technology and network technology to deeply allocate, combine, process, disseminate and sell tourism-related physical resources, information resources, and production factor resources. In this way, it can promote the transformation of traditional tourism to modern tourism, speed up the development of tourism, and improve the production efficiency of tourism. The development of tourism informatization in a broad sense covers the process from (primary) tourism informatization, tourism digitization, tourism intelligence to tourism intellectualization. They are in the same line, not only gradually deepening and upgrading the technical application, but also gradually shifting the development focus from the technical application from the perspective of the supply side to the perspective of the demand side to meet the needs of tourists and enhance their experience core.

2) Connotation and Form of Tourism Informatization

From the current stages of domestic tourism development, the connotation of tourism informatization mainly includes the following aspects.

(1) Connotation of tourism informatization.

① Intergration of information service.

Through the tourism public information service platform, it provides tourists with online service integrating tourism public information query, tour guide, tourism product reservation, tourism complaint and handling, etc., to achieve the integration of tourism public information service.

② Precision marketing.

Tourism destination and tourism enterprise use the Internet, social media, third-party platforms and other channels to collect market data of customer sources, carry out targeted marketing, realize precise marketing and personalized recommendation of product and service, and improve the efficiency of marketing.

③ Industrial operation data.

Through the informatization construction of tourism enterprise, it strengthens the full data management of business processes, strengthens the data connection between the government and enterprise, strengthens the analysis and utilization of data resources, and improves the application level of tourism informatization.

④ Industry management intelligence.

It uses green, intelligent and ubiquitous information technology to strengthen the management of the tourism industry and improve the scientific and intelligent level of tourism management. Through the construction of the tourism e-government system, it promotes the opening and sharing of data resources of relevant government departments, establishes a sharing directory of tourism government information resources, realizes the sharing and coordination of government resources, and improves the efficiency of industry management.

(2) Form of tourism informatization.

Tourism informatization covers a wide range and is rich in content. Its main manifestations include tourism enterprise informatization, tourism e-commerce, tourism e-government and so on.

① Tourism enterprise informatization.

Tourism enterprise informatization mainly refers to the internal information construction of various tourism enterprises such as tourism product suppliers, accommodation and service enterprises, tourism transporters, tourism intermediary service enterprises, tourism commodity development and sales enterprises. It adjusts and reorganizes the organizational structure and business process of the enterprise by building and using the information infrastructure, information network and information system, realizes the data and networking of the enterprise operation, and improves the operation and management efficiency and competitiveness of the enterprise.

② Tourism e-commerce.

Tourism e-commerce refers to the electronic and networked construction of e-commerce platforms or transactions related to tourism activities. It aims to use the Internet and other ICT technologies and related electronic equipment to publish, transmit and exchange basic tourism information and tourism business information, publicize tourism destinations, tourism enterprises and market tourism products. Meanwhile, it strengthens the direct communication between the main players in the tourism market, conducts pre-sales and after-sales services of tourism, and conducts electronic tourism transactions.

③ Tourism e-government.

Tourism e-government refers to the informatization of tourism management department business. Its focus is to streamline, optimize, integrate and reorganize its internal and external management and service functions through the use of modern network communication and computer technology, and then to implement it online for breaking the constraints of time, space and departmental separation. Ultimately, it will provide the public and itself with integrated colleges, high-quality, clean management and services.

7.1.2 Informatization Management of Tourism Destination

1) Content of Informatization Management of Tourism Destination

For tourism destination management agencies, the main contents of tourism destination information management include tourism industry management, public service management, marketing management, tourist management, tourism resources and environment management.

(1) Informationization of tourism industry management.

The informatization of tourism industry management in tourism destination mainly involves tourism government affairs office and tourism industry supervision. The informatization of tourism government affairs mainly includes business collaboration (electronic and grid-based business handling, official document circulation and information exchange), approval collaboration (processed and grid-based administrative approval), statistical coordination (automatic reporting, statistics, replacement and sharing of data through grids) and emergency coordination (rapid emergency command, dispatch and emergency information interconnection). It is mainly to interconnect the office systems of tourism management departments at all levels and tourist attractions or tourism enterprises in tourism destination, fully integrate and share business information and industry data, and realize the transition from paper material flow to electronic file flow. It transfers the complicated and trivial management work from the field to the online, thereby improving the management efficiency and management level and saving manpower, material resources and financial resources. The informatization of tourism industry supervision refers to the comprehensive supervision and management of the tourism industry through dynamic monitoring of tourism enterprises, collection and investigation of tourism complaints, tourism law enforcement, as well as the evaluation and public sharing of credit information and unlawful behavior information of practitioners and related practitioners. Moreover, it maintains the order, norms and service quality of the tourism market, and guides the healthy and orderly development of the tourism industry in the tourism destination.

(2) Informatization of tourism public service management.

The informatization of tourism public service management in tourism destination mainly involves the construction and management of public service systems consisting of public information services, public transportation services, public safety services, and public infrastructure. It mainly realizes the horizontal coordination of management departments through informatization means (the tourism management department, the tourism destination transportation, public security and other departments carry out labor division and cooperation according to different functions) and vertical coordination (the tourism management departments at all levels and tourist attractions or tourism enterprises according to different responsibilities for labor division). It builds tourism comprehensive information service platform (such as tourism public information service platform website, tourism call center), tourism information service facility (such as multimedia information query terminal, touch screen), public environment monitoring system (such as intelligent monitoring in public places) and pan-network (such as public WiFi) to realize the informatization of tourism public service and its monitoring and management. Its purpose is to provide all kinds of tourists and tourism enterprises with comprehensive, accurate and timely tourism public information service.

(3) Informatization of marketing management.

The informatization of tourism destination marketing management refers to relying on information technology to carry out various forms of online marketing and management activities. In terms of media, it mainly relies on tourism destination portals, mobile Apps, social media (such as WeChat and Weibo), tourism vertical websites and other new media. Functionally, it is mainly reflected in network information management and public opinion analysis, network marketing channel management and evaluation, online marketing activity implementation and management, tourism e-commerce promotion and regulation, etc. With the advantages of modern Internet marketing, it realizes the co-ordination, globalization and precision of tourism destination marketing.

(4) Informatization of tourist management.

The informatization of tourist management mainly involves tourist quantity management, tourist behavior and tourist feedback. In terms of tourist quantity management, it realizes early warning and regulation by establishing tourist demand forecast model and public environment monitoring system. In terms of tourist behavior management, it collects tourists' dynamic data through location-based services, sensing technology, video surveillance and other technologies, and establishes an early warning and management mechanism. In terms of tourist feedback management, it provides information, networking, and interactive communication channels to sense and process tourists' opinions in a timely manner.

(5) Informatization of tourism resources and environment management.

It is about utilizing remote sensing technology (RST), geographic information system

(GIS), radio frequency identification(RFID), infrared sensing, video surveillance and other means to remotely and real-timely monitor the current situation, and timely implement resource and environment maintenance and protection measures based on monitoring data.

2) Impact of Informatization Management of Tourism Destination

(1) Changing the supply chain structure of tourism destination.

The continuous improvement of the informatization degree of tourism destination will promote the transformation of the tourism supply chain structure from linear to network then to dynamic network. For example, with the continuous improvement of the informatization of tourism destination, the components of Zhangjiajie's tourism destination supply chain have increased from the original three elements of the most basic tourism suppliers, tourism intermediaries and tourists to five elements including the government and the community. Meanwhile, the types of travel intermediaries have expanded from the original traditional travel agencies to various types including traditional travel agencies, individual reception departments and travel e-commerce websites.

(2) Affecting the distribution channel of tourism destination.

The wide application of information technology promotes the evolution and development of the tourism market in the changes of transaction costs, the comparison of the costs of different transaction channels and the ebb and flow of various forces. Information technology also leads to the re-intermediation of the distribution channel of tourism destination in the process of continuous disintermediation, and continues to affect the tourism market order, market transaction rules, and market structure of tourism destination. Meanwhile, with the widespread use of mobile Internet and mobile payment software, this influence is also increasing.

(3) Innovating management service for tourism destination.

The application of information technology is a significant source of business innovation in tourism destination, including tourism resource management, ecological environment management, marketing, tourism public service and other management business innovation, which all depend on the extensive application of information technology.

(4) Supporting the realization of all-for-one tourism.

Tourism destination informatization is a vital fulcrum to realize all-for-one tourism, and they interact on each other. All-for-one tourism needs the support of all-for-one tourism informatization, and its characteristics of full-process service, all-round experience, all-element integration, all-industry integration, and all-space tourism can be implemented through the construction of a smart tourism system. And tourism informatization reflects its own value through global tourism.

(5) Enhancing the image of tourism destination.

The information management of tourism destination enables the integration of resources and elements such as scenic spots, hotels, transportation, communications, entertainment, and culture within the scope of tourism destination. It can meet the needs of tourists and provide tourists with more convenient, higher‐quality and more personalized services and experiences, thereby optimizing the image of tourism destination perceived by tourists and promoting word‐of‐mouth communication. In addition, relying on the informatization of marketing management, the image of the tourism destination can be better spread to the tourists.

(6) Increasing the competitive advantage of tourism destination.

As a factor of productivity, information technology itself has extensive penetration and value‐added. Meanwhile, information technology plays the role of "catalyst" and "booster" for the effectiveness of other tourism factors that constitute productivity. Through information management, network information flow guides business flow, capital flow and personnel flow, which can not only add new vitality to the tourism industry, but also promote the performance of all relevant elements, improve the operation efficiency, and further increase the competitive advantage of tourism destination.

(7) Reshaping the interaction and connection of the tourism industry between regions.

The development and construction of tourism destination informatization has a spatial spillover effect. The unreasonable spatial layout and competition of information infrastructure will bring negative spatial spillover effects and prevent the coordinated growth of the tourism economy in the region. The improvement of information technology consumption in tourism destination can produce positive spatial spillovers and promote the development of the tourism industry in adjacent areas. Hence, promoting the coordinated development of regional tourism informatization will help speed up the integrated development of regional tourism and improve the competitiveness of regional tourism.

3) Trend of Informatization Management of Tourism Destination

The development trend of tourism destination information management is mainly reflected in the following points: system standardization and normalization; improvement of basic database; acceleration of new technology application and innovation; intelligent, systematic, and intensive management.

(1) System standardization and normalization.

It refers to the establishment of a tourism informatization standard system covering tourism websites, tourism consulting centers, tourism service hotlines, food, accommodation, travel, shopping, entertainment and other tourism service formats. It accelerates the formulation of various national standards, industry standards, local standards and enterprise standards involving tourism information resources, and promotes mutual connection and complementarity. It selects some provinces, municipalities, tourism destinations and related enterprises with relatively mature conditions and abundant resources to carry out the pilot work of tourism information resource standards, summarizes the construction experience of tourism information resource standards, intensifies the propaganda and promotion of the pilot work, and gives full play to demonstration effect of the pilot work.

(2) Improvement of basic database.

It should establish and improve the basic tourism database system covering tourism statistical yearbook database, tourism enterprise direct reporting database, domestic tourism sample survey basic database, inbound spending survey basic database, tourism industry basic database, etc. It establishes and improves the industry data collection and sharing platform, formulates a unified data collection and sharing platform, formulates unified data collection, aggregation, sharing and exchange standards, and realizes the collection, aggregation, processing and sharing of government data, enterprise data and social data.

(3) Acceleration of new technology and application and innovation.

Tourism destination accelerates the promotion of new generation information technology (such as mobile Internet, Internet of things technology, tourism electronic payment, wearable technology, Beidou system, artificial intelligence, computer simulation technology, social network, tourism big data, tourism cloud computing) in the applications of tourism industry. It constantly innovates new tourism models, expands new tourism supplies, expands new tourism areas, and builds new tourism engines. It strives to achieve breakthroughs in meeting tourists needs, improving tourism quality, and leading comprehensive innovation. Meanwhile, it provides power support for the transformation and upgrading of the tourism industry, improving the quality, and enhancing the efficiency.

(4) Intelligent, systematic and intensive management.

Tourist destination should speed up the construction of a intelligent tourism system, and guide the development concept to change from technology supply-oriented to tourism demand-oriented. It proposes to improve the breadth and depth of the application of various intelligent technologies and intelligent equipment for tourism needs in the tourism industry, to create a "people-oriented" intelligent tourism destination management and service platform, and to realize comprehensive intelligence, systematization and intensification of tourism destination management activities, and form a large number of intelligent tourism cities and intelligent tourism enterprises with strong leading role and prominent demonstration significance.

7.1.3 Tourism Destination Information System

1) Introduction of Tourism Destination Information System

(1) The tourism destination information system (DIS).

DIS is a human-led with the use of computer hardware, software, network communication equipment and other office equipment to carry out mobile phone, transmission, processing, storage, update and maintenance of tourist information in order to improve benefits and efficiency. The purpose is to support an integrated human-machine system that supports high-level decision-making, middle-level control, and grass-roots operations of tourism organizations. Its service objects mainly include tourism administration departments, tourism enterprises and public users.

(2) Tourism administration departments.

Via the tourism destination information system, the local tourism administration departments can manage tourism enterprises, tourism resources, tourism transportation, etc., within its jurisdiction, and count various tourism-related data. It can organize tourism destination marketing and enhance communication with tourism enterprises, tourism consumers and tourism media. It can also provide various tourism services and relevant policy information to the public in a timely manner.

(3) Tourism enterprises.

For travel agencies, hotels and other tourism enterprises, they not only use the tourism destination information system to complete their internal management, but also can promote the enterprise on the tourism destination website, provide enterprise and product information, promotional information, communicate with tourists, and accept consumer inquiries and reservations, etc. For tourist attractions, it can use the information system to carry out digital scenic spot management, network marketing, online ticket sales, and provide various information services related to tourist attractions, such as electronic commentary, tour guide, queue management.

(4) Public users.

Public users refer to tourists or potential tourists, as well as potential tourism project investors. Via the tourism information system, tourists can learn about tourist attractions, tourist routes, tourist costs, and information on tourist service facilities related to tourism destinations, and make tourist reservations. In addition, investors can also learn about investment project information from the tourism destination information system.

2) Application Types of Tourism Destination Information System

(1) Destination marketing system (DMS).

DMS is a tourism informatization application system and an open systematic architecture. It is also a comprehensive application system for tourism promotion and tourism service based on the Internet, combining database technology, multimedia technology and network marketing technology. DMS mainly provides tourists with comprehensive tourism destination information via websites, including tourism resources, tourism facilities, tourism events, weather, transportation, tourism enterprises, tourism products and prices. And by building an e-commerce platform, DMS provides communication and transaction services for tourism destination administration departments, tourism enterprises and tourists in the generating regions. In addition, DMS has established a complete process of tourism information collection, release and update, complete information technology standards and management specifications, and a complete tourism information and service quality assurance mechanism. The use of DMS can effectively collect, organize and integrate tourism destination information, establish an effective market feedback mechanism for the tourism industry, carry out overall planning and effective publicity for the image of the tourism destination, and provide various marketing services for local tourism enterprises.

(2) Tourism destination geographic information system (GIS).

The application of GIS in tourism destination is a technical system for collecting, storing, managing, computing, analyzing, displaying and describing the geographical distribution data of the spatial environment of tourism destination with the support of computer hardware and software systems. The tourism destination geographic information system mainly provides geographic information services, including tourism electronic maps (positioning, navigation and other services), tourism destination resource management, tourism planning assistance, environment monitoring and protection, and management decision support.

(3) Tourism destination e-government system.

The tourism destination e-government system is a networked management information system for tourism government affairs office and tourism industry management realized by the tourism destination administration department based on tourism management network and business database of the tourism destination. In terms of system composition, the tourism destination e-government system usually includes the tourism government affairs office system and the tourism industry management information platform. The tourism government affairs office system is usually composed of the tourism e-government network of the tourism destination and the office automation system. The tourism e-government network of tourism destination promotes the interoperability of business systems of various departments, builds a high-quality, efficient, fair and inclusive government service information system, and improves the development and utilization of tourism government information resources. The office automation system realizes the electronic and networked processing of official documents of tourism administration departments at all levels, optimizes the government office process, and improves office efficiency. The tourism industry management information platform has formed an information system structure with unified data and hierarchical authorization management, and has the functions of convenient and efficient tourism resource data survey, industrial operation monitoring and emergency command.

(4) Tourism destination public information service system.

The tourism destination public information service system is a comprehensive service system that provides a variety of tourism information services, which is composed of a comprehensive tourism information service platform and corresponding tourism information service equipment and software. The comprehensive tourism information service platform is composed of tourism information websites, tourism consultation platforms, tourism service hotlines, and multimedia information query terminals. It is a unified and open tourism public platform of information release, consultation and tourism complaint, which provides information inquiry, complaint acceptance and product promotion services. Tourism information service equipment includes information service terminals such as touch screens, mobile clients and wireless network coverage provided free of charge for tourists in places such as tourism consultation centers, tourism distribution centers and tourism service centers. Tourism information service software is an information service application such as tourism official Weibo, WeChat public account, mobile Apps and other information service applications opened by tourism destinations, scenic spots, hotels and restaurants. In terms of service content, tourism public information service involves not only the government-oriented urban service system, tourism information service system, tourism transportation system, tourism distribution center and other subsystems, but also involves market-oriented service subsystems such as culture, catering, and accommodation.

7.2 Intelligent Tourism

7.2.1 Introduction of Intelligent Tourism

1) Concept of Intelligent Tourism

Intelligent tourism is the continuation and advanced stage of tourism informatization. It is a new concept developed on the basis of "Smart Planet" and "Smart Cities". IBM pioneered the "Smart Planet" business plan in 2008. The core of the plan is a smarter approach to changing the way of governments, companies and people interacting with each other by leveraging a new generation of information technology for increasing the clarity, efficiency, flexibility and responsiveness of interactions. After that, the concept of "Smart Cities" was derived and became the concrete practice of "Smart Planet" in urban construction and management. Intelligent tourism is the corresponding concept after "Smart Cities".

Although there are many definitions of intelligent tourism, it can be considered that intelligent tourism is based on a new generation of information communications technology

(ICT). It can meet tourists' personalized needs by providing high-quality and high-satisfaction services, so as to realize the systematization and intensive management changes of the sharing and effective utilization of tourism resources and social resources.

2) Related Framework

(1) The framework of intelligent tourism.

The framework of intelligent tourism shown in the following Figure 7-1 consists of technology layer, application layer, industry layer and association layer.

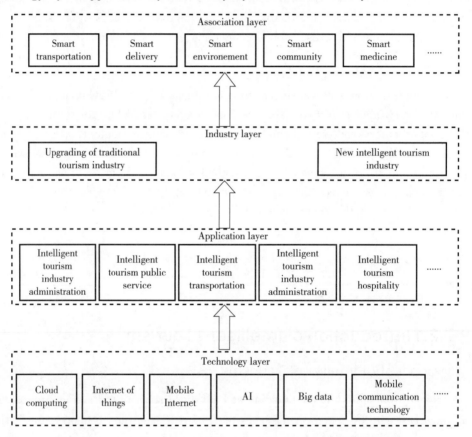

Figure 7-1　The frame work of intelligent tourism

① Technology layer.

The technology layer of intelligent tourism is to apply various intelligent technologies (including the Internet of things, cloud computing, mobile Internet, artificial intelligence, big data, mobile communication technology, etc.) to realize the construction of the underlying foundation of intelligent tourism.

② Application layer.

The application layer of intelligent tourism refers to the applications generated by the integration of technology layer and tourism elements, including intelligent tourism industry administration, intelligent tourism public services, intelligent tourism marketing, and intelligent tourism reception system.

③ Industry layer.

The industry layer of intelligent tourism refers to the transformation and upgrading of the tourism industry and the enrichment of the industry brought about by the penetration of intelligent elements in the tourism industry, including the application of intelligent elements in traditional tourism industry and sector, as well as new cultural industry, creative industry and technology service industry.

④ Association layer.

The association layer of intelligent tourism means that intelligent tourism as a significant part is interrelated with other parts of smart cities, as a significant part of them. On the one hand, the construction of the intelligent tourism system, like other smart industrial systems, relies on the perception layer and technology layer of the smart cities to realize the sharing of basic resources; on the other hand, due to the high relevance of tourism industry, the construction of the intelligent tourism system also needs to rely on the intelligent platforms and databases formed by other smart industries (such as smart transportation, smart logistics, smart environment) to realize the sharing of information resources.

(2) The technology framework of intelligent tourism.

The technology framework of intelligent tourism shown in the following Figure7-2 generally includes five layers, namely the perception layer, the transmission layer, the basic service layer, the application service layer and the information presentation layer. Meanwhile, it mainly consists of two technology guarantee systems of information security and information standard.

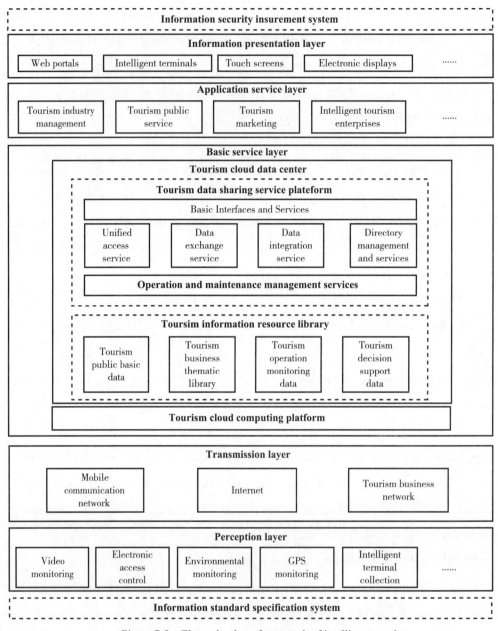

Figure 7-2　The technology framework of intelligent tourism

① Perception Layer.

It collects front-end perception information and data in various fields of the tourism industry through video monitoring, smart sensor collection, tourist smart terminal feedback, information collector reporting, and data sharing by horizontal government departments (such as transportation, meteorology, industry and commerce, environmental protection, public security, fire protection, and health).

② Transmission Layer.

It mainly realizes the unified, reliable and safe transmission of sensor data, video data, alarm data, management data and other tourism information data among tourism enterprises, scenic spots, district and county tourism departments, city and provincial tourism committees (bureaus).

③ Basic Service Layer.

This layer mainly provides basic support for upper‐layer smart services. Among them, the tourism cloud computing platform mainly provides hardware resources and supporting resources for the intelligent tourism platform, ensures the processing capacity and system security of the platform, and realizes the automatic completion of computing problems such as massive tourism information processing and query. The cloud data center is the data foundation of the entire tourism informatization, which realizes the unified collection, storage, processing, sharing and exchange of tourism information data.

④ Application Service Layer.

It mainly includes intelligent tourism public service application for tourists, intelligent tourism industry management application for tourism authorities, intelligent tourism marketing application and enterprise management application for the whole industry chain.

⑤ Information Presentation Layer.

This layer mainly includes web portal, intelligent terminals, touch screens, electronic displays, etc. It mainly provides multi‐terminal integrated tourism public information services and tourism destination marketing services for web terminals, smart mobile terminals, touch screens and other display terminals through the media information release platform.

⑥ Information Standard Specification System.

It mainly regulates tourism information data standards, application standards, technical standards, management standards, etc., through the national or tourism industry -related information standardization system.

⑦ Information Security Insurement System.

In accordance with the requirements of e‐government information security, it establishes information security strategies, security technology prevention systems, and management guarantee systems to achieve information and system confidentiality, integrity, availability, controllability, and non-repudiation.

7.2.2 Intelligent Tourism Destination

1) Introduction of Intelligent Tourism Destination

An intelligent tourism destination requires that the tourism activities of the tourism destination enable the governments, enterprises, tourists, and community residents to perceive each other, so that the data of various information systems of the tourism destination can be seamlessly connected and transferred. Data becomes the productivity of tourism activities in tourism destination. The government visualizes all tourism activities through the tourism management and control platform of tourism destinations, including scenic spots and rural tourism spots, forming an ecosystem in which tourism data, information and knowledge of tourism destination can be transferred intelligently.

The characteristics of intelligent tourism destination mainly include service personalization, subject diversification and close connection.

(1) Service personalization.

In terms of service personalization, it refers to relying on the basis of big data to provide corresponding targeted products and services for each tourist, fully reflecting the intelligence of the tourism destination.

(2) Subject diversification.

Differing from individual constructions such as smart scenic spots and smart hotels, the development and construction of intelligent tourism destination start from the whole and provides tourists with "one-stop" tourism information service. Therefore, it also requires intelligent tourism destination to integrate more administration agencies, service agencies and service facilities to achieve coordinated operation. The subjects involved in intelligent tourism destination are more diverse and complex.

(3) Close connection.

On the one hand, intelligent tourism destination requires the governments, enterprises, tourists, and community residents to establish perceptual connection with each other; on the other hand, an intelligent tourism destination is an organic whole with a unified combination of tourism elements, requiring the coordinated development of resources, information, facilities, and services.

2) Content of Intelligent Tourism Destination Construction

The construction of intelligent tourism destination is mainly reflected in three aspects: tourism services, tourism management and tourism marketing.

(1) Intelligent tourism services.

It mainly includes information services for tourists and various tourism business services for tourism enterprises. Intelligent tourism takes the concept of "host-guest sharing" as the starting point, and improves tourism experience and tourism quality with the use of information technology. It is mainly reflected in that tourists can feel the ubiquitous and personalized service experience brought by intelligent tourism in the whole process of tourism information acquisition, tourism planning decision-making, tourism product booking and payment, enjoying, reviewing and evaluating tourism. It is also reflected in allowing tourists to obtain information conveniently and quickly through intelligent information organization and presentation, helping tourists to better arrange travel plans and form travel decisions, making tourists smoother, more comfortable and more satisfied in the travel process, and bringing better travel security and travel quality assurance for tourists. Moreover, it also opens the application interface of the intelligent tourism destination management and service platform to tourism enterprise in tourism destination.

(2) Intelligent tourism management.

It mainly involves service management and market management. Firstly, through information technology, intelligent tourism can timely and accurately grasp the tourist activity information and the management information of tourism enterprises, and realize scientific decision-making and scientific management. Simultaneously, it promotes the transformation of tourism industry regulation from traditional passive processing and post-event management to process management and real-time management. Secondly, intelligent tourism forms information sharing and collaborative linkage with public security, transportation, industry and commerce, health, quality inspection and other departments, and combines tourism information data to form a tourism forecast and early warning mechanism to improve emergency management capabilities and ensure tourism safety. Thirdly, intelligent tourism management refers to the effective handling of tourism complaints and tourism quality issues, and maintaining the order of the tourism market. Finally, intelligent tourism encourages and supports tourism enterprises to widely use information technology to improve management level, enhance the competitiveness of products and services, and enhance the interaction among tourism administrative departments, tourists, tourism enterprises, tourism resources and the environment for efficiently integrating tourism resources and promoting the overall development of tourism destination.

(3) Intelligent tourism marketing.

Intelligent tourism marketing refers to the process of posting various texts, pictures, video information of tourism destinations and product information of tourism enterprises to potential tourists through various media and network communication channels. It is manifested in the display and dissemination of information on various marketing elements and means. On the one hand, intelligent tourism uses tourism public opinion monitoring and data analysis to mine tourism hot spots and tourist interest points, and guide tourism companies to plan corresponding tourism products, and formulate corresponding marketing themes, thereby promoting product innovation and marketing innovation in the tourism industry. On the other hand, intelligent tourism analyzes the content and models of communication that tourists are interested in by accumulating tourist data and tourism product consumption data, thereby gradually forming a data-supported enterprise self-media marketing platform.

3) Intelligent Tourism Destination Management System

Intelligent tourism destination management system is a model of the integration and development of tourism destination and modern technological innovation, and it is the development trend of tourism destination management. The management system construction of intelligent tourism destination mainly covers administration departments, tourists, tourism enterprises, tourism resources and environment management.

(1) The administration management department system of intelligent tourism destination.

Firstly, it is necessary to build an integrated command, dispatch and management platform with office digitization and intelligence as the core, to provide a unified means of information release, to realize the access, command and dispatch of tourism destination management events, and to supervise the responsible personnel in all aspects of the event and evaluation, remote operation, control and management of various equipment in tourism destination. Secondly, it establishes an intelligent tourism emergency response system to realize the early warning, processing and intelligent recovery of tourism disasters and abnormal situations.

(2) Tourist management system for intelligent tourism destination.

Firstly, it realizes precise management and dynamic management of tourists. It adopts technologies such as location-based services, Internet of things, sensor recognition, and video surveillance to collect tourists' traffic data and dynamic data in real time, so that tourism administration departments can carry out tourist evacuation and emergency regulation at any time. Moreover, it integrates data from other departments to identify, classify and analyze the identity and source of tourists, and assist tourism administration departments and tourism enterprises to make management decisions. Secondly, it establishes an intelligent public service system for tourists, provides comprehensive information services such as transportation, security, finance, culture, catering, accommodation, and accepts complaints and feedback from tourists.

(3) Tourism enterprise management system of intelligent tourism destination.

It establishes a unified monitoring and dispatching system. Through the collection of dynamic data of tourism enterprises, it can grasp the dynamic changes of its type, level and quantity distribution at any time, and form the supervision and command and dispatch of tourism enterprises in tourism destination. And based on enterprise data analysis, it guides and supports enterprises to develop e-commerce application in an all-round way through their own business process re-engineering, helping them develop towards an intelligent business field.

(4) Tourism resources and environment management system of intelligent tourism destination.

Firstly, it establishes sound tourism resources and environment monitoring system. It uses remote sensing technology (RST), geographic information system (GIS), radio frequency identification (RFID), infrared sensing, video surveillance and other technologies to conduct remote and real-time monitoring of tourism destination resources and environment, and timely maintain necessary resources according to the analysis results. Secondly, it sets up identification and early warning device in the vicinity of key tourist resource areas to issue warnings to tourists who view damage to tourism resources. Thirdly, based on the real-time collection of passenger flow information, it measures the real-time environment capacity through the load analysis of the environment carrying capacity, and timely warns and takes measures to guide tourists.

Case Study

"Cloud" Touring Xi'an Beilin Museum and Promoting Traditional Culture Online

Chapter Summary

With the rapid development and broadly adoption of information technology, it is significant for related government departments and enterprises of tourism destination to take into account about how to involve IT utilities nowadays.

 Issues for Review and Discussion

1. What are narrow and broad definitions of tourism informatization?
2. What are the aspects included in the connotation of tourism informatization?

Exercises

Chapter 8
Sustainable Development of Tourism Destination

Knowledge Graph

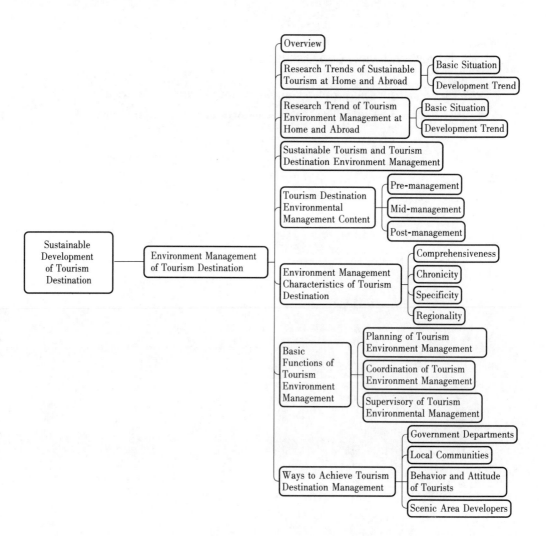

Chapter 8 Sustainable Development of Tourism Destination

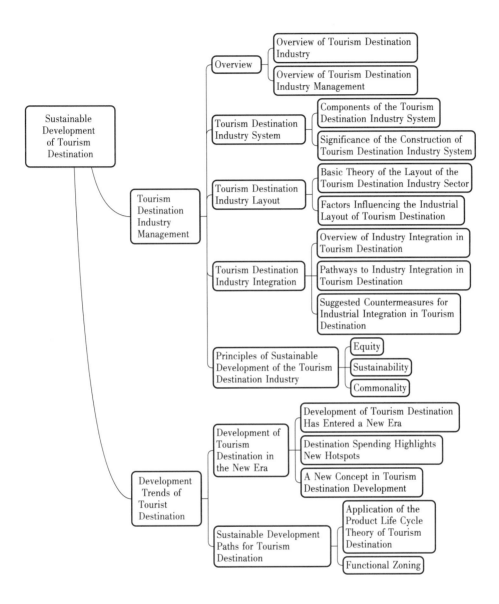

Learning Objectives

(1) Understand the connotation of sustainable development of tourism destination and the development trend in China and abroad.

(2) Grasp the classification of tourism destination industry, tourism destination industry characteristics, and tourism destination industry management characteristics.

(3) Understand the composition of tourism destination industrial system.

(4) Master the influencing factors and basic models of tourism destination industrial layout and clarify tourism destination industry integration paths.

Introduce Case

The Fourth Grand Canal Cultural Tourism Expo Was Held in Suzhou

Technical Words

English Words	中文翻译
tourism industry	旅游产业
sustainable development	可持续发展
industry management	产业管理
tourism industry system	旅游产业体系
tourism industry integration	旅游产业融合

8.1 Environment Management of Tourist Destination

8.1.1 Overview

In recent decades, world tourism has developed rapidly. However, with the rapid development of tourism, overexploitation of tourism will have a serious negative impact on the local environment: the predatory development of tourism resources, the extensive management of tourist areas, the morbid expansion of tourism facilities construction, the improper disposal of waste, the destruction of wildlife habitat, the reduction of biodiversity, etc. They are increasingly threatening the sustainable development of local areas and also affecting the further development of local tourism. These problems cause people's high attention to the sustainable development of tourism.

In the 1990s, many foreign experts put forward the concept of sustainable tourism, the essence of which is to maintain the integrity of environment resources and culture, and give the residents of tourist areas fair opportunities for development. Specifically, it is to enhance people's understanding of the environmental and economic effects of tourism and strengthen their awareness of ecological and environmental protection, promote the equitable development of tourism, improve the quality of life of residents in tourist reception areas, provide tourists with high quality of tourism life, and protect the future social tourism resources or industrial development of the ecological environment. The concept of sustainable tourism ensures the sustainable development of tourism. In the process of tourism development, we should always maintain a high degree of alert to the social, cultural and economic environment, and make positive impact for the local social, economic and cultural aspects as far as possible through reasonable tourism development activities.

Tourism environment management refers to the use of law, economy, administration, planning, science and technology, education and other means to exert influence on all behaviors and activities that may damage the tourism environment, coordinate the relationship between tourism development and environment protection, and deal with tourism-related departments in the national economy. Social groups, enterprises and institutions and individuals involve in environment issues, so that tourism development not only meets the needs of tourists, but also protects tourism resources, prevents environment pollution and destruction, and realizes the organic unity of economic, social and environmental benefits. The protection of tourism environment is mainly to solve the problem of man-made pollution and destruction of tourism environment. Therefore, the protection of tourism environment through tourism environment management is essentially to limit people's behaviors and activities that damage the tourism environment and promote to protect the tourism environment.

There is a close relationship between sustainable tourism and environment. To correctly handle the relationship between them in the process of tourism development and management, it needs to be controlled and coordinated through environment management. The environment management of tourism destination is aimed at sustainable tourism. From the perspective of environment protection, the natural environment of tourism destination is actively managed, effectively guided and monitored in real time to provide tourists with a beautiful and comfortable tourism environment. At present, the research on environment management of tourism destination at home and abroad is not well combined with tourism, and there is a lack of integration of the scientific development concept of sustainable tourism into environment management. Therefore, studying the relationship between sustainable tourism and environment management is conducive to providing a theoretical basis for the environment management of tourism destination, and better guiding the implementation of environment management of tourism destination to promote the sustainable development of tourism destination.

8.1.2 Research Trend of Sustainable Tourism at Home and Abroad

1) Basic Situation

From 24 to 28 in April 1995, United Nations Educational, Scientific and Cultural Organization(UNESCO), United Nations Environment Programme(UNEP) and World Tourism Organization(WTO) convened the World Conference on Sustainable Tourism Development in Lanzarote, Canary Islands, Spain, which was attended by more than 600 representatives from 75 countries and regions. The conference established the basic ideas and theories of tourism sustainable development, and finally passed *Tourism Sustainable Development Charter* and *Tourism Sustainable Development Action Plan*. This conference marked the birth of the concept of sustainable tourism. Subsequently, *Manila Declaration on the Social Impact of Tourism, Agenda 21 for the Tourism (Travel) Industry Towards Environmentally Sustainable Development* and so on were constantly deepening the concept of sustainable tourism.

China's research on sustainable tourism started in the late 1980s. Since the concept of sustainable tourism was put forward, China's sustainable tourism theory has also been unprecedentedly developed through several international conferences and various declarations adopted by the conference. Among them, the most important theoretical research on sustainable tourism development is the National Natural Science Foundation of China (NSFC) "Ninth Five Years Plan" Key Project Research on the Theory and Practice of Sustainable Development of China's Tourism Industry chaired by Professor Guo Laixi. The results of the research not only have achievements in tourism theory, but also can directly serve the national and regional macro decision-making and scientific, systematic and standardized services of industrial development. At present, the theoretical research of sustainable tourism has become a hot topic in China.

2) Development Trend

Since the promulgation of *Tourism Sustainable Development Charter* and *Tourism Sustainable Development Action Plan* (hereinafter referred to as "*Charter and Action Plan*"), foreign countries have had a common understanding of sustainable tourism, and studied and developed sustainable tourism in their respective tourist attractions in accordance with *Charter* and *Action Plan*. Since Professor Guo Laixi's research on the theory and practice of sustainable development of Chinese tourism, many scholars and experts have begun to study the concept of sustainable tourism, and have transitioned to practical research, such as environment impact assessment.

There are obvious differences between domestic and foreign scholars on the research focus of sustainable tourism. Foreign scholars focus on practical application, while domestic scholars mainly focus on theoretical research, even if it is applied research, the elaboration of the theory is often too long. Therefore, on the whole, there is still a certain gap between Chinese research on sustainable tourism and international research. For example, many theories in the study of the concept of sustainable development often cannot get rid of the framework of foreign theoretical research. However, Chinese sustainable tourism theory research has certain advantages. Since Scientific Outlook on Development was put forward, sustainable tourism, as a form of scientific concept of development, has a solid theoretical and policy support. It fully reflects the Chinese characteristics while studying the sustainable development of many scenic spots in China. Therefore, while absorbing foreign advanced theories, enriching sustainable tourism research with Chinese characteristics is the direction that Chinese scholars and experts need to pay attention to.

8.1.3 Research Trend of Tourism Environment Management at Home and Abroad

1) Basic Situation

Since tourism activities and tourism development have a great impact on tourist attractions and local environment, tourism environment management is mainly aimed at tourism destination. There are many monographs in this field abroad, such as Ralf Buckley's *Nature-based Tourism, Environment and Land Management* which discussed the relationship between tourism and society, culture and environment in detail, and put forward some views on tourism environment management. In addition, the book *Environmental Management and the Competitiveness of Nature - Based Tourism Destinations* by Twan Huybers and Jeff Bennett studied the relationship between tourism and environment in detail, and put forward a preliminary idea of managing environment from the perspective of tourism. At present, there is little literature on environment management from the perspective of tourism. Most scholars focus on the environment impact of tourism development and the environment management of tourism destination from a theoretical point of view. In his article *Tourism Development and Environment Management*, Fu Wenwei elaborated Chinese tourism environment management system and current situation and put forward some suggestions for environment management. Lin Yueying made a detailed introduction to the concept of tourism environment management in his article *On Tourism Environment Management*, and elaborated the characteristics and functions of tourism management. The microscopic research includes Feng Haiyan's *Preliminary Study on Environment Management of Tourist Attractions*, which mainly studied the specific environment management content and implementation methods of tourist attractions.

2) Development Trend

At present, domestic and foreign scholars generally believe that environment management of tourism destination is a part of environment management, which is the management of tourism destination environment under the framework of environment management. This consensus can clearly explain the content and scope of tourism environment management, but it lacks a description of the purpose of tourism environment management. The purpose of tourism environment management is to ensure the normal operation of tourism. After the concept of sustainable tourism is put forward, the goal of tourism environment management is to ensure the sustainable development of tourism in the early, middle and late stages of development. This goal shows that tourism environment management has gone beyond the scope of ordinary environment management, but fully embodies the characteristics of sustainable tourism. However, the current domestic and foreign research only focus on the means of management, policy development, and have not yet stood at a higher level of tourism environment management.

8.1.4 Sustainable Tourism and Tourism Destination Environment Management

Sustainable tourism is a broad concept, which requires the development of tourism to ensure the coordination and unity of the three goals of local society, economy and environment. The social goal is to protect the local cultural heritage, enhance the cultural pride of the local people, provide understanding and communication opportunities for people from different regions and cultural backgrounds, and provide tourists with high-quality tourism products; the environment goal is to improve the way of land use, from consumptive use to constructive use, improve the ecological environment, strengthen the public environmental and cultural awareness, promote the protection of the environment and culture, and protect the ecological and cultural environment on which the future tourism product development depends; the economic goal is to increase employment, expand product market, increase economic income, improve local infrastructure and improve the quality of life in the region.

Tourism destination environment management is a discussion on the sustainable development of tourism under the framework of sustainable tourism. Because the development of tourism will bring positive or negative effects to the society, economy, cultural and natural environment of the tourist area, the management of these effects constitutes the main body of environment management in tourism destination.

8.1.5 Tourism Destination Environment Management Content

Tourism destination environment management has different descriptions according to different division methods. According to the functions, tourism destination environment management includes environment planning management, environment quality management and environment technology management. Based on the development process of sustainable tourism, this section divides the environment management of tourism destination into pre-management, mid-management and post-management, so as to more intuitively reflect the environment management.

1) Pre-management

Tourism destination environment management is not just a simple post-maintenance management of tourism destination after the end of tourism development. At the beginning of tourism development, it is necessary to effectively manage and plan the environment. The pre-management of the tourism environment mainly refers to the investigation and analysis of the local tourism environment, including natural environment background investigation, social and economic environment background investigation, and the calculation of the carrying capacity of the tourism environment derived from it. In the past, many tourism development activities have made detailed and specific investigations on the local nature, society, economy and culture in the early stage. According to these investigations, the carrying capacity of tourism environment has been measured, but a complete system has not been formed yet. Coordinating these tasks and incorporating them into the pre-management of tourism environment management are conducive to making a correct, comprehensive and systematic evaluation of the local background of tourism development and helping to choose a reasonable sustainable development model.

Tourism carrying capacity is one of the important criteria to measure sustainable tourism and an important tool to describe the environment of tourism destination. The carrying capacity of tourism environment includes social carrying capacity, natural carrying capacity, economic carrying capacity and residents' psychological carrying capacity. According to the bucket principle, the factors that restrict the development of tourism in tourism destination are judged. Based on the natural environment background report and the social environment background report, the environment carrying capacity of the tourism destination under different space and time scales is measured, and the current situation of the tourism environment of the tourism destination is comprehensively described, which provides guarantee for the middle and later management of tourism environment management.

2) Mid-management

After a detailed background survey of tourism destination, tourism development has entered the medium-term development stage based on tourism planning. There will be a large number of construction projects in this stage, and it is also the most obvious stage of tourism development on environment impact. Therefore, the mid-management of the tourism environment directly affects whether the development of the tourism destination can move forward with the goal of sustainability. Mid-management includes tourism environment quality assessment, tourism activities on the environment impact analysis and tourism development environment impact monitoring.

(1) Evaluating tourism environment quality.

Evaluating tourism environment quality should be included into the middle of tourism environment management, because many tourist areas often have beautiful background environment quality, but the ecological environment is so fragile that a little development will cause irreparable damage to the environment of tourist areas. Therefore, the significance of tourism environment quality evaluation is to describe the tourism environment quality in the process of development and use the platform of environment quality evaluation to evaluate the environment quality change of tourism destination, and provide data support for the whole medium-term tourism environment management.

(2) Analysis of the impact of tourism activities on environment.

When evaluating the quality of tourism environment, it will be found that the impact of tourism activities on the environment is not a simple destruction, but has both advantages and disadvantages. Therefore, the environment impact analysis of tourism activities is based on the evaluation of tourism environment quality to study the impact of tourism activities on the environment of tourism destination. The study of these effects can provide a rational analysis for the tourism development process and provide targeted objectives for tourism environment management.

3) Post-management

Post-management of the tourism destination environment is a central part of the overall environment management. Pre-management and mid-management provide good data support and impact analysis for post-management respectively, while post-management addresses the impact of tourism activities on the tourism environment after tourism development.

The environment impact of tourism is managed. The management of the environment is also enriched by the maintenance of the tourism destination, the dynamic monitoring of the tourism environment information system and the establishment of an early warning system for the tourism environment.

(1) Environment protection in tourism destination.

Environment protection in tourism destination is also known as tourism environment management in the traditional sense, which manages the water, air, noise, solid waste and protects the flora and fauna, to maintain the environment quality of existing tourism destination, and through the joint collaboration of government environment protection departments and the management of scenic spots, to carry out comprehensive management of the environment in tourist attractions. For example, the separate collection and management of solid waste within the scenic area, the establishment of fixed water quality monitoring points, the placement of noise pollution warning signs and the establishment of patrols for the protection of flora and fauna will all ensure the normal circulation and discharge of water, air, noise and solid waste within the scenic area on a daily basis.

(2) Dynamic monitoring of environment information in tourism destination.

Traditional environment management in tourism destination is often done through on-site surveys. This can be adequate in the early and middle stages of environment management, but as the development of tourism destination progresses, long periods of data collection and analysis are required.

The analysis then requires a lot of human and material resources. Therefore, through the use of GIS technology, the construction of tourism environment information system can well achieve the dynamic monitoring of the environment quality of the entire tourism destination. The main components of the tourism environment information system include the dynamic distribution of tourists and the environment background data. By monitoring the distribution of tourists, it is possible to visually analyze the areas with the highest incidence of environment events in tourism at that moment in time. The monitoring of environment background data provides real and effective data for the evaluation of tourism environment quality and the impact of tourism activities on the environment at a later stage of tourism environment management, and allows the use of GIS technology to build tourism distribution models and dynamic models of tourism environment quality.

(3) Early warning system for the tourism destination environment.

Tourism destination environment early warning system can be said to be the tourism environment late management alarm bell, in the tourism environment there are major problems, such as the number of tourists surge, major environment pollution events affecting the scenic environment, these problems can be based on the tourism environment early warning measures developed in advance to adjust and repair. Therefore, the tourism destination environment early warning system is mainly based on the tourism environment carrying capacity and the development of the tourism environment quality warning line of that tourist place, forming a set of tourism environment carrying capacity as the main theoretical basis of the system. For example, after a surge of tourists or major environment pollution events, the tourism destination environment early warning system can maintain the tourism environment according to the established management and restoration measures to ensure that the tourism environment is restored to its original state in the shortest possible time.

8.1.6 Environment Management Characteristics of Tourism Destination

1) Comprehensiveness

Due to the industrial characteristics of tourism itself, such as the number and breadth of sectors and units involved, the production and consumption of products, the tourism environment involves not only the natural ecological environment, such as the atmosphere, water bodies, soil, organisms, many of which are natural tourism resources in their own right, but also the human and social environment in which there are both human tourism resources, such as cultural relics, monuments, folklore, culture and art, and tourism social environment such as safety and health, convenience and comfort, and relaxation of the tourism destination and the tourist dependency, folklore, culture and art. Therefore, the field of tourism environment management involves political, economic, social, natural, scientific and technological aspects, and the scope of tourism environment management involves tourism, transportation, culture, cultural relics, environmental protection, industry and commerce, health, public security, industry, agriculture, forestry, water conservancy and other departments. In addition, the prevention and control of environment pollution invovles society, economy, culture, ecology and other aspects of the system engineering, any single approach or measure cannot work, they must take law, economy, administration, planning, science and technology, education of the supporting approach, and combining with the integrated prevention and control to achieve success. In this way, tourism environment management is highly integrated.

The management of the tourism environment with the aim of sustainable development requires the correct evaluation and management of the natural environment and the comprehensive and systematic management of the various factors that may affect tourism development and tourism activities.

2) Chronicity

The environment management of tourism destination is integrated throughout the development and operation of the destination. Environment research is incorporated into environment management at the early stages of development, and long-term management is carried out from tourism development to the later stages of tourism activities, ensuring the harmonious development of tourism development, tourism activities and the tourism environment throughout.

3) Specificity

The management of the tourism environment with the objective of sustainable development also has its own specificities. Due to the beautiful environment quality of some tourism areas, as well as the relatively high carrying capacity of the tourism environment, a relatively large number of tourism development activities can be carried out.

Development activities have no impact on the tourism environment for a short period of time, but over time, their environment effects gradually emerge. Traditional tourism environment management is no longer able to ensure sustainable tourism development because it lacks control over tourism development and tourism activities as a whole and throughout the entire process. Sustainable tourism environment management is about limiting and managing current tourism development activities in a gradual and long-term way to ensure the sustainability of tourism development and tourism activities.

4) Regionality

As the state of the tourism environment is influenced and constrained by the geographical location, climatic condition, population density, transport condition, economic development, industrial layout, social civilization, tourism resources and the degree of development and environment capacity of the destination and tourism-dependent area, the means adopted and the content implemented for tourism environment management will vary from region to region. Therefore, tourism environment management has a clear regional dimension.

8.1.7 Basic Functions of Tourism Environment Management

The basic functions of tourism environment management refer to those inherent functions in the tourism environment itself. Although the subject of tourism environment management is multicultural, there are broadly three basic functions of tourism environment management: planning, coordination, supervision.

1) Planning of Tourism Environment Management

Regulation and planning are arrangements that people make for future activities. The difference between them is that regulation is longer, generally over a year, and focuses on defining the objectives to be achieved by future activities, and the steps to achieve them and important measures, while planning is shorter, generally under a year, and focuses on concretizing planning objectives and implementing realistic, concrete and feasible measures and action programs. There is a spatial and temporal gradual process of the tourism environment pollution and tourism resources damage. If there is a long time accumulation of the scope of tourism resources damage and tourism environment pollution, it is difficult to change and restore to a good state in a short period of time, the cost is tragic, and some tourism resources and their environment suffered damage and pollution are impossible to recover. Therefore, we should not only take some emergency measures to deal with the immediate pollution and damage to the tourism environment, but also develop long-term planning and plan to determine the objectives of tourism environment protection to be achieved in a certain period of time and the corresponding steps and major measures to be taken, so as not to repeat the painful path of "pollution first, treatment later" in other industries.

Planning is the most fundamental function of tourism environment management, which is the basis and guarantee of tourism environment protection work and activities. Planning for tourism environment management is developed and implemented by the various different tourism environment management functions. Environment planning made by environment management functions at all levels should take full account of tourism environment protection and include tourism development in the economic and social development plan and program of the same level of government, taking full account of the importance of the tourism environment to tourism development, national economy and social development. Development planning for the tourism industry and its related industries should reflect the contents of the environment protection plan of governments at all levels. Development planning for tourism and related enterprises and institutions should also reflect the environment protection contents covered in the plan of the competent departments.

2) Coordination of Tourism Environment Management

The coordination of tourism environment management means that all the various industries, units and individuals related to tourism environment protection are organically combined so that they can form a synergy to achieve the desired goals of tourism environment management. The role of the coordination function in tourism environment management is to reduce the disconnection and contradiction between the various aspects and elements of tourism environment protection, and to establish a normal relationship between the top and the bottom, and between the various sectors and individuals, so that they can work together in unison and in a coordinated manner to achieve the goals of tourism environment protection. In this sense, the management of the tourism environment is actually a kind of cross-management. For example, the environment protection, forestry and public security departments manage rare species and wildlife, and the tourism, industry and commerce and taxation departments manage the tourism market order. As the content and scope of tourism environment management is extremely broad, and its subjects are presented as diverse, coordination is objectively required. The protection of the tourism environment can hardly be achieved by the tourism and environment protection departments alone. In some cases, coordination is required at the appropriate level of government. For example, in the West Lake scenic area in Hangzhou and the Baiyun Mountain scenic area in Guangzhou, various departments and units built hotels and guesthouses, destroying the natural ecological environment of the scenic area, and in the end the municipal government stepped in to coordinate the work. Therefore, coordination is an important function of tourism environment management.

3) Supervisory of Tourism Environmental Management

It is not enough to have rules, coordination and division of labor in the management of the tourism environment. To ensure that the plans are implemented, there must be strong monitoring. Supervision includes monitoring and supervising. The supervision function of tourism environment management means that the management body monitors the managed behaviors and results in tourism and related activities for deviations from the management objectives, as well as supervising the relevant units and individuals to comply with and implement the regulations, plans, rules and standards of tourism environment protection.

To achieve the supervision function of tourism environment management, there must be two basic conditions. The first one is a sound basis for the implementation of supervision, mainly including tourism environment planning, regulations, rules and standards, etc. The second one is to have the authority of the management body to be able to justify the implementation of the supervision function given by the state.

The supervisory function of tourism environment management cannot only be directed at the results of the process of tourism and its related activities, but should also be carried out throughout the whole process of the regulated activities. For example, the bad phenomenon should be stopped at the beginning and solved in a timely manner, because the work will be much more passive and difficult when the problem is exposed. The costs of environment damage and management will be even greater. Therefore, it is important to monitor and supervise the whole process of the tourism environment and its related activities to help protect it.

8.1.8 Ways to Achieve Tourism Destination Management

Traditional environment management of tourist attractions is mostly narrow ecological environment management, that is, only from the perspective of the scenic area itself to solve the environment pollution problem, without open and macroscopic consideration from the perspective of the tourism experience and without taking into account the requirements of the stakeholders of the scenic area on the tourism environment, so the environment management work is still limited to the scenic area project itself, the "initiative" can not be extended to the external environment of the scenic area. In order to achieve environment management at a more macro level and in a more comprehensive scope, it is necessary to build a scenic environment management system with the participation of the stakeholders of the tourist attractions. The so-called stakeholders are "any individual and group who can influence the achievement of the objectives of the enterprise or who can be influenced by the process of achieving the objectives of the enterprise" (Freeman, 1984). From the perspective of scenic environment management, scenic area stakeholders mainly include government departments, local communities, tourists and scenic area developers, etc. They have an interactive and mutually influential relationship with the scenic environment(as shown in Table 8-1). The realization of environment management in tourist attractions depends on the activities of the respective stakeholders and the coordination of the relationships between them.

Table 8-1 The relationship between scenic environment and stakeholders

Stakeholders	Key points of interest	Examples of the relationship with the scenic area environment
Government departments	Economic and social benefits	On the basis of obtaining certain economic and social benefits, we should strive to obtain certain environmental benefits and realize regional sustainable development.
Local communities	The improvement of living standard, the improvement of living environment	The local community living environment is a part of the tourism environment.
Tourists	A pleasant travel experience	Tourists satisfy their tourism needs in the scenic spot environment and exert influence on the scenic spot environment with their tourism behavior.
Scenic area developers	The highest return on investment	The scenic area environment is used to obtain the expected return on investment, and its business activities play a key role in the scenic area environment.

1) Government Departments

Among the various stakeholders in a tourist attraction, the government departments play a macro‐regulatory and leading role. They regulate and guide the behaviors and activities of other stakeholders through legislation, taxation and administration, thus achieving environment management of the tourist attractions.

2) Local Communities

Local communities are not only the most affected stakeholder in the area, but also the most influential in environment management in the area. Environment management in tourist attractions must take into account the issue of community participation and actively encourage local communities to participate in environment management, to play their role in environment management supervision and maintenance, and at the same time to strengthen environment education for the communities, to shoot public service announcements, and to create a good tourism human environment.

3) Behavior and Attitude of Tourists

The behavior and attitude of tourists are key factors in the environment management of scenic areas, emphasizing that tourists should be responsibly for the environment. One of the keys to managing tourists is to determine the correct tourism capacity. Attention should be paid to capacity control within the area as well as to the balance of hot and cold tourist routes within the region. Another important element is the adoption of effective methods and techniques to educate tourists about the conservation of the landscape and the environment. In addition, tourists must respect the folklore, the cultural traditions and the religious beliefs of local communities.

4) Scenic Area Developers

Scenic area environment management is an important purpose of sustainable tourism. In the case of destination developer, the principles of sustainable tourism are to be observed at all stages of their operations, including energy and water consumption, waste disposal, product development, marketing and transportation, and other aspects of tourism. Sustainable tourism depends both on the development strategy of the destination itself and, to varying degrees, on the marketing strategies and business tactics of the destination developers. In particular, developers need to manage relationship with the local communities by developing private projects while providing public facilities and services to meet the needs and aspirations of the communities.

8.2 Tourism Destination Industry Management

8.2.1 Overview

1) Overview of Tourism Destination Industry

The tourism industry is a comprehensive industry that provides transportation, sightseeing, accommodation, catering, and hotels for tourists by virtue of tourism and entertainment services. Tourism business is mainly composed of three parts: tourism, passenger transport and hotel industry. They are the three pillars of tourism. Tourism is also known as smokeless industry and intangible trade. As a new and advanced form of social consumption, tourism often combines material life consumption with cultural life consumption. The advanced form of social consumption in the narrow sense mainly refers to travel agencies, tourist hotels, travel cars and ship companies, and various industries related to tourism. The broad sense of tourism, in addition to specialized tourism business departments, also includes tourism-related industries.

(1) Tourism industry.

National Statistical Classification of the Tourism and Related Industries (2018) defines the basic scope of tourism and related industries. Tourism in this classification refers to the activities of tourists, i.e. their travel, accommodation, dining, sightseeing, shopping and entertainment. Tourists are those who travel for sightseeing, recreation, visiting friends and relatives, culture and sports, health care, short-term education (training), religious pilgrimage, or for official business purposes, and they travel outside their usual environment for duration of less than one year. At the same time, this classification divides the tourism destination industry into two main parts: tourism and tourism-related industries. Tourism refers to the collection of activities that directly provide services such as travel, accommodation, dining, sightseeing, shopping to tourists; tourism-related industries refer to the collection of activities such as providing tourism support services and government tourism management services to tourists on their trips.

The tourism industry is divided into seven categories: tourism travel, tourism accommodation, tourism catering, tourism excursion, tourism shopping, tourism entertainment and tourism integrated services, which are classified as follows.

① Tourism travel: tourism railway transport (railway passenger transport, passenger railway stations), tourism road transport (urban tourism public transport services, road passenger transport), tourism water transport (water passenger transport, passenger ports), tourism air transport (air passenger transport, sightseeing air services, airports, air traffic management), other tourism travel services (passenger ticket agents, tourism transport equipment rental).

② Tourism accommodation: general tourism accommodation services (touristm hotels, general hostels, other tourism accommodation services), recreational tourism accommodation services.

③ Tourism catering: tourism meal service, tourism fast food service, tourism beverage service, tourism snack service, tourism catering delivery service.

④ Tourism excursion: park tours (city park management, tourist attraction management, eco-tourism tours, amusement parks), other tourism tours (heritage and non-physical park management, museums, religious services, martyrs' cemeteries, memorials, tourism exhibition services, agricultural tourism and leisure tourism).

⑤ Tourism shopping: travel tools and fuel shopping, travel goods shopping.

⑥ Tourism entertainment: tourism and cultural entertainment (cultural performance tourism services, performance venue tourism services, tourism indoor entertainment services, tourism photography and printing services), tourism and fitness entertainment (sports venue tourism services, tourism fitness services), tourism and leisure entertainment (bath tourism services, health tourism services, other tourism and leisure entertainment services).

⑦ Tourism integrated services: travel agencies and related services, other tourism integrated services (tourism event planning services, tourism e-platform services, tourism business management services).

(2) Tourism-related industries.

The tourism-related industries are divided into two categories: ancillary tourism services and government tourism management services, which are classified as follows.

Ancillary tourism services are divided into tourist travel sevices (tourist rail travel, tourist road travel, water travel, tourist air travel), tourist handling services, tourism financial services (tourism-related banking, tourism personal insurance, tourism property insurance, other tourism financial services), tourism education services (tourism secondary vocational education, tourism higher education, tourism training), other tourism auxiliary services (tourism security, tourism translation, tourism entertainment and sports equipment rental, tourism daily necessities rental, tourism advertising) and other types; government tourism management services are divided into government tourism affairs management and foreign-related tourism affairs management.

Tourism project, from initial planning to design and construction, and then to opening for business and visitors to play, requires the close cooperation of all these links. The tourism industry has a cross-sectoral complexity and a multi-sectoral approach to service consumption, with a strong interdependence between tourism products and the need for each link to provide security. Therefore, the tourism industry is more of a "pan-tourism industry structure based on the tourism industry itself and linked to the primary, secondary and tertiary industries such as health and sports, culture and arts, finance, public services and other related industries".

The tourism destination industry is a comprehensive industry that provides goods and services for the tourism activities of tourists by virtue of the tourism resources and tourism facilities of the destination, and in addition to the general characteristics of the economic industry, the tourism destination industry also has its own unique characteristics. In addition to the general characteristics of an economic industry, the tourism destination industry has its own unique characteristics.

① Openness.

In the context of the knowledge economy, soft elements such as technology, intelligence, creativity and network are the core drivers for the development of the tourism industry. Under the role of these soft elements, the tourism industry is constantly integrating with new things, making the scope of the modern tourism industry highly open. From the supply of tourism resources, tourism resources are no longer limited to traditional natural resources such as mountains and rivers or human tourism resources such as monuments and sites, social phenomena, economic activities, and folklore can be transformed into tourism resources, leading to the emergence of new tourism products such as exhibition tourism, film and television tourism, wellness tourism and space tourism. The infinite supply of tourism resources has pushed the boundaries of the tourism industry to extend indefinitely. The dynamic nature of tourist demand and the regional characteristics of tourism supply also lead to uncertainty in the boundaries of the tourism industry.

② Regionality.

The development of the tourism industry must be based on tourism resources, tourism infrastructure, and the tourism industry of a country or region.

Development is influenced by the character, the level of development, the conservation of the tourism resources of the place, the transport, the accommodation and the communication facilities of the place and the tourism.

The tourism industry is constrained by factors such as the construction of supporting facilities, and has strong regional characteristics. The development of the tourism industry is constrained by the regional economic development environment, while the development of tourism will promote local economic growth, optimize the local industrial structure as well as increase employment and labor income.

These particularities of the tourism industry show that factors such as the level of tourism infrastructure development, the rationalization and advanced structure of the tourism industry, the government's industrial coordination function and the supply of public service products have an important impact on the competitiveness of the tourism industry.

2) Overview of Tourism Destination Industry Management

(1) Concept of tourism destination industry management.

Tourism destination industry management is the process of planning, organizing, coordinating, communicating and controlling the tourism industry in order to design and maintain a favorable environment for achieving the objectives of destination industry development and regional macro-control. Tourism destination industry management is sometimes understood as tourism industry management.

The first level is through the tourism organizations and industry associations which plan, coordinate and communicate the production and operation activities of the various sectors and promote the development of the industry. The second level is for national government agencies to plan, coordinate and guide the various sectors by setting various fiscal and financial policies to determine the development direction and objectives of the various sectors in tourism, especially the key sectors. Coordination among them is mainly through close communication among industry associations and cross-industry trade federations and government departments.

(2) Characteristics of tourism destination industry management.

The main subjects of tourism destination industry management are tourism administration departments and tourism industry organizations at all levels. Therefore, tourism destination industry management has the following main characteristics.

① Comprehensiveness.

The management of the tourism industry has an comprehensive character. Tourism is a highly interrelated industry with six major tourism.

The elements of "food, accommodation, transport, tourism, shopping and entertainment" make the management of the tourism industry very extensive, and the management of the tourism industry is not only within the tourism sector, but also in other related sectors.

② Broadness.

The scope of tourism industry management has broad characteristics. Tourism activities are activities involving multiple regions and sectors, thus tourism industry management involves a wide range of active departments and tourism administrative departments are difficult to coordinate. In reality there is a more serious "multiple government" phenomenon.

③ Dynamicity.

Tourism industry management is dynamic in character. Tourism industry management is a dynamic management, involving the whole process of tourism enterprise operation. For example, in the case of travel agencies, tourism industry management forms a dynamic management process from the approval of license, collection of quality deposit, annual inspections, complaint handling and the treatment of unqualified enterprises.

④ Innovation.

Tourism industry management is characterized by innovation. With the arrival of the "Internet+" and the information age, the Internet, cloud computing, big data, the Internet of things and other new things, the development of modern information and communication technologies has brought new development opportunities for the change, transformation and upgrading of traditional industries, and the vigorous development of smart tourism is a product of the times that tourism has emerged from the current scenario, providing new ways and methods for innovative management of the tourism industry.

(3) Contents of tourism destination industry management.

① Regulation and management of the tourism industry.

It refers to the implementation of the Party's cultural work guidelines and policies, the study and formulation of cultural and tourism policies and measures, and the drafting of cultural tourism laws and regulations. At present, there is an imbalance between the total supply and demand of tourism in China, the structure of tourism competition is more intense and disorderly, the market is relatively chaotic, and there is a strong demand for maintaining order in the tourism industry both inside and outside. Therefore, the construction of the legal system of the tourism industry should be accelerated, and the supervision and enforcement of the tourism industry should be strengthened to create a favorable environment for the development of the tourism industry.

② Tourism industry service management.

With the gradual maturation of China's market mechanism, the direct intervention of the tourism administration on tourism enterprises should be gradually reduced, and the focus of industry management should shift to providing industry services for the healthy development of the tourism industry. These industry services include the followings.

a. Tourism information service.

This includes tourism information statistics and dissemination, the construction of tourism information markets and information platforms, etc. This is an important aspect of industry management to serve the industry as a whole and provide public goods.

b. Tourism promotion service.

It includes the promotion of tourism products as well as the image of the country and the tourism destination.

c. Tourism relationship coordination service.

Tourism involves many industry sectors and tourism management functions involve many government departments, and tourism administrative authorities should do a good job of coordinating these intricate relationships.

d. Tourism education and training service.

Education and training for industry practitioners are important guarantees for the sustainable development of an industry, as education and training have strong externalities and quasi-public goods attributes, tourism industry management departments should increase investment in this area and encourage the participation of market players through appropriate mechanism.

e. Standardized tourism service.

Tourism standardization is important for regulating the business behavior of tourism enterprises, clarifying the relationship between the rights and obligations of tourism enterprises and tourism consumers, and forming a unified tourism market, etc. Tourism authorities and tourism industry associations should increase their efforts to develop and implement tourism industry standards.

③ Tourism industry planning and management.

Governments in all countries are committed to the preparation and implementation of tourism planning. Tourism planning is an important guiding document for the development of tourism, and is an important tool for governments at all levels to determine the direction of tourism development, achieve tourism development goals and layout of tourism productivity, and implement macroeconomic regulation. It's an important tool for controlling and guiding the behavior of companies.

④ Supervision and management of the tourism industry.

As a "smoke-free industry", tourism has developed into a sunrise industry. The efficient and rational development of the tourism industry not only adjusts and optimizes the industrial structure, but also contributes to the harmonious development of society. The government, as the competent authority for the tourism industry, has the responsibility of regulating the industry. In the process of developing and using tourism resources, government departments should effectively supervise and control the behavior of enterprises, so as to reconcile short-term and long-term interests, individual interests and public interests, and lay the foundation for the sustainable development of tourism.

(4) Measures of tourism destination industry management.

The management tools are linked to the management subjects and their specific forms are profoundly influenced by the nature of the management subjects themselves. The main bodies of tourism industry management are the relevant government departments and private industry management organizations. The government's industrial management department mainly establishes a tourism management measure system centered on administrative means; private enterprise management organizations, mainly centered on services, rely on association charters and rules to establish a tourism management measure system. Specifically, Chinese current industry management mainly has the following instruments.

① Tourism market access measures.

In order to ensure the basic quality of tourism operators and practitioners and the quality of tourism products, Chinese tourism management authorities have formulated and implemented corresponding tourism policies and regulations and established a tourism market quasi-personnel system, mainly including the travel agency licensing system, the tour guide qualification certificate system, and the tourist spotting and hotel star rating system. The tourism market associate system is achieved by granting administrative approval powers to the relevant competent authorities.

② Tourism market supervision and management measures.

For operators and practitioners who have entered the tourism market, the management of Chinese tourism industry has also developed a set of mechanisms to regulate and monitor their conducts, for example, the tourism complaint system, the travel agency quality deposit system, the annual inspection and review system, and the tourism market special rectification system. The tourism market supervision and management system concentrates on the government's use of administrative power to regulate and restrain the behavior of market players.

③ Tourism market guidance and service measures.

In addition to compulsory administrative measures, China has also developed a number of systems and practices to guide the behavior of tourism enterprises and serve the tourism market, such as the formulation and introduction of tourism planning at all levels, the development of tourism standardization, tourism marketing and tourism information services. The tourism market guidance and service tools reflect the transformation of government functions and industrial management, they are more adapted to the development of Chinese market economy system, and they should be further strengthened in the future.

8.2.2 Tourism Destination Industry System

Chinese modern tourism industry system is tourism management system and tourism scenic system. The travel agency system is a system jointly constituted by the political development and tourism system of China, and has a complex internal relationship. It jointly maintains the development of the tourism industry system.

1) Components of the Tourism Destination Industry System

Specifically, the modern tourism industry system consists of three main systems: tourism authority management system, tourism operation system and tourism preservation system.

(1) Tourism authority management system.

This is the core system of the modern tourism industry system, which consists of the national government tourism authority, the main tourism departments of the people's governments and the tourism industry associations at all levels. The national tourism authorities include tourism management departments established by governments at all levels, whose main responsibilities are to coordinate the development of tourism, formulate development policies, plans and standards, draft relevant laws and regulations and supervise their implementation, guide tourism work within their jurisdictions, organize the census, planning, development and protection of tourism resources, formulate market development strategies for domestic tourism, inbound tourism and outbound tourism within their administrative jurisdictions and organize their implementation, and organize the overall image of tourism. The authorities are also responsible for the overall management of tourist attractions, travel agencies and other tourism services and practitioners, regulating their business activities and assuming responsibility for regulating the order of the tourism market, supervising and managing the quality of services and safeguarding the legitimate rights and interests of tourism consumers and operators. In short, the tourism authorities represent the state and the government, exercising the powers assigned to them by the state to ensure that the entire tourism industry carries out its work in a stable and orderly manner. In addition, in some places there are tourism industry associations, which are social groups in the tourism industry formed by tourism authorities at all levels, tourism enterprises and institutions, tourism-related departments, as well as people from all walks of life, experts and scholars who are passionate about tourism, with the responsibility of promoting the self-regulation and development of this industry. The tourism management system is well-defined and managed, and is a strong pillar to ensure the rapid development of the tourism industry in individual regions. With the support of the government authorities, the tourism industry associations can play a good role to jointly undertake the management functions and responsibilities of the tourism entity enterprises.

(2) Tourism operation system.

The tourism operation system includes two main categories: tourist attractions and travel agencies. Many tourist attractions are the bodies of tourism products in the traditional sense, and the services they provide are an important tourism product in modern tourism. In the traditional sense, almost all tourism activities are based around the natural and social tourism resources of tourist attractions which provide a certain space for tourism activities to unfold. Their geographical layout within different cities or territories constitutes the spatial structure of tourism. Tourism spatial structure refers to the degree of spatial aggregation and the state of aggregation formed by the interaction of tourism economic objects in space, it reflects the spatial attributes and interrelationships of tourism activities, and it is the projection of tourism activities in geographical space and an important indicator of the state of regional tourism development, it involves the development of tourism products and is the main market for tourism consumption. Whether the layout of tourism spatial structure in a certain region is reasonable or not directly affects the development of the local tourism industry. In terms of the management of scenic spots, at present, there are three main models: the government-exclusive management model, the leasing contract or buyout model, and the modern enterprise system for operating scenic spots model. The main source of income is the entrance fee, in addition to other services. There are a large number of tourist attractions with different activities, which are closely related to people's willingness to travel. The internal construction and structural characteristics of the tourist attractions are also important elements that affect the income from their operations. They are at the heart of the tourism industry system and all tourism activities revolve around them. The tourism management system deals with them through various legal, economic and administrative means, and the travel agency designs, develops and sells tourism products for the tourists.

(3) Tourism preservation system.

The tourism preservation system is a system of transport, hotels and restaurants, entertainment and shopping, and other services together, and their common feature is to provide the various services needed by tourists to help travel agents realize the value of tourism products and make them appreciate.

① The transport services sector provides the necessary transport to realize the tourism product.

Travelers have to use modern transport to travel from one area to another to enjoy tourism services. Transport is not only the basis and prerequisite for the development of the national economy, but also for the development of regional tourism, and it is of great importance for improving the accessibility of tourism destination. In the modern tourism industry, the transport sector should be able to provide various means of transport in a timely manner according to the needs of the tourism sector, creating convenient transport conditions, allowing tourists to enjoy convenient and fast transport services, minimizing transport costs and providing more profit margins for travel agents. Travel agencies are cooperating well with the Ministry of Transport. They can use their advantages to create more economic increment for the transport sector.

② Hotels and restaurants are important parts of life for travelers to enjoy according to tourism services.

Tourism is a part of life, tourism cannot be separated from food and accommodation. Letting tourists feel the warmth of home is the consistent requirement of tourism work. To improve the quality of tourism services, we have to take more efforts on diet and living. In terms of living, room design principles are quietness, comfortableness, safety, well-equipped facilities, cleanliness and hygiene, the scale and style of furniture should be consistent with the size and shape of the rooms, and they should strive to provide customers with high quality services within their reach: standardized management, well-trained staff, everywhere reflecting the style of etiquette. In terms of diet, they should be able to provide some local specialties according to the taste of tourists and pay attention to the reasonable collocation of nutrition in line with the requirements of modern nutrition, so that tourists can get a different kind of life enjoyment. They should also let tourists enjoy the beautiful scenery of the tourist attractions and feel the subtle care of life.

③ Entertainment and shopping are important elements of high-level spiritual enjoyment in tourism activities.

To enrich the content of tourism activities, it is necessary to emphasize spiritual enjoyment, which is the main purpose of the travel industry. Tourism entertainment including the various culture events and some exhibitions can increase the rate of repeat visits to tourism destination. This can be seen as one of the hot spots for tourism innovation in recent years. This requires destination governments or enterprises to develop more and richer culture or sporting activities and create tourism-themed activities based on some local cultural characteristics and the needs of modern society, so as to attract more tourists and increase local tourism revenue.

2) Significance of the Construction of Tourism Destination Industry System

(1) Providing a basis for the overall development of the industrialization of tourism.

An understanding of industrialization requires an understanding of the concepts of "industry" and "industrialization". An industry is an economic group engaged in the production of similar materials or services, and is a collection of economic activities of enterprises with certain attributes. Most scholars believe that the interaction between the demand for tourism and the supply of tourism leads to a series of economic phenomena and relationships in the economic activity of tourism, thus forming a tourism industry. From the perspective of demand, the tourism industry refers to tourism products or tourism services with similar or closely competitive and substitution relations with each other; from the perspective of supply, the tourism industry refers to tourism products or service activities of similar economic nature with similar production technology, production processes and other characteristics. In *Modern Chinese Dictionary*, "Hua" is interpreted as "to add to a noun or adjective to form a verb, indicating transformation into a certain nature or state", with the meaning of transformation and evolution. Industrialization refers to the process whereby a non-national economic sector or industry, which provides a particular type of labor or result under certain conditions or in a certain historical period, transforms itself from a non-industrial sector to an industrial sector by adjusting its scale, organization and objectives of activity through the transformation of commodity-money relations, and becomes a sector or organic organization of the national economy. Industrialization consists of two basic requirements, the change from non-industry to industry and the qualitative change that involves an expansion of scale and an evolution of structure. Further, the industrialization of tourism means that tourism should develop a degree of scale that is generally recognized by society, achieving a change from a quantitative collection to a qualitative change, and truly becoming an important part of the national economy classified by a certain standard.

At present, Chinese tourism industry has completed the transition from non-industry to industry and is in the process of industrialization. For the individual, tourism is a form of consumption and experience, "a short intellectual experience with social, leisure and consumer attributes that the individual spends for the primary purpose of seeking pleasure ". The process of industrialization of tourism is very long , it follows the laws of the industry life cycle (investment period, growth period, maturity period and decline period) and the development logic of continuous adjustment, transformation and upgrading of the industry structure. At present, the development of Chinese tourism industry is faced with universal problems, for example, "the stability of the growth of the tourism market needs to be further consolidated, the tourism industry is developing in a relatively sloppy manner, the institutional mechanism is relatively lagging behind, the legal environment still needs to be improved, the market order is not regulated enough, and the support of talents and technology is insufficient".

Through the excavation of the theory of tourism industry system and the exploration of the practice of tourism industry system, actively seeking the scientific development path of tourism industrialization and striving to discover the low-cost and high-efficiency promotion method, we will achieve important theoretical and practical significance to the development of tourism industry in the country and even the region. The construction of a tourism industry system, a comprehensive and systematic grasp of the vertical development and horizontal development of Chinese tourism industry, targeted adjustment of the quantity, quality and structure of the tourism industry, feasible and scientific improvement plans all can also be put forward to gradually promote the industrialization process of the tourism industry.

(2) Providing ideas for independent tourism industry boundaries.

The tourism industry is the product of a certain stage in the development of the social division of labor and social productivity. In terms of the history of the industry and the nature of the industry, the tourism industry does not exist from the beginning. In the case of China, during the difficult period when the national economy was underdeveloped and food and clothing were not available, tourism was a luxury for the majority of urban and rural residents. In the 1980s, it was common to hear the phrase "Tourism sets the stage, the economy sings" and "Tourism gives a lead to production". These statements reflected the fact that the tourism industry was only a supporting actor in economic development during that period. Since then, with the overall economic strength in Chinese, the demand from residents and government attention, the contribution of the tourism industry to the regional economy, polity, society and culture has increased. The tourism industry has shown a clear role in increasing foreign exchange, balancing international income and expenditure, accelerating currency remittance, promoting economic development, absorbing labor and relieving employment pressure.

The basic objective of the study of the tourism industry system is to provide a basis for the independence of industry boundaries, to identify them clearly, and to find a way to promote their scientific development in practice. In the case of China, the first issue to be addressed in promoting the development of tourism is awareness, fundamentally addressing the misconception of some experts and scholars and government officials that the tourism industry is a subsidiary and secondary sector. Secondly, the importance of the tourism industry needs to be unified with the independence of the tourism sector, and the confusion between the boundaries of the tourism industry and other industries needs to be addressed at the source. Finally, it is necessary to consider how to separate the tourism industry and how to establish a professional and exclusive statistical database applicable to the tourism industry, so as to change the lack of data support for the scientific development of the existing industry and the lack of basis for scientific decision-making.

(3) Providing a path to a larger and stronger tourism industry.

To develop and strengthen the tourism industry requires an understanding of the main factors influencing its development and a grasp of the basic components of the tourism industry system. In terms of the customary classification of industrial economics, the factors affecting the development of the tourism industry include demand, supply, external trade, institutional policy, development strategy and environment. Demand and its structure influence the production service and production structure of the tourism industry, while the investment structure, accumulation and consumption structure, individual consumption structure, and the ratio of intermediate to final demand are important components of the development of the tourism industry. In the case of the investment structure, the investment in road transport infrastructure has greatly improved the accessibility of the country and the conditions for the development of the tourism industry. The increase in personal consumption expenditure on clothing, food, accommodation, transport, culture and entertainment will have a direct impact on the development of the tourism industry sector such as transport, food and accommodation, and entertainment.

To make the tourism industry bigger and stronger requires an understanding of the basic mechanism of the operation of the tourism industry and the process of realizing the construction of the tourism industry system. The market mechanism is the key that drives tourism development, relying on the interaction of market factors such as price, supply, demand and competition to automatically regulate the production and operation activities of tourism enterprises and institutions and to achieve proportional and coordinated socio-economic development. Dynamism is the key mechanism that drives tourism development and is the evolutionary movement of the tourism industry system in accordance with specific constraining relationships. Motivational mechanisms are spontaneous and intrinsic forces within the industry, manifesting themselves in complementary division of labor, reduced transaction costs, knowledge sharing, external economies, economies of scale and network innovation. Incentives arise from the conscious planning and regulation of the industry by the organizations involved, in the form of external competition, brand awareness, collaborative development and cluster policies. Making the tourism industry bigger and stronger requires a grasp of the phased development of ideas for the construction of the tourism industry system. Broadly speaking, the development of the tourism industry needs to extend the scope of the tourism industry and promote the integration of tourism with the primary industry, secondary industry and modern service industry; it needs to improve the support role of other industries to the tourism industry and improve the construction of industrial supporting facilities; it needs to actively and effectively cooperate among regions and expand the tourism brand effect; it needs to promote each other among related industries and give full play to the role of industrial ripple and correlation effect; various tourism resources need to be integrated and utilized to improve the optimal allocation rate of resources. The overall quality level of the tourism industry needs to be improved to enhance consumer satisfaction. Standing in the perspective of tourism industry system construction, bigger and stronger tourism industry needs to pay attention not only to the economic benefits of tourism industry, but also to the social benefits of tourism industry; not only to care about the scale construction of tourism industry, but also to care about the structure optimization of tourism industry; not only to care about the development of tourism industry itself, but also to care about the supporting development of industries with a large degree of connection with tourism industry; not only to focus on the tourism product, but also to focus on the quality of tourism products.

To sum up the influencing factors above, the operational mechanism and development ideas to build the tourism industry system should grasp the important content, based on the industry system view from the exploration of tourism development path, so that they can give full play to the role of the elements in different periods, enhance efficiency in the resource division, achieve structural optimization of the goal in the overall competitiveness of the industry, and effectively promote the tourism industry bigger and stronger.

(4) Providing a guide to action for quality tourism economic development.

How to guide the tourism industry to a scientific, orderly and sustainable development model to drive regional economic development and provide a guide to action for a strong tourism economy are both the original intention and the goal of building a tourism industry system. The impact of tourism economy on the national economy is multi-path and multi-level. Experts and scholars believe that the tourism industry has a direct or indirect effect on the national (regional) economy, mainly in the following ways: the tourism industry can increase foreign exchange earnings and balance the payments; accelerate the return of currency and reduce market pressure; promote and drive the development of related industries; provide employment opportunities and stabilize social order; promote community development and narrow the community gap; strengthen civil understanding and maintain world peace; expand international cooperation and accelerate social progress; facilitate the construction of a strong tourism industry system. It also facilitates scientific and cultural exchanges and promotes the development of human civilization.

In comparison, the theoretical development of the primary and secondary sectors of the three industries is relatively advanced, while the tertiary sector lags a little behind, and the theory of the tourism industry is very underdeveloped. For example, the industry multiplier effect is a key element of industry research, and industry and manufacturing are relatively advanced in these areas with mature analytical techniques and special databases to support data analysis. The tourism industry is lagging behind in terms of research on the multiplier effect, and the quality of research results and studies cannot be compared to those of the primary and secondary industries. The lack of results is one reason, and the lack of analytical data is another. The tourism industry is not included in the *Industrial Classification for National Economic Activities(GB/T 4574—2017)* , which makes it difficult to understand the tourism linkage model. There are some results on the relationship between tourism and economic development in some of the faster and better developed regions of the country (e.g. Guangzhou, Beijing) , but most regions have not followed up. So there are gaps among them. In addition, some of the few existing research results are based on research assumptions, which carries some risk and reduces the credibility of the model. The uncertainty of the positioning and the status of the tourism industry, the differences in definitions of tourism activities between government agencies and industry organizations have progressed to reduce the credibility of the industry.

Therefore, promoting the construction of a tourism industry system, theoretically clarifying the relationship between tourism industry development and regional economic development, and factually demonstrating the role of tourism industry development in promoting the regional economy are inevitable for the construction of "strong tourism economy", and are also the first tasks in the path selection of "strong tourism economy".

8.2.3 Tourism Destination Industry Layout

1) Basic Theory of the Layout of the Tourism Destination Industry Sector

A tourist site is a spatial unit of tourism activity whose constituent elements include tourist attractions and tourist towns which are made into tourist spaces by transport routes. This level of reasoning is an explanation of how industries are laid out in a tourist area, including the layout and construction of tourist attractions and tourist towns, and the handling of the relationship between tourist attractions and tourist towns, involving theories such as tourism location theory, growth pole theory, tourist land life cycle theory and tourist central place theory.

(1) Location theory.

The word "location" is derived from the German word "Standort", which was translated into English as location in 1886.

The theory of location, also known as the theory of standing or standardization, first appeared in economics in the early 19th century.

In the early 20th century, the German economist Weber developed the theory of the location of industrial areas, and in the 1930s, the German geographer Chris Taylor developed the theory of central places based on the location of settlements and markets. A little later, another German economist, Liaoš, used Chris Taylor's theoretical framework to develop the market location theory of industry. Japanese scholars have made in-depth studies on the application of location theory in tourism development planning, and developed the more mature tourism location theory.

The application of location theory in tourism is reflected in the fact that location theory is a guide to regional tourism and destination development strategies. Location conditions reflect the ease with which people can undertake tourism, thus affecting the size and accessibility of the tourism market and ultimately determining the economic benefits of tourism. In some cases, despite the abundance of tourism resources, tourists will not choose this destination to a large extent due to poor locational and economic conditions. Therefore, when formulating a tourism development strategy, it is important to analyze the factors of each location first (including nature, resources, transportation, market, manpower, economy, agglomeration, etc.), then study the locational characteristics of the area, determine reasonable strategic objectives, decide on the development intensity and progress, and seek locational advantages without blind planning.

(2) Growth pole theory.

The growth pole theory was first developed by the French economist Francois Perroux. According to Francois Perroux, the main driving force of economic development is innovation, and innovation always tends to be concentrated in certain special leading industries which promote the development of other industries through a series of effects and become the growth poles of industries. From this, we can see that Perroux's growth poles are mainly the growth poles of industries, rather than the growth poles of space.

Perroux's colleagues and students applied Perroux's growth pole theory to regional space, notably the French economist Bourdeville who saw growth poles as spatial agglomerations of dominant propulsive industries. He believed that the growth poles even moved away from the concept of industry altogether and turned into geographical growth poles.

A regional growth pole has three meanings.

① It is a spatial agglomeration of interrelated leading industries.

② It is a spatial agglomeration of propulsive industries and their related industries.

③ It is a center that drives economic growth in the surrounding hinterland.

The application of growth pole theory to tourism is reflected in the fact that a growth pole is a spatial agglomeration of tourism and related industries, which can manifest itself within a region as a tourism site or a tourism area. Growth poles have an agglomeration effect, where tourism productivity factors are first laid out. At the same time growth poles also have a diffusion effect, when growth poles develop to a certain stage, there will be strong competition and diseconomy of scale, which then shows an obvious diffusion effect. Growth poles will drive the development of edge areas, and the spatial layout of the tourism industry will spread to the surrounding area.

(3) Tourist land life cycle theory.

The life cycle of a tourism product is also called the life cycle of a tourist place by some authors. In the late 1930s, Gilbert studied the growth process of British seaside resorts. In the 1960s, the German geographer Chris Taylor studied the evolution of tourist villages along the Mediterranean coast and divided the life cycle of tourist villages into three stages: development, growth and decline.

The leading researcher on the life cycle of tourism destination was the famous Canadian geographer Butler who proposed a model of the evolution of the life cycle of tourism destination. In his model, the level of development of a tourism site varies over time, before the development of tourist attractions, the number of tourists was close to zero. When the destination is initially developed, a few visitors to the destination appear. As the development progresses, the number of visitors to the destination grows, but this growth is not endless; rather, like the development of anything, it reaches a stage of maturity and maintains a stable number of visitors, before moving from maturity to decline, the number of visitors to the destination begins to fall. At this point, if the positioning and development measures of the destination are reoriented, the number of visitors to the destination may grow a second time, otherwise it will decline significantly.

The use of the life cycle of tourism sites can be reflected in the spatial layout of the tourism industry in three ways.

① Analyze the stage in which the life cycle of a tourism site is located and guide the development of new products and the adjustment of strategic directions.

② To choose the right time for spatial diffusion. When the tourism site has reached a mature stage of development in order to maintain this good state of development, internal adjustments can be made to carry out a new image positioning and upgrading of the tourism industry, or we can choose a best time to expand outward spatially. For example, the establishment of the Great Jiuzhai international tourism zone: one aspect is to expand the market to form a brand; the other aspect is to develop Jiuzhai, Huanglong Scenic Area to a mature stage.

③ Adjust the scale of the spatial layout of the industry. A certain stage of life development of a tourist place corresponds to a certain number of visitors for tourism. The scale of the spatial layout of the tourism industry can be expected to be adjusted according to the number of visitors being a function of the stage of life development of the tourism place.

(4) Tourist central place theory.

Both the spatial model of peri-urban tourism with the city as the core, and the long form of tourism based on the organization of tourist routes reflect a strong theory of the tourist center. The founder of this theory was Chris Taylor, but he did not use an evolutionary approach to the study of the characteristics of industrial centers in commercial service centers and therefore he did not develop an ideal spatial model of the role of tourism. The spatial model which was proposed by Chris Taylor is not much of a guide to the actual spatial grouping of tourism. Some Chinese scholars in 1987 showed that the final pattern of the spatial organization of tourist places should be similar to the K=3 system in Chris Taylor's central place theory.

2) Factors Influencing the Industrial Layout of Tourism Destination

Through theoretical analysis and the practice of tourism development in tourism destination, we found that the spatial layout of the regional tourism industry is subject to the influence and constraints of various factors which are mainly resource factors, location conditions, market factors, socio-economic factors and policy factors.

(1) Resource factors.

Tourism resources, also known as tourism attractions, are natural and historical site and cultural environment that are attractive to tourists, as well as man-made creation that are used directly for tourism and recreational purpose. Generally speaking, resource factors have a greater impact on areas where tourism development is at an initial stage, and as tourism development increases, the impact of resource factors on the development of tourism sites decreases. Resource factors influence the spatial layout of regional tourism in the following ways.

① Quality of tourism resources.

There is a correlation between the quality of tourism resources and tourist behaviors. Chen JianChang et al.(1988) pointed out that for tourism-oriented destinations, tourists who travel on a large scale across countries and provinces generally choose only international and national tourism destinations. In addition to international and national tourism destinations, tourists who travel on a medium scale within the province also choose provincial tourism destinations. Those who only visit small-scale destinations within cities and counties choose all levels of destinations. In other words, high quality tourism places attract more and larger range of tourists, while low level tourism places attract fewer and smaller range of tourists. The quality of tourism resources directly influences the regional tourism layout, with high quality tourism sites often being prioritized for development and becoming the center of regional tourism, i.e. the key nodes of the regional tourism network. Low quality tourism sites are generally undeveloped or minimally developed in the early stage of regional tourism development and are only patronized by local residents due to the low value of their resources.

② Distribution of tourism resources.

The distribution of tourism resources refers to its combination state in space. The size of the attractiveness of tourism resources can be expressed in two states: one is the level and quality of tourism resources; the other is the combination and distribution of tourism resources, i.e. tourism resources' general combination of better form of tourism attractions will also show a strong attractiveness.

The distribution of tourism resources is either concentrated or dispersed. Concentrated resources are easy to develop and help to save tourists' time, distance and energy costs, so that they can obtain greater benefits at a lower cost, so areas with concentrated resources will undoubtedly become priority areas for tourism development, which is reflected in the spatial layout as an alternative to growth poles. The distribution of tourism resources determines the pattern of regional development, for example, the Chongqing section of the Yangtze River Three Gorges, which in the past was generally characterized by a "three points and a line" pattern, with the "three points" being Fengdu Ghost Town, Shibaozhai and Baidicheng, while the "line" refers to the Yangtze River. The regional tourism layout is influenced by the distribution of tourism resources and is mainly laid out in the "three points", which is also an inevitable spatial break in the tourism technology economy.

In regional tourism planning and construction, the spatial layout of tourism should be based on the distribution of tourism resources, recognizing the influence of the distribution on the spatial layout, so that the spatial layout of regional tourism is compatible with the distribution of resources.

(2) Location conditions.

The intensity and direction of tourism flows determine the spatial layout of tourism places. And among the conventional factors that affect the intensity and direction of tourism sources, in addition to tourism resource factors, another one is the location conditions of tourism attractions. It is generally believed that the resources factor is the primary factor influencing the spatial layout of regional tourism, but Niu Yafei believed that the location conditions of the tourist attractions can influence the layout of the tourist attractions more than the tourist resources factor. In any case, we agree that the location of the tourism area is the key factor.

Location conditions affecting the spatial layout of regional tourism can be expressed in two ways: traffic conditions and natural conditions. Tourism industry has regional and immovable characteristics, tourists must undergo spatial displacement to the tourist place in order to use tourism products, so the accessibility of tourism attractions often becomes the bottleneck of tourism development. Under the same conditions of tourism resources level, the tourist attractions with good traffic locations are the first favored by the regional tourism industry, and there is a close connection between the regional tourism industry layout and the traffic routes. Tourism natural conditions refer to the sum of various natural factors of tourism destinations and dependent places, and are the natural environment complex composed of atmosphere, water, biology, soil, rock and so on in the tourism area. Tourism natural environment not only determines the distribution of tourism destinations and has an important impact on the accessibility of tourism areas, traffic routes, networks, etc., but also has an important impact on the formation, characteristics and distribution of tourism objects. For example, the arid natural environment in the northwest of China, the formation of deserts, gobi, Yardang landforms and other natural tourism landscape, as well as the corresponding human landscape such as oasis agriculture; Qinghai‑Tibet region alpine natural environment, the formation of high mountains, snowfields, glaciers, wet and cold vegetation and alpine animals, etc.; the natural environmental characteristics of Yunnan, Guizhou, and Fujian lines are humid and hot climate with abundant mountainous terrain and wide dissolution range; the natural environment of Inner Mongolia is characterized by a hot and humid climate, mountainous terrain and widespread soluble limestone, resulting in typical karst landscapes and beautiful mountain scenery.

① The locational relationship between the touristm destination and the external source.

The relative relationship between the tourism destination and the external source of tourists refers to the distribution of the source of tourists on the map of the tourism destination and their distance from each other. As a rule, the more densely the source places are distributed and the closer they are to the tourism destination, the more likely it is that a large and stable flow of visitors will be formed. In essence, this is the law of distance decay at work.

② Internal locational conditions of the tourist site.

The status and role of each destination in the regional destination system are different, with external flows often flowing first to destinations with high resource ratings and better location conditions, and then, if possible, to other destinations within the region. A similar situation exists for intra‑regional sources of visitors. The location conditions within the tourism area are characterized by the proximity of the tourism area to the regional sources of tourists and the traffic conditions. Generally speaking, the closer the tourism destination is to the regional source center and the more convenient the transport conditions are, the better the internal location conditions will be, and the tourism destination with good internal conditions will be given priority in development.

③ Spatial relationship between a tourism destination and a tourist place.

The spatial relationship between a tourist destination and a tourist place is essentially a relationship of interaction, which refers to the position of a tourist place within a certain regional context in the distribution of regional tourist flows. This position is undoubtedly influenced by other tourism destinations in the region, and in particular by neighboring tourism destinations.

(3) Market factors.

Market factors influence the spatial layout of regional tourism in two ways: the demand characteristics of tourists and the spatial behavior patterns of tourists in tourism destination.

The demand characteristics of tourists are composed of a series of complex attributes, including the classification of tourists, the characteristics of the source market (including the level of economic development, cultural differences, consumption habits, special preferences for tourism products, etc.), the consumption characteristics of tourists in the tourism destination (such as consumption levels, consumption composition, length of stay, consumption choices) and other factors. This set of factors are the characteristics of tourists that are expressed statically and dynamically when making decisions and consuming tourism products, and they fundamentally influence the development of regional tourism products, the internal structure of the tourism industry, the scale and grade of tourism, and the spatial mix and distribution of tourism. Only a spatial layout of the tourism industry based on the characteristics of tourist demand can achieve the normal functioning of the tourism economy and the sustainable development of regional tourism.

The spatial behavior patterns of tourists in tourist places are mainly expressed as the spatial flow of tourists in the region, i.e. the flow characteristics of tourists in tourist attractions, which is the overall embodiment of the demand characteristics of tourists in tourist places. In the region, the geographical distribution of tourism resources and the level of economic development are uneven, some places are rich in tourism resources and have high grade, while others have lesser tourism resources, this uneven distribution of resources is bound to cause the unevenness of tourism demand in space, which is the result of the market's choice of tourism supply. The difference in the number of people received by each tourism destination is the result of the flow of tourists in the region, the tourism destination that receives more tourists may become a growth pole, where the tourism industry is concentrated and laid out; the tourism destination that receives fewer people becomes a marginal area with a less developed tourism industry. In addition, it is important not only to focus on the results of the spatial flow of tourists, but also to analyze the process by which such results are formed, so that it is possible to distinguish the following issues: ① the imports and exports and routes within the region; ② the ultimate tourism destinations and transit tourist places; ③ the spatial relationship between tourist places in terms of tourist flows, i.e. the correlation between tourist places; ④ the flow of tourists on tourist routes. Once these issues are clarified, the regional tourism layout can be targeted.

(4) Socio-economic factors.

The level of regional socio-economic development provides favorable and unfavorable conditions for the development of tourism and is directly related to the development and layout of regional tourism.

① Analysis of economic factors.

Economic factors affect the spatial layout of tourism in a number of ways, including the level of economic development of the source country or destination and the level of economic development of the destination.

The level of economic development of the source country or destination is related to the ability to travel and the level of tourism consumption. International experience shows that the motivation to travel is widespread when per capita gross national product (GNP) reaches 1,000 dollars, and most economically developed regions in China have reached or exceeded this level of per capita value with strong potential source markets. The strong economic strength of the source area generates a strong demand for tourism, which drives the development of regional tourism and promotes the expansion of the development area, thus developing the spatial layout of regional tourism from a point to an axis and then to a mature network, and perhaps even to a tourism board similar to a contiguous urban area.

The economic capacity of developed destinations provides the necessary infrastructure, transport conditions, financial capacity and level of service management for the development of tourism. Tourism is a highly dependent sector and its development must depend on the development of the national economy and other related industries. Generally speaking, tourism is more developed in areas where the national economy is better developed, whereas in poorer areas, regardless of the abundance of tourism resources, the limited level of economic development places significantly constraint on tourism development. Studies have shown that in poorer areas, the initial investment in the tourism industry is generally low without economic value. As investment in infrastructure such as transportation increases, investment in the tourism industry gradually becomes more profitable, and the return on investment in the tourism industry far exceeds the investment. This shows that the initial development of tourism in poorer areas is often difficult due to the impact of investment benefits. For this reason, the government should play a leading role in the development of tourism in poor areas and do a good job in the first phase of the construction of infrastructure such as transport and communication, to create a good environment for the investment of tourism enterprises.

② Analysis of social factors.

There are many social factors that influence the spatial layout of regional tourism, but here we will only discuss the impact of national leave system on the spatial layout of regional tourism. 21st century has seen a general shortening of statutory working hours, an increase in public holidays and an increase in the amount of time people have to spend on leisure. The establishment of a paid holiday system and the introduction of double holidays have given a strong impetus to the development of regional tourism. In China, for example, city dwellers have begun to use short trips as their main choice of leisure activity on their double days off, and as a result, tourist sites around cities have been effectively developed, expanding the regional tourism network.

(5) Policy factors and others.

At this stage, Chinese tourism industry is a government-led industry, and government investment behaviors and policy factors will have a significant impact on the spatial layout of tourism.

The development of tourism must be based on the development of other industries, such as transportation, communication, water and electricity. To develop tourism, transport need to be the first development. Transport and other infrastructure investment is large, the beginning of the return is not obvious and the payback period is long, so generally these should be invested by government. The government's limited financial revenue determines the need to be selective when investing in transport and other infrastructure, generally those with high levels of resources and good location conditions of tourism infrastructure bottlenecks are solved first. From this process, it can be seen that the government's investment behavior has a strong guiding effect on the investment of enterprises.

In order to attract tourism developers, some local governments have developed a number of preferential policies, such as tax breaks, low cost land transfers and simplified procedures. Generally speaking, tourism investment is more active in places with good policy conditions, and the tourism industry is better developed. Other factors such as politics, culture and special events can also influence the spatial distribution of tourism.

8.2.4 Tourism Destination Industry Integration

Since the 1970s, the rapid development and diffusion of high technology have led to the blurring of the boundaries of industries that originally had a division of labor, and the interpenetration and integration of industries to form new industrial forms, which have emerged as new growth points for the economy. Economists have proposed the theory of industrial convergence to explain this phenomenon. The tourism industry is also showing signs of convergence, driven by this wave. As a comprehensive industry, the integration of tourism with other industries has its own intrinsic necessity and external necessity for development. As an innovative form of tourism development, tourism industry integration has injected vitality and vigor into the development of Chinese tourism industry. "Tourism+" as a representative of the industry integration development model has become a new form of tourism industry development and a hot spot of inside and outside industry.

1) Overview of Industry Integration in Tourism Destination

Different scholars have different perceptions on the definition of industrial integration, and a unified conclusion has yet to be formed. Regarding the concept of "industrial integration", the common understanding in China refers to the intersection of different industries, and with the final integration, it gradually forms a new industry dynamic development process. According to the Japanese industrial economist Masu Uekusa, it refers to the change in the competitive relationship between two enterprises as a result of technological progress and deregulation. The *Green Paper on the Convergence of the Telecommunications, Media and Information Technology Sectors, and the Implications for Regulation* published in 1997, in the *Green Paper* the European Commission pointed out that industrial convergence refers to the integration of industries in terms of alliances, mergers, technology network platforms and markets. American scholars Greenstein and Khanna considered industrial convergence as an economic phenomenon, which is the contraction or disappearance of industrial boundaries by firms to accommodate industrial growth.

In summary, industrial convergence is a technological convergence that occurs at the boundaries of industries or at the intersection of different industries as a result of technological progress and deregulation, which reshapes new identities and triggers new market demands. This in turn results in a change in the competitive relationships between firms, thus possibly redrawing the boundaries of former industries.

2) Pathways to Industry Integration in Tourism Destination

The pathways of tourism industry integration refer to the various forms of integration between tourism and other industries in the development process under the role of industry integration dynamics. Due to the different functions, technical advantages and characteristics of various industries, as well as the differences in the way they are linked to the tourism industry, the pathways of integration with the tourism industry are also different.

(1) The "modular embedded" integration pathway.

The "modular embedded" integration pathway means that tourism is embedded in other industry chains in the form of value modules, becoming a value-added point in the chain and giving other industries a tourism function. This effect is illustrated by the development of hybrid businesses and the outsourcing of tourism services. Taking travel management as an example, travel companies provide specialized advice, systematic management and full service for all types of business trips, conferences and exhibitions, incentive travel and business visits, nesting the former travel agency business into the overall operation of other companies. The modular development model implies an upgrade of economic resources, with high-level resources such as organization, network, reputation and social capital becoming the dominant factors, transcending the previous driving factors of tourism development, accelerating the close links between tourism and the network society and achieving a transformation and upgrading of tourism.

(2) The "horizontal expansion" integration pathway.

The "horizontal expansion" pathway of integration refers to the way in which the tourism industry expands and integrates with other industries such as the primary and secondary industries, as well as with the tertiary industry in addition to tourism. Tourism is a demand-led industry, and the variability of demand requires the variability of products, so the tourism industry has to explore and create a wider range of elements with tourism value, and continuously integrate these elements into its own industry, so that tourism methods and products are constantly innovated, and the value space is expanded with variable profit models. For example, the rich and varied forms of tourism such as industrial and agricultural tourism are that the tourism industry makes the resources of other industries enter the tourism industry through horizontal expansion, so that the tourism resources continue to expand and enrich. The main feature of this fusion approach is the continuous integration of resources from other industries with the link of tourism resources expanding, while the other links in the tourism industry chain change little or remain unchanged.

3) Suggested Countermeasures for Industrial Integration in Tourism Destination

(1) Deregulation of industries and improvement of cross-border governance mechanism.

The tourism industry is a competitive industry. The government should deregulate the industry so as to attract more talents, capital, technology and other resources to enter the tourism industry and promote the renewal of the tourism industry. Of course, in the process of industrial integration, there will be conflicts arising from different rules, resources and distribution of interests, so it is necessary to improve the cross-border governance mechanism in order to coordinate the contradictions of various local interest subjects whose behaviors do not match in the industrial integration. The cross-border governance mechanism emphasizes the continuous interaction among various interest subjects to implement the management of public affairs based on recognized goals in order to achieve an effective allocation of resources based on the achievement of goals. To this end, the following aspects can be considered: firstly, to establish an organization above the industry members, to regulate the behavior of the members, to set policy objectives and use policy tools to achieve the goal of improving the competitiveness of the industry; secondly, to establish an effective incentive mechanism to achieve the maximum balance of interests of the members, to establish of special funds with different contents according to the needs; thirdly, the restraint mechanism should be improved, mainly by the improvement of a series of regulations and systems to achieve restraint and supervision of the behavior of the relevant interest subjects.

(2) Strengthen industrial collaboration and enhance policy guidance effect.

Due to the diverse and dynamic nature of tourism demand, the integration of the tourism industry can occur in any industry. Therefore, it is important to strengthen the information communication and collaboration between industries to find the possibility of innovative products from them, while paying more attention to technological advances and changes in demand. In this regard, it is important to explore the possibility of joint policies that can facilitate the integration of different industries. For example, in the integration of agriculture and tourism in the development of high-tech agro-tourism and agro-tourism based on farming, the Ministry of Agriculture and Rural Affairs of the People's Republic of China and the China National Tourism Administration jointly issued an industrial policy to encourage farmers to develop new types of agricultural tourism. In the new situation of diversification of consumer demand, the various industrial sectors should break the thinking of sectoral division and seek a broader space for industrial development with an open concept, and look at the industrial development situation beyond this industry and promote the upgrading of industrial structure with the introduction of a linked policy of industrial sectors. In order to promote the needs of the initial development of tourism industry integration, we can consider the preparation of industrial integration planning and the introduction of industrial integration standards according to the needs of industrial development to guide industrial integration actions. For example, we can introduce and select national industrial and agricultural tourism demonstration base rapidly according to the needs of the integration of the three industries, if we can further promote such practices to such aspects as exhibition tourism, sports tourism, it will better promote industrial integration.

(3) Fostering enterprise groups and improving the innovation capacity of enterprises.

As the main body of industry integration, the size of the enterprise's strength and the level of its innovation ability are the key factors to realize the integration. Although some of the existing tourism conglomerates have entered the ranks of the fortune global 500, the tourism conglomerates formed by the administrative force as a whole lack real strength and competitiveness. The other and more important aspect of cultivating enterprise groups is that they are able to grow naturally through the trials and tribulations of market competition, so that they are truly innovative and competitive. At present, the lack of innovation ability of tourism enterprise groups has not only the problem of insufficient strength, but also the problem of imperfect market order and poor protection of intellectual property rights, so cultivating enterprise groups is more important than cultivating competitive market environment and system, and one of the important things is to improve the legal and regulatory construction to protect the innovative behavior of enterprises and innovation interests. At the same time, encouragement policies such as the establishment of an industrial innovation reward system should be used to encourage and advocate the continuous learning and innovative behavior of enterprises. The government and the market should play different roles at different stages of industrial integration. Once the integrated industries have passed the infancy stage, the government should promptly change from being a micro-promoter to a macro-manager, allowing the new integrated industries to compete, grow, enhance and grow under the laws of the market economy.

8.2.5 Principles of Sustainable Development of the Tourism Destination Industry

There are three main principles of sustainable development: equity, sustainability and commonality, and the sustainable development of the tourism destination industry must comply with these three principles.

1) Equity

(1) Meaning.

The principle of equity has two dimensions: firstly, sustainable development must build equity within humanity as a whole. This includes both inter-generational and intra-generational equity. Inter-generational equity refers to the reasonable determination and distribution of rights, obligations and benefits between the present generation and its descendants in terms of resource use and ecological and environmental conditions. For future generations, we have the responsibility not only to pass on material and spiritual civilization, but also to maintain a good ecological civilization. Intra-generational equity is equity between the present generation and others. If the distribution of resources within a generation is not fair, there will be a polarization between the rich and the poor, which will only result in the destruction of the harmonious relationship between man and nature. If the present generation cannot achieve equity in the distribution of resources among themselves, it is inconceivable that they will really care about the interests of distant future generations. Only by dealing with the relationship among various interest groups in a fair manner can a consensus be formed in the minds of the general population of the present generation, and only then can the enthusiasm of all parties be truly mobilized to build and maintain a harmonious relationship among man, nature and society. It can be said that without fairness and harmony among contemporary people, there will be no fairness and harmony between people and nature.

① Intra-generational equity.

The sharing of tourism resources between residents of tourism destinations and visitors to the source of tourism is equity. Sustainable development in tourism destinations requires that the basic tourism needs of tourists are met and that local residents are given the opportunity to fulfil their right to a better life. Therefore, fair distribution and equitable development rights for all segments of the population involved in tourism activities in tourism destinations should be addressed as a particular priority for sustainable development in tourism destinations, combining the elimination of waste in terms of over-consumption of tourism resources and poverty eradication. Different people have different needs for tourism resources. Residents of tourism destinations who live there but have not exploited tourism resources are generally relatively economically poor, and their demand for tourism resources is limited by the level of economic income, they usually meet basic needs through the external presentation of resources; visitors to source destinations who are far from tourism resources but are economically wealthy have environmental or developmental needs for the resources of the destination. It should be acknowledged that the different needs of these two groups of people place different demands on the resources of tourism destinations in terms of conservation, development or utilization. In past development processes, these two demands have often appeared as opposites, and are difficult to reconcile, and more often than not, it is the "occupier" of the destination resources who has the advantage of location, thus allowing basic needs to prevail and destroying the destination resources.

② Inter-generational equity.

Inter-generational equity means equity between generations. People in tourism destinations must recognize that local tourism resources are limited and that the vast majority of them are non-renewable. Over-exploitation and unrestricted consumption will inevitably cause irreparable damage to existing tourism resources, resulting in the deterioration of the tourism environment, which undermines the right of future generations to use the tourism resources, thus causing the future generations to lose out on the benefits. It is important to emphasize here that the principle of inter-generational equity has been neglected in previous social science theories. This is one of the fundamental differences between the principle of equity in the sustainable development of tourism destinations and the traditional view of social development.

(2) Dilemmas.

The main dilemmas facing the principle of equity include two aspects.

① The conflict between poverty eradication and the search for development.

The overriding principle of intra‐generational equity between residents of tourism destinations and visitors to tourism sources emphasizes the eradication of poverty, since the root causes of environmental and ecological damage are primarily poverty‐based. However, in countries and regions that are less economically developed but richer in tourism resources, the eradication of poverty depends on the construction and renovation of large‐scale infrastructure and the increase in the level of industrialization. As these countries or regions are lagging behind in terms of labor productivity, technology, management and capital, the construction and renovation of infrastructure and the improvement of industrialization are often achieved through a crude development approach, which makes it difficult to guarantee the sustainable use of resources and environmental protection. Poverty eradication in developing countries can be achieved through economic aid from developed countries to developing countries, but in reality, due to national and ethnic interests, economic aid from developed countries to developing countries often comes with harsh political conditions, which makes it difficult to achieve.

② The phenomenon of cultural invasion.

The local culture of tourism destinations, especially those that use human tourism resources as a tourist attraction, can bring considerable economic benefits to the tourism industry. But traditional ethnic tourism, in terms of development, management and tourism methods, may have a negative impact on the local ethnic culture, especially when the foreign culture brought by tourists. Under the influence of the idea of quick success and profit, tourism development overly depends on economic purposes in order to cater to the consumer interests of tourists in the development of resources. Due to a lack of genuine understanding of the essence of local ethnic culture, too many cultural scenes imitate local social life, leading to the staging, commercialization, and vulgarization of ethnic culture. The large‐scale development of some ethnic cultural tourism resources has led to the gradual disappearance of the cultural value of the resources, such as tourism souvenirs that can reflect the local tourism characteristics and culture. The negative impact of tourism activities on the traditional culture of ethnic groups is mainly manifested in the impact of the foreign culture brought by tourists on the traditional culture of ethnic areas, resulting in a change in the ideology and values of local residents, which in turn affects their behavioral habits and eventually leads to the assimilation or disappearance of certain cultural characteristics. The original cultural closed circle is broken by tourism, and the foreign culture influences the original cultural environment and leads to cultural changes.

2) Sustainability

(1) Meaning.

The principle of sustainability is the most fundamental principle of sustainable development in tourism destinations, which determines and influences the other basic principles, and it can be said that the other principles are at its service. The principle of sustainability emphasizes that the resources and environment of a tourism destination are the primary conditions for the survival and development of its inhabitants, the survival and development of the inhabitants of a tourism destination cannot be discussed without them. The sustainable use of tourism resources and the maintenance of sustainable ecosystems are the primary conditions for the sustainable development of tourism destinations. The core of the sustainability principle is that the economic and social development of a tourism destination must not exceed the carrying capacity of the resources and the environment.

Most environmentalists understand that sustainability means the declining reserves and other types of natural resources losing in the course of development are inexistence, even the natural resource base maintaining and increasing for human welfare are possible. A significant proportion of tourism resources, such as the natural and cultural heritage resources of tourism destinations, as non‐renewable resources cannot be explained in terms of sustainability by applying the above criteria, but should be interpreted in economic terms: maintaining the natural and historical cultural heritage resource base at a level that will allow future generations to obtain at least the same level of output as the present. The sustainability of natural and historical cultural heritage resources is simply understood as requiring them not to be destroyed in the course of development and that they are preserved in a stable manner for transmission to future generations, i.e. static sustainability.

(2) Dilemmas.

The main dilemmas facing the principle of continuity include four aspects.

① The contradiction between tourism development and zero growth in the level of consumption of tourism resources.

According to the principle of sustainability in the development of tourism destinations, the sustainable use of tourism resources emphasizes that the stock of tourism resources remains relatively unchanged, in which the consumption of non‐renewable tourism resources should cease, while for renewable tourism resources, the rate of resource consumption should be equal to or less than the rate of regeneration of such resources. But the reality is the opposite. In the case of non-renewable tourism resources, the poorer countries will not cease to use or consume them for developmental reasons, and the resource‐owning countries will not cease to exploit them for developmental reasons. In the case of renewable tourism resources, people will hope for new resources to emerge, so they will not reduce the use and consumption of existing resources, and in the absence of macroeconomic regulation, the rate of use of such resources is likely to exceed the rate of their regeneration. Thus, there is an irreconcilable contradiction between the need for economic development and zero growth in resource consumption levels.

② Environmental extremes and the "tragedy of the commons".

The core of the principle of sustainability in the development of tourism destinations is that economic and social development must not exceed a certain carrying capacity of tourism resources and the environment. If an environmental limit is set in accordance with the maximum carrying capacity of nature, the cycle of the entire ecosystem can be maintained by the purification capacity of the natural ecosystem itself up to the environmental limit. However, if the level of environmental pollution exceeds this limit, the cycle of the system will be broken and the environment will deteriorate. In reality, due to the lack of awareness and the need for development, most countries and regions do not set this extreme value, and even if they do, it is only a formality and is not really implemented. At present, within a country, there is no limit to the total amount of sewage discharged for a problem like water pollution, and when the problem is so serious that it endangers the survival of its people, it can be corrected through government action (the price paid for such corrective action is high); but when environmental problems involve more than one country, the "tragedy of the commons" arises, as in the case of Black Sea water pollution, carbon dioxide emission, air pollution, etc. These have now become the biggest problems threatening the survival of mankind.

③ The contradiction between the infinite human desire and the finite nature resources.

The human desire is endless and is expressed in the demand for tourism, such as the need for adventure and other tourism needs. The satisfaction of these needs is largely dependent on the consumption of more resources. In the book *There Is No End to History* published in 1997, Wei Jianlin proposed that developed countries account for only 23% of the world's population, but consume 75% of energy, 79% of commercial fuels, 46% of logs, 78% of panels, 72% of steel production, 75% of carbon dioxide emissions and 90% of CFCs (chlorofluorocarbon), its population is growing very slowly, but it consumes 35-50 times more energy per capita than developing countries. This view of consumption and consumption patterns needs to be reformed. At the same time, the earth's natural resources are finite and at the present rate will one day be depleted by mankind.

④ The contradiction between the blind growth of population and the limited resources.

An implicit premise of sustainable tourism destination development that cannot be ignored is that the population of a destination (both in terms of the number of tourists and the number of local inhabitants) is essentially static, maintaining the total amount of resources in order to ensure that the well-being of future generations does not decline. In the case of population growth, this can only be achieved by increasing the human resources base, and this is difficult to achieve. Therefore, sustainable development of tourism destination is difficult to achieve in the context of population growth.

3) Commonality

(1) Meaning.

Sustainable development requires the common participation of the general population, which objectively prescribes people's subjective consciousness. First of all, it is necessary to look at the relationship between human development and social development in a dialectical manner. Human development is always closely related to the process of society, and they are two aspects of the same historical process with consistency and unity. Only a full understanding of this dialectical relationship of interdependence can be conducive to correctly dealing with the conflict between the macro goals of social protection and individual interests, and can help us consciously sacrifice local interests to preserve social resources and the environment. Secondly, the theory and practice of sustainable development require the social and practical subjectivity of each individual. This requires not only that human beings realize that a good resource environment is the basic prerequisite and condition for human survival and development, but also that all people living on the earth have a common responsibility to protect the earth, and that everyone needs to fulfil their rights and obligations and participate in the broadest sense.

Different tourism destinations in different countries and regions of the world, due to their different history, economy, culture and levels of development, have different policies and implementation steps for sustainable development. However, the overall objective of a sustainable development strategy for tourism destinations is the same and unified, i.e. the relationship between the protection of the environment and the development of tourism should be dealt with from a practical point of view in all countries and regions. The holistic nature and the interdependence between countries and regions dictate that to achieve the overall objective of sustainable development in tourism destinations, concerted national and even global action must be sought.

Sustainable development of tourism destinations, as a common goal for tourists and residents of tourism destinations, embodies the principles of equity and sustainability, and requires joint action to achieve. The natural and historical heritage of the world is the common heritage of all mankind, and its preservation is not only the responsibility of a region or a country, but a shared obligation of the entire international community. For this reason, UNESCO and other international organizations have drafted and adopted a series of important legal instruments to promote the protection of the cultural heritage of mankind by the international community. Since 1840, when the French architectural expert Mérimée proposed the *Historic Buildings Act*, the principle of commonality in the protection of the historical and cultural heritage of mankind has been gradually recognized

Case Study 8-1

Vinetree to Promote Responsible Travel

Case Analysis 8-1

throughout the world, and has since been established in the Athens, Venice, Machupi and Washington Charters which all contain specific provisions on the protection of historical and cultural heritage. To this end, UNESCO has drawn up *the World Heritage List* under the *Convention Concerning the Protection of the World Cultural and Natural Heritage*, with the aim of bringing global attention and protection to *the World Heritage Sites*. As of June 2009, the 33rd Session of the World Heritage Committee had 890 world heritage properties on *the World Heritage List*, and China's total number of World Heritage properties is 38.

(2) Dilemmas.

① The conflict between environmental integrity and national interest.

On the one hand, the spread of environmental pollution has no regional boundaries or even national boundaries, and shows commonality and globalism, thus creating interdependence between regions and countries; on the other hand, different regions or countries have different history, economy, culture and levels of development, and their specific goals, policies and implementation steps for sustainable development differ greatly, and the interests pursued by each region and country are different. It is therefore difficult to unify actions to protect the environment. The enthusiasm for sustainable development is now largely fueled by the environmental concerns of developed countries and regions, but even among the major developed countries, national interests make it difficult to agree on actions quickly. According to the World Resources Institute (WRI), for example, the United States had the highest cumulative emissions in the world from 1850 to 2004, with a cumulative per capita emission of 1,105.4 tones. According to the U.S. Energy Information Administration (EIA), as of 2006, the US accounted for 41% of the world's cumulative emissions. However, the United States does not meet its obligations in this regard, which demonstrates the practical difficulties of joint international action.

② The contradiction between the relative independence of tourism destinations and the coordination between different regions.

The principle of equity emphasizes the right of countries and regions to develop their own tourism resources in accordance with their own national and regional environment and development policies. On the one hand, for the interests of the tourism destination, many countries or regions, especially the less developed countries or regions, will focus more on their own economic growth in order to improve people's income when the pressure of development outweighs those of the environment. On the other hand, the principle of commonality emphasizes the cooperation between countries and regions in the preservation of the ecological environment. In reality there is a certain contradiction and conflict between these two things.

8.3 Development Trend of Tourism Destination

8.3.1 Development of Tourism Destination in the New Era

1) Development of Tourism Destination Has Entered a New Era

Socialism with Chinese characteristics has entered a new era, which means that all walks of life have ushered in a new period of development. The people's lives are getting better and better as the domestic development is flourishing, and after being satisfied on the material level, people are paying more and more attention to quality in their pursuit of spirituality. Tourism, as a means of spiritual enjoyment, is developing in a new direction in line with the changing needs of the people. Likewise, the new era will see creative development in tourism destination.

(1) The age of self-travel.

With the evolution of the stage of economic development and the improvement of the national income level, China has entered the era of scale of automobile production and consumption. According to data released by the National Bureau of Statistics of China, the country's civilian car ownership in 2017 was 217.43 million, an increase of 1.86% over the end of the previous year, of which 186.95 million were private cars, an increase of 1.99%. International experience shows that the automobile era, the highway era and the era of casual travel go hand in hand. The growing number of car owners who travel by car has extended from the areas around their place of residence to medium and long distance areas, and off-site car rentals have also appeared in many tourism destinations. Self-drive tours are not only developing rapidly in the economically developed eastern regions of China, but are also becoming popular in the economically backward western regions. According to the *Self-drive Tourism Development Report of Western China 2018*, the number of self-drive trips in China reached 3.1 billion in 2017, an increase of 17.4% compared to 2016, accounting for 62% of the total number of domestic trips. The average distance travelled by car was 464 kilometres and the average number of days spent in travelling was 2.39 days. Travel has become a necessary part of residents' daily lives and an important expression of the people's right to enjoy rest. Self-drive trips, self-help trips, individual trips, bicycle rambles and theme trips are becoming fashionable, and the Chinese tourism market is entering the era of self-travel in all its aspects.

The advent of the self-tourism era is both a challenge and an opportunity for the future development and management of tourism destination. On the one hand, the arrival of the self-tourism era means that the tourism demand is stimulated in one step, and the behavior of tourists shows a more obvious autonomy, which provide opportunities for the development of tourism micro and small enterprises and online tourism enterprises; on the other hand, the individualized behavior of the self-tourism era is more difficult to regulate due to its decentralized nature, which poses a greater challenge in terms of adapting the supply of tourism public services to individualized development, and the pursuit of eco-tourism products may have a negative impact on the fragile environment. Tourism destinations should make efforts in terms of planning, management and services, strengthen the construction of caravan camps and tourism public product systems, accelerate the creation of smart destinations and strengthen the construction of all-area tourism destinations, make efforts in terms of scientific and rational visitor management and services, and build a multi-dimensional and all-area tourism supply system.

(2) The "internet+" era.

The 21st century is a digital, networked and knowledge-based society, and the information industry will become the focus of national competition and a strategic pillar industry for the country, directly affecting the survival and development of the country in the new century. E-commerce based on digitalization and networking will change traditional trade patterns, provide the driving force for the management of tourism destination in the new era of economic development, and become an important growth point for the development of national economies in all countries.

For the traditional tourism industry, taking the path of "Internet+" development is in fact giving full play to the comprehensive advantages and driving force of tourism and actively using the Internet to promote changes in the development model of tourism, improve the effectiveness of services, and promote the transformation and upgrading of tourism. The "Internet+" era requires a higher degree of information and intelligence in the tourism industry, and also presents an opportunity to cultivate new industries, shape new business models and expand development space. The construction of wisdom museum cities are all developed in the context of the "Internet+" era.

(3) The era of great health.

In the 21st century, China has entered the era of "Healthy China 2030", without universal health, there is no overall well-off. The report of the 19th CPC National Congress put forward the concept of Comprehensive Health, outlined the blueprint of a healthy China, and put forward the idea of deepening institutional reform to ensure a healthy China care. The concept of Comprehensive Health is a global concept, which is based around every person's clothing, food, housing, transportation, birth, old age, sickness and death for a comprehensive origin.

With the launch of the "Healthy China 2030" strategy, the health industry has become an important engine for the development of the service industry under the new normal, and at the same time, the era of mass tourism has also arrived. The pursuit of healthy and spiritual needs became one of the indispensable goals of tourism, so the pursuit of diversified and personalized tourism experiences and services will gradually become the main demand of people's leisure tourism. Health and wellness tourism is gradually becoming a regular mode of mass tourism. In the era of health, the demand for health and wellness is no longer just about treatment, but about prevention, treatment, restoration and recuperation. As recreation is a new way of life, the era of Comprehensive Health has given rise to recreation tourism, advocating a healthy and civilized way of life and production, and making green tourism, low-carbon tourism and responsible tourism more popular. We should speed up the construction of deep-breathing towns, and promote the rapid development of tourism models such as retirement holidays, recreation and health holidays, sports holidays, family holidays, family-friendly holidays, scientific research adventure holidays, and conference and business holidays.

(4) The "tourism+" era.

"Tourism+" is a new productive force that can not only give better play to the pulling, integrating and enhancing power of tourism, but also provide a tourism platform for the development of related industries and sectors, give rise to new business models, and enhance the development level and comprehensive value of related industries and cities. And that is the quality and effectiveness of the development of the tourism industry. For a long time, tourism has been perceived as a simple consumer sector, and as an isolated industry. In fact, the contribution of tourism to the national economy is not only consumption, but covers three major areas of consumption, investment and export. Tourism is an important industry that enhances national happiness, improves national health and promotes social harmony, and is also a new economic growth point with the function of optimizing regional layout, coordinating urban and rural development and promoting new urbanization. "Tourism+" is the key to open the door of a strong tourism country, with the function of "building a platform, enhancing value, promoting sharing and improving efficiency". In the era of "tourism+", the boundaries of tourism have expanded, and the integration of the traditional tourism industry with other industries has gradually deepened and expanded, allowing the value of the industry to be reconstructed. The "tourism+" era requires tourism to integrate deeply with industry, agriculture, culture and other industries, to recreate the value chain of the tourism industry, to optimize the development space of the tourism industry, to extend the lifeline of tourism, and to meet the needs of different people for tourism.

2) Destination Spending Highlights New Hotspots

(1) Rural tourism is in high demand.

According to the Ministry of Culture and Tourism Monitoring Center data measurement, in the first half of 2018, the national rural tourism receipt was 770 billion yuan, accounting for 31.4% of the total domestic tourism revenue; rural tourism received

1.37 billion people, accounting for 48.6% of the total number of domestic tourism. Rural tourism means that tourists are immersed in a rich historical and cultural atmosphere and poetic natural scenery to experience novelty, shock, nostalgia, leisure and comfort. Rural tourism represents individuality, luxury, freedom, return, wellness, leisure, social interaction and business tourism, and is becoming a strong growth point after city tourism, foreign tourism, scenic spot tourism and exhibition hall tourism. More and more families would like to take their children to the countryside in their private cars to experience rural life and the richness of nature, and more and more elderly people are going to the countryside to look for their childhood memories and relax. The Central Document No.1 has focused on the issues relating to agriculture, rural areas and farmers for many years, from new rural construction to beautiful countryside, technological agriculture and modern agriculture, guiding comprehensive agricultural development to create new industrial dynamics. In 2017, the report of the 19th CPC National Congress put forward the strategy of revitalizing the countryside, providing policy protection for the upgrading of the tourism industry in the countryside, and leisure agriculture and rural tourism continue to be hot spots for tourism development.

(2) Unlimited prospect for industrial integration.

With Chinese tourism product supply system becoming more and more perfect, residents have more choices for their trips. Sports and fitness tours, education tours, technology tours, recreation tours, food tours and other special products launched by various tourism destinations across the country have exploded the tourism market, meeting the differentiated and personalized needs of different tourists. Industry integration brings surprises to tourists and injects positive energy into local economic and social development, allowing local people to share the fruits of development. Cross-border integration is the essential feature of this era, and "tourism+" is an important method and path to achieve new tourism development. Through industry integration, it can produce tourism forms adapted to the characteristics of the new era of tourism and new tour life forms, form new models of study, pension, leisure and fitness, etc., play a huge market power and play a catalytic, optimization, integration, amplification role.

(3) Technology tourism shines.

Thanks to advances in artificial intelligence and digital technology, tourists are better informed about their travels. More and more tourists will use science and technology to understand their destination and surroundings before they go out. In the future, more and more travelers would like to experience VR (virtual reality) before they go out to make a decision. Virtual reality has already gained traction and many travel companies are working hard to exploit the potential of this technology and apply it to the real world. Previously, Song Cheng, Shanghai Disneyland Park and Overseas Chinese Town(OCT) have all announced their affiliation with VR/AR (augmented reality). This new technology for "immersive" interactive experiences has a wide range of applications in the tourism industry. One of the world's largest VR theme park, Oriental Divine Painting, has an atmospheric park with oriental landscapes, rides with Chinese cultural connotations and technological elements, and realistic and fantastical experiences that have left a deep impression on visitors. The park's acclaimed "Liang Shanbo and Zhu Yingtai" and "Nüwa Mending the Sky" are two of the most technically advanced attractions in the world, with "Liang Shanbo and Zhu Yingtai" being the world's largest multi-participant naked eye AR show. The project is based on a classic Chinese love story and uses a new magical illusion stage, augmented reality technology such as optical images and real life performances to tell the traditional Chinese story. VR has only just begun to be introduced into scenic areas and will have a promising future that needs to be continually approached to meet the needs of visitors. According to the International Data Corporation, AI is predicted to drive global tourism receipts to over 47 billion dollors by 2020. Tourism companies that "know where their customers are, where they are going and what they are doing" will be able to take a big slice of the pie.

In addition, innovation and development in information technology are constantly refreshing people's impressions of tourism. In the past, it was common for people to queue up to buy tickets for attractions, even if they didn't know the way around, the local climate and where the local specialties were, etc. Nowadays, an App is what you need to visit a city. Smart Tourism is developing rapidly, bringing real convenience to visitors. In some destinations, smart tourism services such as online booking, smart tour guides and shared evaluation are commonly used after the construction of Tourism Industry Operation Monitoring and Emergency Command Platform.

(4) Fast travel and slow travel with a focus on enjoyment.

The rapid development of society and the fast-paced lifestyle of overload have become the hallmark of modernity and glory of a city. More and more people in the city think they are living in an "accelerated era", life is getting faster and faster, the psychological pressure is getting bigger and bigger, the white-collar class in big cities is generally in a sub-healthy state because they are busy. In addition, the rapid development of high-speed rail has brought great convenience to people's travel, people do not have to spend a lot of time on the way when they go out. In such a social environment, slow living and slow tourism have emerged. Slowness has become a fashionable way of life and behavior around the world. Slowing down the pace makes traveling more enjoyable. More and more young people prefer to travel on their own. Instead of rushing around with inefficiency and pursuing many sights to visit in total, nowadays, people prefer to walk at their own pace, stay in a place, slow down, stroll around leisurely, feel the life of the locals and let their anxious hearts slowly calm down. Slow travel is becoming a new fashion.

3) A New Concept in Tourism Destination Development

At present, Chinese tourism development is facing the background of the era of mass tourism, regional tourism, quality tourism and cultural tourism integration, which brings new opportunities and challenges to the development and management of tourism destinations. Only by optimizing the structure of the tourism industry, activating the integration of multiple resources, creating new consumption points, strengthening the awareness of tourism innovation, increasing tourism investment, transforming government functions, establishing a new view of tourism and improving tourism information services can tourism destinations better meet the needs of today's tourists and continuously highlight the social value of the tourism economy. The advent of the new era has also put forward new requirements for the management of tourism destination.

(1) Innovative management of the tourism system.

Innovative tourism management system mechanism is necessary to adapt to the development of the new era and is an important grasp of the transformation of economic development. The change of the management system of tourism destination should firstly increase the authority of tourism management agencies, coordinate tourism planning, implementation of systems and inter-departmental cooperation, achieve comprehensive law enforcement, common management by all ministries and more standardized market supervision, and improve the overall management level of the tourism industry. Secondly, in conjunction with the context of the times, innovative management mechanisms and institutions, using technologies such as the internet, cloud computing and big data to manage organizations at all levels, can avoid the shortcomings of traditional management while keeping up with the trends of the times.

(2) Upgrading of tourism service.

The report of the 19th CPC National Congress pointed out that the main contradiction in our society has been transformed into the contradiction between the people's growing need for a better life and the unbalanced and insufficient development. This contradiction is reflected in the tourism industry, where quality tourism has come into being. Standardized and regulated tourism services are currently the most needed and necessary for travelers. On this basis, quality and premium tourism services are also created in response to the requirements of the times in order to meet the growing tourism needs of the people. Therefore, tourism destinations should be led by standards related to tourism management services, strengthen the implementation of tourism safety laws and regulations, make efforts to carry out special rectification of the tourism market order, continuously improve the comprehensive tourism supervision system and mechanism, increase the comprehensive supervision of tourism, highlight the focus on tourism management services, safety management of tourism festivals and activities and standardized operation of travel agencies, and continuously improve the standardization of tourism management services. To enhance the overall level of tourism management services, the upgrading of tourism services should adopt innovative ideas, promote standardization, specialization and humanization, and develop tourism industry self-regulatory conventions and service specifications, with a focus on regulating the business and service behavior of tourism units and practitioners, and implement the standardization of tourism services.

(3) Integration and restructuring of tourism resources.

The new era has also put forward new requirements for the integration of tourism resources. For example, the current cultural tourism industry is in full swing from the market growth rate to a series of national policy support, and then to industrial investment effort, so cultural tourism industry has become an important engine to lead Chinese consumption upgrade, pulling the development of the real economy. At the same time, with the establishment of the Ministry of Culture and Tourism of the People's Republic of China, capital from all walks of life has been attracted to the cultural tourism industry, further stimulating the huge investment space and potential hidden in the market. This background and market environment is bound to drive the restructuring of tourism resources. The traditional combination of tourism resources can no longer meet the current needs of the people, we should explore its common connotations based on the refinement of the existing mature tourism products, form synergies through effective integration, provide new tourism concepts for tourists, expand the tourism chain, and thus promote tourism bigger and stronger.

(4) Optimal organization of the tourism industry.

For the optimized organization of the tourism industry, tourism destinations can set up tourism industry promotion centers to strengthen the comprehensive coordination and promotion duties of the tourism industry, coordinate the development of the tourism industry, integrate and optimize the placement of various types of tourism resources, coordinate the promotion of tourism industry projects and the construction of tourism public service systems, safety supervision, etc. Strengthening tourism planning and management duties can effectively avoid blindness in tourism development and promote tourism planning and implementation, so that tourism resources can be used more effectively and rationally. At the same time, it is necessary to reduce the fetters imposed on the development of the tourism industry by the development of other industries, actively build a modern tourism development management system with special features and in line with the national tourism development plan, strengthen the internal linkage of industrial operations, expand the scale of development of the tourism industry and obtain the scale benefits of development.

(5) Purification and upgrading of the tourism market.

The purification and upgrading of the tourism market should firstly establish a comprehensive regulatory system based on the standard of tourists' satisfaction, and secondly, the marketing and market development responsibilities of tourism cities should be strengthened. The rights of scenic spot rating, travel agency management, star hotel rating, guiding solo qualification examination training and tourism administrative law enforcement can be delegated to localities, associations and other executions to promote the downward shift of the tourism law enforcement allotment and strengthen the tourism market supervision function and strength of agencies at all levels. Tourism authorities should establish a sound system of low service regulation of tourism, shifting the focus of regulation to operational regulation. Tourism destination should establish a sound system of integrity evaluation, credibility supervision, disciplinary action for breach of trust and withdrawal from violations for tourism enterprises, and improve the public display system for tourism enterprises and key practitioners, while various forms of interaction with tourists can be used, such as tourism complaint hotlines, WeChat platforms and electronic mailboxes, to listen to tourists' opinions and establish a comprehensive supervision system for the tourism market with tourists' satisfaction as the starting and ending point. Tourism destination should push tourism enterprises into the market, establish a modern enterprise system, participate in market competition, maximize the benefits of the destination's resources, try to separate ownership and operation, and change the government-underwritten and administrative-means-operated business model. At the same time, the cultivation of non-state tourism enterprises should be increased, forming a advance mechanism for the reform of state-owned tourism enterprises and enhancing the momentum of reform of state-owned tourism enterprises.

8.3.2 Sustainable Development Paths for Tourism Destination

To achieve a sustainable future for tourism destination, it is necessary to focus on both theory and realistic practice.

1) Application of the Product Life Cycle Theory of Tourism Destination

The product life cycle (PLC) is a concept in marketing that has been around bewteen the 1920s and 1930s. In 1966, Raymond Vernon, a professor of economics at Harvard University, published his famous paper *International Investment and International Trade in the Product Life Cycle* in *the American Quarterly Journal of Economics*, in which he mentioned the product life cycle theory for the first time. Since its inception, product life cycle theory has been applied to many areas of research and has provided a useful tool for the analysis of certain phenomena. This theory has been applied to the field of tourism, resulting in the "life cycle theory of tourism destination".

Gates (1992) proposed that the sign of the cycle theory can be pushed forward to

Gilbert's article *The Growth of Islands and Seaside Health Resorts in England* in 1939. However, it is generally believed that the cycle theory began with a paper published by W. Christaller in 1963 *Some Considerations of Tourism Location in European: the Peripheral Region—Underdeveloped countries—Recreation Areas*. In his paper, Christaller described his observation that tourism destination experience a relatively consistent process of evolution: discovery, growth, and decline. In 1980, R.W.Butler resystematically elaborated on the cycle theory. He divided the life cycle of a tourism destination into six stages: exploration, involvement, development, consolidation, stagnation, decline or rejuvenation, and introduced a widely used " S "—shaped curve to describe it. In addition, there are methods for dividing the life cycle into five stages (e.g., Plog, 1973). However, foreign scholars often use Butler's six-stage periodic model when citing and studying the periodic theory.

Butler argued that destinations, like products, undergo a "life to death" process, excepting that the number of tourists replaces the sales of household products. Destinations evolve and change because of a variety of factors: changes in tourist preferences and needs; the deterioration and possible renewal of physical facilities and amenities; and the changes (or even disappearance) of the original natural and cultural attractions that made the area attractive in the first place.

(1) Exploration stage.

The exploration stage is characterized by a limited and fragmented number of adventure tourists who have frequent contact with the local population in the destination. The natural and socio-economic environment of the destination has not been altered by tourism. Parts of Antarctica, Latin America and the Arctic Ocean region of Canada are in this stage.

(2) Involvement stage.

The gradual increase in the number of tourists in the involvement stage has attracted the local population to start providing some simple facilities specifically for tourists. Tourists continue to interact frequently with the local population. The tourist season is emerging, advertising is beginning to take place and the tourism market is being defined. Some of the smaller, less developed islands in the Pacific and Caribbean are in this stage.

(3) Development stage.

The development stage resulted in a large and well established tourism market, which attracted significant inward investment. The number of tourists continues to rise and at its peak the number of tourists even exceeds the number of permanent residents in the area. Access to transport, local facilities and tourism destinations have been greatly improved, advertising and promotion have increased the large scale and modern facilities provided by foreign companies have changed the image of the destination. The rapid growth of the tourism industry has made it partly dependent on imported labor and support facilities. This stage should prevent excessive misuse of facilities, which makes national or regional planning programs particularly important. Parts of Mexico, North Africa and the West African coast belong to this stage.

(4) Consolidation stage.

The economic development of destinations during the consolidation stage is closely linked to tourism. The growth rate of visitors has declined, but the total number of visitors will continue to increase and exceed the number of long-stay residents. The scope for advertising and promotion has been further expanded in order to extend the market reach and tourist season, attract more long-distance visitors. Local residents have become resentful of the arrival of tourists. The former facilities are now relegated to secondary status and are no longer desirable. Most of the Caribbean and Northern Mediterranean regions are in this stage.

(5) Stagnation stage.

The stagnation stage has reached or exceeded the maximum capacity of the tourism environment, leading to the creation of many economic, social and environmental problems. A well-established image of the tourism destination still exists, but it is no longer popular. The number of tourists has reached its maximum, making the tourism market largely dependent on repeat visitors, conference visitors, etc.

(6) Decline or rejuvenation stage.

In the decline or rejuvenation stage, tourists are attracted to new destinations, which will lead to a spatially and quantitatively reduced tourist market, leaving only a few weekend holidaymakers or non-staying tourists. A large number of tourist facilities are replaced by other amenities and there is a considerable degree of resale of real estate. This stage saw resurgence in the level of tourism involvement by local residents who purchased tourist facilities at fairly low prices. At this point, the former tourism destinations either become so-called "tourist slums" or completely disconnect from tourism. Another possibility is for destinations to enter a period of regeneration after a period of stagnation. There are two ways. One way is to create a series of new man-made landscapes, but the effectiveness of this strategy will be greatly reduced if neighbouring regions or competitors emulate this model; the other way is to take advantage of undeveloped natural tourism resources and conduct marketing campaigns to attract existing and future visitors. Many destinations in the UK and Northern Europe fall into this category. But it is to be expected that the revived destinations will eventually face decline. Destinations that are unique will not always be attractive because of changing tourist needs and preferences. The only way to make a destination or product competitive in the long term is to update the product in line with changing tourist preferences, as the case with Disneyland, a man-made landscape.

There are five possibilities in the decline or revival stage.

① The redevelopment of the destination is successful, leading to a continued increase in visitor numbers and the destination entering a revival phase.

② It is limited to small-scale restructuring and renovation, leading to continued growth in visitor numbers to a lesser extent.

③ The focus is on maintaining existing visitor numbers and avoiding a decline.

④ Overuse of resources and a lack of environmental protection leads to a decline in the competitiveness of the destination and a sharp drop in visitor numbers.

⑤ War, epidemics or other catastrophic events lead to a dramatic decline in visitor numbers and it is difficult to restore them to their original level.

While the concept of continuous destination development is ideal, it is important to re-emphasize that not every destination has gone through every stage of its life cycle, as exemplified by the creation of "instant destinations". The development of Cancun in Mexico was characterized by a very short exploration and participation phase. In tourism planning, a destination is always a destination, and the idea that water is far from attractive to tourists is too absolute. Butler pointed out that once the maximum capacity of a tourist day has been reached, the overall quality and attractiveness of tourism will eventually decrease. At the same time, the shape of the life cycle curve may change depending on the different characteristics of the destination, such as development rates, visitor numbers, accessibility, government policies and the number of similar competing destinations. It is important for destination planners, developers and managers to recognize that tourism attractions are not infinite and should be treated as a finite, non-renewable tourism resource. The development of tourism destinations should be kept within an affordable range for their potential competitiveness to be sustainable.

2) Functional Zoning

(1) Exploring the functional zoning model of tourism destination.

The functional zoning of a tourism destination is the process of setting specific objectives for the use and management of the various land zones within the destination where tourism activities are carried out. Each zone has clear, understandable and practically achievable objectives (e.g., water conservation, water connotation, excursion and holiday, production, experimentation, fire prevention, ecological protection), and the overall structure pursues the optimization of the integrated socio-economy and tourism use functions of the ecological environment within the scenic area to ensure the sustainable development of the destination.

As early as 1973, landscape planner Richard Forster advocated a concentric pattern of use, dividing the national park from the inside out into core conservation areas, recreational buffers and intensive recreational areas, as shown in Figure 8-1. This zoning model has been endorsed by the International Union for Conservation of Nature (IUCN).

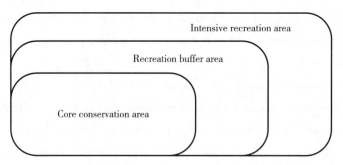

Figure 8-1　Richard concentric functional partition diagram

Other scholars or countries also have their own approaches or theories on the zoning of tourism destination. The followings are representative.

① The functional zoning of French nature parks.

Natural parks in France are generally divided into central conservation areas, peripheral preservation areas and fully protected areas, similar to Richard's concentric circles model. In addition, Gunn proposed a national park tourism zoning model in 1988, which divides parks into key resource reserves, low-use wilderness areas, dispersed recreation areas, intensive recreation areas and service communities.

② The functional zoning approach of Canada national parks.

a. Special protection areas.

No public access is allowed, while appropriate programs and exhibitions are provided outside the area to inform visitors about the characteristics of the area.

b. Wilderness areas.

Wildness areas are the areas that represent the characteristics of natural area and remain unchanged, allowing visitors to have a first-hand experience of the natural and cultural heritage of the park by providing appropriate outdoor recreational activities and a limited number of facilities within the carrying capacity of the ecosystem.

c. Natural environment areas.

Natural environment areas manage as a natural environment, providing outdoor recreation and simple natural facilities for visitors, controlling motorized traffic and preferring public transport that contributes to heritage conservation.

d. Outdoor recreation areas.

Outdoor recreation areas allow a relatively wide variety of services and facilities for visitors to enjoy and appreciate the park's scenery, and allow the use of direct motorized transport.

e. Park service areas.

These are the areas where visitor services and support facilities are concentrated, and where the park's operation and management center is located.

③ The structural division of nature reserves in China.

In China, *the Regulations of the People's Republic of China on Nature Reserves*

(1994) and some major nature conservation works have divided the structure of nature reserves into core zones and buffer zones and experimental zones. The core zones are strictly protected, while the buffer zones can be used for linear tourism. Some of the current tourism destinations in China have been developed with ecological protection in mind and have been clearly zoned during planning, for example, the Changli Gold Coast Nature Reserve is divided into four zones: development zone, research zone, management zone and monitoring zone.

(2) Concentric functional zoning pattern.

Although the specific approach to functional zoning as well as its name may vary due to the different resources and environment within a scenic area, its core elements are broadly the same. We believe that Richard's concentric circles model of functional zoning best represents the essence of functional zoning in tourism destination. The three areas in this model are described below.

① Core conservation area.

The core conservation area is the core of the structure of the tourism destination system, it is an area under absolute protection and least disturbed by human activities, and it is the most intact natural ecosystem with the most wildlife resources concentrated and a section with special protection significance. The core area is responsible for the effective protection of the target, and its size and shape should be able to meet the needs of the protection target. Depending on the actual situation, within a tourist attraction, the core area may be one or several. In the core areas of nature reserves, human activities are strictly controlled and, as a general rule, no unit or individual is allowed to enter the area, even with special permission. Only activities that do not damage the natural state are allowed, such as various resource surveys and dynamic monitoring of ecosystems, flora and fauna resources.

② Recreation buffer area.

The recreation buffer area is an area on the periphery of the core area, interspersed with the surrounding communities, a transition area between the core conservation area and the intensive recreation area. It can either have a clear boundary or be defined to a single extent, but for management purposes it is best to align it with the natural village or the corresponding administrative boundary. This area is in a position to determine the entire.

According to the status of the ecological and environmental characteristics and values of the tourist attraction, apart from a small number of scientific research brackets, strict closed protection must be carried out. Only limited tourist activities are allowed (including control of the number of visitors and types of tourist activities) and only access by foot or simple means of transport that do not cause harm to the environment. The role of the recreation buffer zone is mainly to mitigate the disturbance of the surrounding human activities to the core area, and to gradually expand the influence of the conservation area on the surrounding areas through the protection and restoration of the natural ecosystem and the necessary landscape construction.

The main tasks of this area are: a. to actively carry out ecological construction, carry out restoration and treatment of degraded ecosystems, and realize a virtuous ecological cycle; b. to coordinate the socio‑economic activities of the surrounding areas to avoid damage to the core area and buffer zone; c. to make full use of the species and natural landscape resources of the reserve and develop and utilize them effectively and rationally as tourism resources, so as to vigorously promote the socio-economic development of the surrounding areas; d. to conduct observation and research on vegetation succession, conservation biology of rare and endangered flora and fauna, genetics, and location of flora and fauna development in the nature reserve.

As a general rule, no production facilities may be built in the buffer zone, and tourism and production activities are also prohibited. If it is necessary to enter the buffer zone of a nature reserve to engage in scientific research, teaching practice and specimen collection for non-tourism purposes, an application and activity plan should be submitted to the relevant management agency in advance, and only after approval can the above activities be carried out.

③ Intensive recreation area.

Intensive recreation area is the main activity area for tourists in the tourist attractions. Because of the relative concentration of tourism activities in this area, a large number of tourists and a certain number and type of motor vehicles can be allowed to enter, and tourism reception facilities, including various types of permanent facilities related to tourism, recreation and sports activities, can be concentrated. The area may have a varying amount of agricultural land, villages or production areas for other industries such as forestry, livestock and fishing due to historical reasons. However, the development of the above‑mentioned industries, especially those affecting and damaging the overall landscape of this tourist attraction, should be restricted.

(3) Environmental impact assessment (EIA).

The Environmental Impact Assessment Law of the People's Republic of China has been in force since on September first in 2003. The key steps in an Environmental Impact Assessment (EIA) include: ①determining the nature of the tourism activities that may be generated by the project; ② identifying the factors in the environment that are more affected by tourism; ③determining the initial and subsequent impacts on the environment; ④ developing strategies to control the positive and negative impacts of tourism on the environment.

Chapter 8 Sustainable Development of Tourism Destination

Chapter Summary

Starting from the sustainable development of tourism destination, this chapter analyzes the characteristics of sustainable development of tourism destination, the composition of industrial system of tourism destination and the industrial integration of tourism destination, the industrial characteristics of tourism destination, and explores the internal mechanism of the development of various industries in tourism destination, so as to provide theoretical and practical guidance for the development of local tourism destination.

Issues for Review and Discussion

1. What is the composition of tourism destination industrial system?
2. What are the influencing factors and basic model of tourism destination industrial layout?

Case Study 8-2

Digital Dunhuang—Enable Culture Relics to Be Permanently Rreserved

Case Analysis 8-2

Exercises

参考文献
References

[1] 张启,王红宝,李小静.城市旅游社区发展模式探讨[J].商业时代,2010(32):129-130.

[2] 芮婷婷.旅游目的地的社区化及社区旅游研究[J].大众标准化,2019(12):84-85.

[3] 王超,王志章.我国旅游社区的社会治理模式研究——基于创新生态系统的视角[J].四川理工学院学报(社会科学版),2015,30(1):1-11.

[4] 陈思.城市居民社区参与的现状与思考[J].江苏省社会主义学院学报,2009(6):61-62.

[5] 张波.旅游目的地"社区参与"的三种典型模式比较研究[J].旅游学刊,2006,21(7):69-74.

[6] 李辉,王生鹏,孙永龙.民族地区社区参与旅游发展现状与对策研究[J].西北民族研究,2008(3):136-141.

[7] 阮立新.生态旅游发展中的社区参与问题研究——以江苏省为例[J].经济研究导刊,2020(4):158-160,165.

[8] 王瑞红.我国社区参与旅游发展的问题及对策[J].资源开发与市场,2008,24(8):763-764,683.

[9] 李琼,陈保平.乡村振兴战略背景下石台县乡村旅游扶贫的社区参与现状与对策研究[J].农村经济与科技,2020,31(3):86-88.

[10] 马勇,黄安民.旅游目的地管理[M].武汉:华中科技大学出版社,2016.

[11] Bramwell B.User Satisfaction and Product Development in Urban Tourism[J].Tourism Management,1998(1):35-47.

[12] 保继刚,楚义芳.旅游地理学[M].3版.北京:高等教育出版社,2012.

[13] 林德荣,刘卫梅.旅游不文明行为归因分析[J].旅游学刊,2016,31(8):8-10.

[14] 吴必虎,唐俊雅,黄安民.中国城市居民旅游目的地选择行为研究[J].地理学报,1997,52(2):97-103.

[15] 谢彦君.基础旅游学[M].3版.北京:中国旅游出版社,2011.

[16] 余建辉,张健华.基于经济学视角的中国游客不文明行为探因[J].华东经济管理,2009,23(10):121-124.

[17] 周玲强,李罕梁.游客动机与旅游目的地发展:旅行生涯模式(TCP)理论的拓展和应用[J].浙江大学学报(人文社会科学版),2015,45(1):131-144.

[18] Wilson A, Zeithaml V A, Bitner M J. Services Marketing: Integrating Customer Focus Across the Firm [M]. New York: McGraw Hill, 2012.

[19] Fitzsimmons J A, Fitzsimmons M J, Bordolol S. Service Management: Operations, Strategy, Information Technology[M]. New York: McGraw Hill, 2015.

[20] Kotler P, Keller K L. Marketing Management[M]. London: Pearson Higher Education, 2015.

[21] 王永贵.服务营销[M].北京:清华大学出版社,2019.

[22] 王永贵.市场营销管理[M].北京:中国人民大学出版社,2022.

[23] 邹统钎,王欣.旅游目的地管理[M].2版.北京:北京师范大学出版社,2012.

[24] 张朝枝,陈钢华.旅游目的地管理[M].重庆:重庆大学出版社,2021.

[25] Sonmez S F, Bachmann S J, Alien L R. Managing Crises [M]. South Carolina: Clemson University, 1994.

[26] Gronroos C. A Service Quaility Model and Its Marketing Implication [J]. European Journal of Marketing, 1984, 18 (4): 36-44.

[27] Parasuraman A, Zeithaml V A, Berry L L. A Conceptual Model of Service Quality and Its Implications for Future Research [J]. Journal of Marketing, 1985, 49(4): 41-50.

[28] 范小建.中国农村扶贫开发纲要(2011—2020年)干部辅导读本[M].北京:中国财政经济出版社,2012.

[29] 刘益.欠发达地区旅游影响研究[M].北京:科学出版社,2012.

[30] 丁焕峰.农村贫困社区参与旅游发展与旅游扶贫[J].农村经济,2006(9):49-52.

[31] 冯灿飞.贫困型旅游地文化变迁的动因及规范研究[J].特区经济,2006(5):200-201.

[32] 李蕾蕾.旅游地形象策划:理论与实务[M].广州:广东旅游出版社,2006.

[33] 母泽亮.旅游目的地品牌系统建设研究[J].中国市场,2006(36):14-15.

[34] 欧阳志云,王效科,苗鸿.中国生态环境敏感性及其区域差异规律研究[J].生态学报,2000,20(1):9-12.

[35] 冯卫红,邵秀英.旅游产品设计与开发[M].北京:中国科学技术出版社,2006.

[36] 王桂霞,邱艳庭.国内旅游目的地营销主体模式——基于电子商务时代的探讨[J].市场周刊(研究版),2005(9):40-41,39.

[37] 刘志红.旅游目的地营销主体研究[J].现代经济信息,2010(5):12-13.

[38] 王昕,张海龙.旅游目的地管理[M].北京:中国旅游出版社,2019.

[39] Candela G, Figini P. The Economics of Tourism Destinations 2nd ed [M]. New York: McGraw Hill, 2010.

[40] 邹统钎,陈芸.旅游目的地营销[M].北京:经济管理出版社,2012.

[41] 张维亮,朱孔山.近十年中外旅游目的地品牌研究述评[J].中国管理信息化,2018,21(17):128-132.

[42] 邹统钎.旅游目的地开发与管理[M].天津:南开大学出版社,2015.

[43] 张朝枝,陈钢华.旅游目的地管理[M].重庆:重庆大学出版社,2021.

[44] 李勇.互联网+酒店[M].北京:人民邮电出版社,2021.

[45] 张凌云,乔向杰,黄晓波.智慧旅游理论与实践[M].天津:南开大学出版社,2017.

[46] 陆均良,杨铭魁,李云鹏,等.旅游信息化管理[M].2版.北京:中国人民大学出版社,2015.

[47] 李云鹏,晁夕,沈华玉,等.智慧旅游:从旅游信息化到旅游智慧化[M].北京:中国旅游出版社,2013.

[48] 骆小平."智慧城市"的内涵论析[J].城市管理与科技,2010,12(6):34-37.

[49] 邹建琴,明庆忠,史鹏飞,等.智慧旅游研究:历程、主题与趋势[J].资源开发与市场,2022,38(7):850-858.

[50] 刘军林.智慧旅游的技术图谱、构成体系与现实图景研究[J].牡丹江大学学报,2015,24(11):36-40.

[51] 李君轶,高慧君.信息化视角下的全域旅游[J].旅游学刊,2016,31(9):24-26.

[52] Buckley R, Weaver D B, Pickering C. Nature-based Tourism , Environment and Land Management[M].Wallingford: CABI Publishing, 2003.

[53] Wall G, Wright C. The Environment Impact of Outdoor Recreation[M]. Ontario: University of Waterloo, 1977.

[54] Lea J. Tourism and development in the third world[M]. London: Routledge, 1988.

[55] 保继刚,楚义芳.旅游地理学[M].北京:高等教育出版社,2001.

[56] 崔凤军.论旅游环境承载力——持续发展旅游的判据之一[J].经济地理,1995(1):105-109.

[57] 李心合.面向可持续发展的利益相关者管理[J].当代财经,2001(1):66-70.

[58] 刘玲.旅游环境承载力研究[M].北京:中国环境科学出版社,2000.

教学支持说明

为了改善教学效果,提高教材的使用效率,满足高校授课教师的教学需求,本套教材备有与纸质教材配套的教学课件(PPT电子教案)和拓展资源(案例库、习题库视频等)。

为保证本教学课件及相关教学资料仅为教材使用者所得,我们将向使用本套教材的高校授课教师赠送教学课件或者相关教学资料,烦请授课教师通过电话、邮件或加入旅游专家俱乐部QQ群等方式与我们联系,获取"电子资源申请表"文档并认真准确填写后发给我们,我们的联系方式如下:

地址:湖北省武汉市东湖新技术开发区华工科技园华工园六路

邮编:430223

电话:027-81321911

传真:027-81321917

E-mail:lyzjjlb@163.com

旅游专家俱乐部QQ群号:758712998

旅游专家俱乐部QQ群二维码:

群名称:旅游专家俱乐部5群
群　号:758712998

教学课件资源申请表

填表时间：_____年___月___日

1. 以下内容请教师按实际情况写，★为必填项。
2. 根据个人情况如实填写，相关内容可以酌情调整提交。

★姓名		★性别	□男 □女	出生年月		★职务	
						★职称	□教授 □副教授 □讲师 □助教

★学校		★院/系	
★教研室		★专业	
★办公电话		家庭电话		★移动电话	
★E-mail（请填写清晰）		★QQ号/微信号	
★联系地址		★邮编	

★现在主授课程情况	学生人数	教材所属出版社	教材满意度
课程一			□满意 □一般 □不满意
课程二			□满意 □一般 □不满意
课程三			□满意 □一般 □不满意
其 他			□满意 □一般 □不满意

教 材 出 版 信 息					
方向一	□准备写	□写作中	□已成稿	□已出版待修订	□有讲义
方向二	□准备写	□写作中	□已成稿	□已出版待修订	□有讲义
方向三	□准备写	□写作中	□已成稿	□已出版待修订	□有讲义

　　请教师认真填写表格下列内容，提供索取课件配套教材的相关信息，我社根据每位教师填表信息的完整性、授课情况与索取课件的相关性，以及教材使用的情况赠送教材的配套课件及相关教学资源。

ISBN（书号）	书名	作者	索取课件简要说明	学生人数（如选作教材）
			□教学 □参考	
			□教学 □参考	

★您对与课件配套的纸质教材的意见和建议，希望提供哪些配套教学资源：